MW00358695

Proust, China and Intertextual Engagement

Shuangyi Li

Proust, China and Intertextual Engagement

Translation and Transcultural Dialogue

Shuangyi Li
Lund University
Lund, Sweden

ISBN 978-981-10-4453-3   ISBN 978-981-10-4454-0   (eBook)
DOI 10.1007/978-981-10-4454-0

Library of Congress Control Number: 2017936932

© The Editor(s) (if applicable) and The Author(s) 2017
This work is subject to copyright. All rights are solely and exclusively licensed by the
Publisher, whether the whole or part of the material is concerned, specifically the rights
of translation, reprinting, reuse of illustrations, recitation, broadcasting, reproduction
on microfilms or in any other physical way, and transmission or information storage and
retrieval, electronic adaptation, computer software, or by similar or dissimilar methodology
now known or hereafter developed.
The use of general descriptive names, registered names, trademarks, service marks, etc. in this
publication does not imply, even in the absence of a specific statement, that such names are
exempt from the relevant protective laws and regulations and therefore free for general use.
The publisher, the authors and the editors are safe to assume that the advice and
information in this book are believed to be true and accurate at the date of publication.
Neither the publisher nor the authors or the editors give a warranty, express or implied,
with respect to the material contained herein or for any errors or omissions that may have
been made. The publisher remains neutral with regard to jurisdictional claims in published
maps and institutional affiliations.

Cover credit: © Renato Granieri / Alamy Stock Photo

Printed on acid-free paper

This Palgrave Macmillan imprint is published by Springer Nature
The registered company is Springer Nature Singapore Pte Ltd.
The registered company address is: 152 Beach Road, #21-01/04 Gateway East, Singapore
189721, Singapore

To my parents, who dreamt of a university education

ACKNOWLEDGEMENTS

Writing this book has been an emotionally and intellectually rewarding journey. It would have been unthinkable without the following people, to whom I am deeply indebted. I must thank Prof. Marion Schmid for inspiring this book in the first place and for being the constant reader of my emotions, thoughts, and intellectual works since my time as an undergraduate; Prof. Joachim Gentz for his careful guidance in the areas of traditional and modern Chinese thought, as well as contemporary Chinese fiction, which were almost entirely new to me at the beginning of this project; Maram for being the constant guardian of my general well-being; and my parents and my sister, Linwen Li, Wei Li, Xia Li, who have always believed in me and supported me unconditionally all these years.

This book has benefited from comments and suggestions made by Prof. Peter Dayan and Dr. Sarah Tribout-Joseph from the French Department of the University of Edinburgh, and Prof. Mary Orr whose vast knowledge of critical theory is an intellectual inspiration. My doctoral research, which laid the foundations for this book, was significantly enriched during my stay at the École Normale Supérieure (Paris), where I was able to participate in the seminars organized by the Proust research team at L'Institut des Textes et Manuscrits Modernes (ITEM) and meet many eminent Proust scholars. I received special help from Pyra Wise and Prof. Annick Bouillaguet and had fruitful communications with Dr. Tu Weiqun visiting from the Chinese Academy of Social Sciences. I must also acknowledge Dr. Young-Hae from Yonsei

University in Seoul, Dr. Yuji Murakami from Collège de France, and Dr. Yuri Cerqueira Dos Anjos from the University of São Paulo, for their help with bibliographic details. I would like to thank Dr. Peter Bland-Botham, Dr. Mary Rigby, and Michael Paparakis for their meticulous readings of various sections of the book. A condensed version of Chaps. 1 and 2 from Part I have appeared in *Comparative Critical Studies* (11.2–3 (2014), 295–341), and some materials on François Cheng in Part II have been used for an article in *Forum for Modern Language Studies* (53.2 (2017), 179–199). I am therefore grateful to both journals for giving me permission to recycle the published materials.

Finally, I am very grateful to and proud of my close circle of friends whose paths have crossed mine in various parts of the world, and whose inspiring, cosmopolitan values seem to have come regrettably under attack by our current political affairs: Xiaofan Amy Li, Peter Cherry, Alex Collins, Claire Ménard, Vincent Gélinas-Lemaire, Christian Vázquez Dietiker, Véronique Desnain, Charlotte Bosseaux, Edouard Notte, Fabien Arribert-Narce, and Ileana Daniela Chirila. I deeply appreciate our intellectual discussions, and I thank you for your courage and encouragement, as well as your drinks, chocolate, dinners, banter, laughter, dance moves, and parties.

CONTENTS

ABBREVIATIONS

For greater clarity in in-text citations, the following abbreviations of primary texts have been adopted in this book. Full publication details of the editions cited can be found in the general bibliography.

RTP I–IV
: The new Pléiade edition of *À la recherche du temps perdu* (1987–1989) in four volumes

PT I–VI
: The Penguin English translation of *La Recherche* as *In Search of Lost Time* (2002) in six volumes

FT I–III (or the *First Translation*)
: The first Chinese translation of *La Recherche* in full in three volumes (1989–1991)

ES (or the *Essential Selection*)
: The abridged Chinese translation of *La Recherche* (1992) by SHEN Zhiming

XT I–IV (or *Xu's Translation*)
: The new unfinished individual Chinese translation of *La Recherche* (2005–2015) by XU Hejin in four volumes

ZT I, II, V (or *Zhou's Translation*)
: The new unfinished individual Chinese translation of *La Recherche* (2004–2012) by ZHOU Kexi

Huhan
: YU Hua's Chinese novella *Zai xiyu zhong huhan* (1991)

Cries
: The English translation of *Huhan* as *Cries in the Drizzle* (2007)

Cris	The French translation of *Huhan* as *Cris dans la bruine* (2003)
DT (or *Le Dit*)	François CHENG's *Le Dit de Tianyi* (1998)
RB	The English translation of *Le Dit* as *The River Below* (2000)
TY	The Chinese translation of *Le Dit* as *Tianyi yan*

I need to add a special note on the use of capitalization for Chinese surnames, as well as their order of appearance in relation to first names. According to the Chinese convention, surnames are usually placed in front of first names. However, some Chinese authors have chosen to present their names in the Western convention (i.e. first name followed by surname). In some cases, this choice reflects the author's insistence on or attitudes to their Chinese or Western identities and readerships. This is why I have kept the original order of appearance of Chinese names in this book (e.g. François CHENG, Yinde ZHANG, and GAO Xingjian). To avoid confusion, I have capitalized the Chinese surnames at their first appearances in this book.

LIST OF TABLES

CHAPTER 1

Introduction

Proust neither visited China, nor did he write substantially on China. The present book traces the strictly *literary* journey that Proust's work made to China and back by means of translation, intertextual engagement, and the creation of a transcultural dialogue through literature. Compared to other Far Eastern countries such as Japan and Korea, where Proust's *À la recherche du temps perdu* was translated respectively between 1953 and 1955 and between 1970 and 1977, scholars in China working both within and outside French Studies have been galvanized more belatedly into researching Proust. Only over the past three decades have they given intense scrutiny to his work. These researchers launched their rather urgent attempts to recuperate the foreign canon, which had not yet received its merited national recognition largely because of its ideological contradiction to the 'socialist realism' that dominated art and literature in Mao's China between 1949 and 1976. The first integral Chinese translation of *La Recherche*, based on the old Pléiade edition (1954), was a collaborative work among fifteen scholars, published between 1989 and 1991,[1] more than 70 years after the original publication of *Du côté de chez Swann*. This sudden explosion of interest in Proust has been partly reflected in the ongoing translation of both academic and popular Western books on Proust, ranging from Samuel Beckett's *Proust* (1990), Gilles Deleuze's *Proust et les signes* (1964), J.-Y. Tadié's *Proust et le roman* (1971), and Gérad Genette's *Figures III* (1972), to Alain de Botton's *How Proust Can Change your Life* (1997) and Maryanne Wolf's *Proust and the Squid* (2007). An enhanced interest

© The Author(s) 2017
S. Li, *Proust, China and Intertextual Engagement*,
DOI 10.1007/978-981-10-4454-0_1

in Proust, together with the more recent publication of the Flammarion (1984–1987) and the new Pléiade (1987–1989) editions of Proust's work in France, as well as numerable flaws in the *First Translation*, finally necessitated new translations: since 2000, two Chinese publishing houses have commissioned two competing new individual translations of *La Recherche*, the first volumes of which appeared respectively in 2004 and 2005.[2] In addition, other translation projects have taken place in the meantime. These include an abridged edition of *Du côté de chez Swann*, a very bold 'essential selection' which condenses *La Recherche* into one single volume (1992), the translations of Proust's other works such as *Contre Sainte-Beuve* (1992), and a selection of Proust's miscellaneous essays and novelistic writings (1999). While bringing back a 'cultural other', literary translation is almost always conditioned by 'agendas in the receiving situation, cultural, economic, political' (Venuti 1995, 14). Why were Proust's works translated into Chinese so late? Why are they being translated and retranslated so intensively merely a decade later? How have they been received? These questions set the starting point of our investigation.

Mirroring the Chinese translation of Proust's works, Proust Studies did not properly commence in mainland China until the 1980s.[3] A few years after the economic reform and opening up of China, Proust was primarily reintroduced as a European Modernist or proto-Modernist writer of 'stream of consciousness'—however debatable the latter term may sound to us today when applied to Proust's work—along with Virginia Woolf and James Joyce. The critical interest in Proust's work throughout the 1980s was thus preoccupied with the literary style of 'stream of consciousness', as well as the application of psychoanalytic theory in literary studies.[4]

Of course, the publication of the *First Translation* at the beginning of the 1990s itself constitutes a major achievement of Proust Studies in China. But perhaps more *critically* significant are the two prefaces included in this integral translation, one translated from André Maurois's French preface to the old Pléiade edition of *La Recherche*, and the other written by the Chinese scholar LUO Dagang. Maurois defines the two major themes of *La Recherche* as 'time' and 'memory'. While supplying more biographical details such as Proust's poor health and eventual retreat from society life, especially in relation to Proust's literary vocation, Luo additionally gives an overview of Proust's place in French literary history since Montaigne and Balzac. He also compares Proust's work—albeit rather sweepingly—to the classical Chinese novel *Dream of the Red Chamber* (mid-eighteenth century). The critical issues outlined in these two prefaces have become a ruling passion in the Chinese academic and—to an even greater extent—Chinese creative writers' reception of Proust from the 1990s until today.[5] Despite the increasingly diversified approaches to Proust's work in China over the past decade or so, time and memory have stood out as the most developed areas of scholarly enquiry, and Chinese Proustians have also demonstrated strong recourse to Chinese conceptual tools, bringing 'Chinese critical features' to the world of Proust Studies. A long line of Chinese aesthetic and philosophical traditions provide capacious room to accommodate Proustian time and memory, which is emblematized by the Chinese title for *La Recherche* as literally *Pursuing the Memory of Time/Years as (Fleeting) Water/River* (追忆似[逝]水年华).[6] The hermeneutic richness of this Chinese title—invoking the Confucian definition of 'time' as 'water' and the Daoist association of 'water' with 'virtue'—which will be repeatedly examined in this book—seems to accord tacitly with most Chinese critics' and translators' introduction of Proust to China as essentially a writer of '*stream* of consciousness'.

Other no less important issues such as anti-Semitism, sadomasochism, and homosexuality are categorically neglected in the Chinese reception of Proust's work. The subject of homosexuality, for example, culturally dissociated from the resonances of 'sin', 'hell', and 'divine punishment' that it holds in the Christian tradition, has generated no particular reaction from the Chinese readership and met with political indifference in post-Mao contemporary China (in all likelihood because it does not directly contradict any particular communist ideology or constitute any subversive power as far as the ruling regime is concerned).[7] Anti-Semitism is seen as culturally irrelevant or even incomprehensible in the Chinese context, and hence hardly noticed in Proust's text.

If Chinese scholarly approaches to Proust's work are still inevitably bound by certain methodological and epistemological concerns over issues such as the comparability between Proust's fluid definition of time and the Chinese metaphysical conception of 'water/river', and between Proustian psychological realism and the Buddhist vision of disillusionment, contemporary Chinese and Franco-Chinese writers interested in Proust are given free rein to appropriate *La Recherche* and displace Proust to the Chinese context in their fictional works. In this regard, I have selected three well-established contemporary mainland Chinese writers—Wang Xiaobo 王小波 (1952–1997), Yu Hua 余华 (1960–), (Zhou) Wei Hui (周) 卫慧 (1973–)[8]—and one Franco-Chinese writer, François Cheng 程抱一 (1929–), whose works constitute a significant part of the present corpus.

Out of the numerous contemporary mainland Chinese writers who have commented on or made references to Proust in their writings, Wang's, Yu's, and Wei's intertextual engagements with *La Recherche* stand out as the most 'systematic' and consistent. They represent three successive generations as well as different schools of authors whose writing careers took off after the economic reform. Having lived through the Cultural Revolution (1966–1976), both Wang and Yu became active in the Chinese literary scene in the 1980s. However, the two writers had rather contrasting upbringings and literary backgrounds. Wang served as a 'rusticated youth' (*zhiqing*, 知青) during the Cultural Revolution (i.e. a young person with a secondary or higher education, sent to the countryside by force to 'help' peasants cultivate the land). After Mao's death, he returned to Beijing and finished his university degree. He then spent 4 years in the United States, completing a master's degree in Far Eastern Studies (1984–1988). His creative works, including the novella featuring Proust 'Fleeting Years As Water', manifest a mixed sense of dark humour and intellectual pleasure. Perhaps because of his experience living and learning in the West, Wang's essays in the late 1980s and early 1990s demonstrate a rather independent and individual approach to social and ethical debates on topics ranging from homosexuality, feminism, and Chinese cinema to the environment.[9] His wife, Li Yinhe, is an eminent Chinese sociologist of Gender and Sexuality Studies. The couple co-authored the book-length study of contemporary Chinese male homosexuality *Their World*, the first of its kind in mainland China (Li and Wang 1992). This work was to enhance the translators' understanding of Proust's sexual discourse in *La Recherche*, as manifested in the current new translations.

Different from Wang's scholarly background, Yu was brought up in the family of a countryside physician. With no knowledge of any language other than Chinese, Yu became a voracious reader of foreign literature in translation, through which he became acutely aware of literary style and writing techniques. He then quickly became a key member of the Chinese literary movement known as 'Chinese Avant-garde Literature' (*zhongguo xianfengpai wenxue*, 中国先锋派文学), which briefly flourished in the 1980s. The subjects of his first novel, *Zai xiyu zhong huha* (在细雨中呼喊, translated into French as *Cris dans la bruine*) (1991), resonate strongly with the themes in Proust's *La Recherche*: time and memory. Primarily because of his literary achievement in this novel, he was later named Chevalier de l'ordre des Arts et des Lettres by the French Ministry of Culture.

Born in the late 1970s, the diegetic concerns of the woman writer Wei, representative of the literary group known as 'The New Generation' (*wanshengdai*, 晚生代), have come far out from the shadow of the Cultural Revolution and official communist propaganda. In stark contrast to Wang and Yu's creative works, which are still thematically and diegetically grounded in the 'national trauma' of China's recent history, Wei's stories are entirely preoccupied with the new culture of urban consumption in the 1990s. She deliberately flaunts female sexuality in her fictional works, which has led to some of them being banned in China and consequently generating media sensationalism in the West. Wei's Francophilia is well known and she explicitly cites Proust in her works probably more than any other Chinese writer. However, Proust often appears in some rather intriguing contexts (such as in 'The Pistol of Desire' and 'Tough Guys Don't Dance'), a detailed analysis of which reveals not only Wei's personal reinterpretation of Proust but also the postmodern reality of a particular branch of contemporary Chinese urban literature with, to appropriate Karl Marx's expression from the *Communist Manifesto*, a 'cosmopolitan character'.

As far as their relation to Proust's work is concerned, perhaps the most obvious difference between the three mainland Chinese writers and Chinese writers in exile in France is the latter's ability to read Proust in French. In fact, their acquaintance with *La Recherche* precedes its Chinese translation. This latter group includes the French academician François Cheng, the Nobel Prize laureate Gao Xingjian (1940), and the Prix Femina winner Dai Sijie (1954). They were all born in China and emigrated to France during their adulthoods. While they use the French language as their creative medium, these writers' strategies to intertextually engage with Proust's work superficially resemble those adopted by mainland Chinese writers. Sweeping references to Proust appear variably in their essays and creative works. However, these Franco-Chinese writers are much more self-conscious of their cultural assimilation into France, as well as their fundamental intention to aesthetically reorient both Chinese and Western literary and artistic traditions. As Gao (2004, 25–26, my translation) reflects: 'la lecture de Proust et Joyce—dont la quête du conscient et du subconscient, ainsi que la conception de l'angle de narration m'ont beaucoup aidé—m'a incité à étudier les différences entre les langues occidentales et chinoise' ('my reading of Proust and Joyce—the quest for the conscious and the subconscious, and the conception of narrative angle helped me a great deal—prompted me to study the differences between Western and Chinese languages').

Among the three, Cheng's engagement with Proust stands out as the most thorough. The importance of Proust's work as an intellectual and artistic model for Cheng, especially in relation to his novel *Le Dit de Tianyi* (1998), is best captured in the author's own words: 'ma démarche, sans prétention de ma part, est très proche de celle de Proust: avec cette langue, j'ai pu repenser ma vie, et repenser ma pensée, autrement que si j'étais resté en Chine' ('my approach, with no pretension on my part, is very close to that of Proust: with this language, I was able to rethink my life, rethink my thought, differently from if I had stayed in China') (2005, 370–371, my translation). Cheng's cultural enterprise goes beyond *intercultural* concerns, which are predominantly configured according to the self/other paradigm that presumes two distinct cultural entities. His creative take on Proust in *Le Dit* not only reflects an active convergence of cultural differences but, perhaps more significantly, embodies a new kind of transnational, transcultural literary aesthetic, whereby the prefix 'trans-' is understood both in the sense of 'boundary *crossing*' and '*transcendance*' (Cheng's own word).[10] Cheng's idea of transcendence is, furthermore, in tune with the discourse of transculturalism that is, to borrow Noemí Pereira-Ares's (2015, 477–478) words, 'frequently endowed with an ethical dimension or cultural attitude which seeks to promote more harmonious ways of understanding our contemporary cultural order, moving away from postcolonialism's emphasis on the nation state'. Through his protagonist's voice, Cheng repeatedly announces the intention to take on the role of a cultural ambassador and to establish transculturalism as a fundamental principle of artistic creation. Increasingly it becomes the artist's *responsibility* to propagate the discourse of transculturalism. This echoes a key 'operative' aspect and '*active factor*' in Wolfgang Welsch's (1999, 200) conceptualization of transculturality. In order that there is cultural transcendence, there has to be cultural 'dialogue'—another key word that lies at the heart of Cheng's intellectual ambition and aesthetic vision. He insists that such cultural dialogue should be 'equal', 'reciprocal', and 'mutually beneficial' (Qian 1999, 12).[11] Cheng's fictional dialogue with Proust goes beyond a kind of 'Proustian rewriting', where the posterior writer crea-tively introduces and elaborates specific critical perspectives from which Proust's work can be differently interpreted and understood. As far as Cheng's *démarche proustienne* (Proustian approach) is concerned, *La Recherche* is only a point of departure—rather than a destination—from which Cheng effects his intercultural transaction. More concretely, in *Le Dit* such intercultural transaction involves self-conscious construc-tions of intellectual, artistic, and historical 'parallels' or 'equivalents' from both Western and Eastern cultural heritages. Given the temporal distance between *La Recherche* and *Le Dit*, Cheng's 'dialogue' signifies what Wai Chee Dimock (1997, 1062) in her 'theory of resonance' for-mulates as 'an interaction between texts and their future readers, com-plicated by the dynamics of historical change and by the interpretive energies thus released'.[12] Cheng's 'dialogue of transcendence' should not be understood along the line of Hegelian dialectics with its empha-sis on the dynamics of opposition, contradiction, and negation in order to arrive at a higher truth—Hegel's thesis, antithesis, and synthesis. Rather, Cheng's 'dialogue' strongly echoes Bakhtinian dialogism, espe-cially in the sense that it allows seemingly incompatible elements to co-exist, interact, and interplay within different perspectives of equal value, so that they can produce new languages, ways of seeing, and realities. In fact, this ambition to transcend cultures primarily through the linguistic medium is widely shared in the world community of translingual writ-ers, as Steven Kellman (2000, 23–24) duly observes: 'refusing to be con-strained by the structures of any single language, translinguals seem both to acknowledge and to defy the claims of linguistic determinism. It is precisely because they recognize the power of particular languages that they attempt to transcend them.'

Proust's relation with the Far East, whether aesthetic or spiritual, has never ceased to fascinate generations of Proust scholars. As early as 1952, Georges Cattaui (1952) was making comparisons between Proustian spirituality and a mixed group of both Western and Eastern mystics. Barbara J. Bucknall (1969, 173–203) subsequently devoted an entire chapter to the exploration of the affinity between Proust's 'religion of art' and notable Eastern schools of thought such as Hinduism and Buddhism. More recently, the subject of Proust's *japonisme* was treated in Luc Fraisse's (1997) rather brief but nevertheless insightful study, and the same subject was more extensively examined in Junji Suzuki's (1997) doctoral thesis. The subject was then picked up again by Jan Walsh

Hokenson (2004, 204–224), in the context of a much wider exploration of aesthetic exchange between France and Japan.

Compared to Proust's *japonisme*, the writer's partaking of *chinoiserie* is fleeting and fragmentary, and indeed *chinoiserie* in Proust is sometimes indistinguishable from *japonisme* or *japonaiserie*. Christine Froula's (2012) essay 'Proust's China' is one of the very few more extensive studies of Proust's relation to China, primarily through the discussion of Chinese artefacts (hence punning on 'china') in Proust's work. In the past decade, most scholarly works engaging with 'Proust and China' have focused on 'China's Proust', i.e. the reception of Proust's work in China. This is also the main research direction undertaken by the present book.

Yinde Zhang's (2003, 109–132) section in *Le Monde romanesque chinois au XXe siècle* entitled 'Proust: de la traduction à la réécriture' comments on a few general lexical, syntactical, and stylistic issues raised in the *First Translation*, and offers a swift factual account of Proust's reception history in China, followed by an exhaustive collection of intertextual references made by a large number of contemporary mainland Chinese writers in their respective essays and fictional works.[13] Many of these ideas are recapitulated in Huang Hong's (2013) article 'Proust retrouvé'. Written in Chinese, Tu Weiqun's (2012) article surveys the critical and academic reception of Proust in China. However, most of these critics' observations are empirical and introductory—rather than theoretical and analytical—in nature.[14] *Le Monde romanesque*, for example, as its full title suggests, is preoccupied with the Chinese literary and intellectual history of the twentieth century at large. The example of Proust only adds to the critic's more general surveys of the 'réception de la littérature française en Chine' and the 'intertextualité franco-chinoise'. In fact, this lack of a conceptual approach to 'Proust and China' in current scholarship has been explicitly acknowledged by Huang (2013, 304): 'China is making up for the lost time, Proust's adventure in the Middle Kingdom has just began. Translations and retranslations, studies and rewritings, an entire sociology of the reception of Proust's oeuvre remains to be done'.

This book seeks thus to fill the current blind spot in criticism by addressing the 'Proustian adventure' in China in a more systematic way. It sets out to see Proust through a cross-cultural and comparative prism, exploring how certain Proustian themes and techniques have been variably reframed, rethought, and reoriented by translators and writers alike against the backdrop of Chinese philosophical and aesthetic traditions as well as contemporary sociological discourses. The analytical focus is on the cross-cultural dialogue between Proust's *La Recherche*—the *hypotext*—and its multiple Chinese translations and novelistic *hypertexts*[15] (written in either Chinese or French), a dialogue underpinned by a wealth of ideologically inflected textual relations: mistranslation, appropriation, adaptation, citation, parody, pastiche, and rewriting.

La Recherche and its posterior (Franco-)Chinese hypertexts naturally bear a certain relation of *influence*. But, in contrast to the common assumption of influence studies, this book proceeds to trace the Proustian influence from the hypertexts to the hypotext, rather than in the reverse order. Approaching Proust's literary legacy from the perspective of Chinese translation and the (Franco-)Chinese authors' creative engagement with his work entails lateral thinking, which, to appropriate Mary Orr's (2003, 84–85) formulation, 'like an incoming tributary, generates something which was not there previously, whether qualitatively or quantitatively'. Orr's concept of 'positive influence' is particularly useful for my investigation of the various literary relations between Proust and Chinese culture, through which I hope to illustrate the 'further and more holistic transformational impact' (85) that such cross-cultural engagements with the canon could exert on the ways we negotiate and rethink the cultural heritages of China and the West. 'Positive influence', according to Orr, is a 'facilitation of informed imagination':

> [It] aims at a variety of responses, not more of the same. It is therefore intrinsic to understanding change, revolt, regress and progress, depending on factors such as, for example, censorship or ideological control […] Beyond tradition, positive influence thus tackles mimetic and anti-mimetic ends and means and can enlist a variety of stimuli. (85)

Furthermore, Orr's insistence on the hydraulic etymology of the word 'influence' serendipitously reminds us once again of the Chinese title for *La Recherche* as *Pursuing the Memory of Time/Years as Water/River*:

> Influence is quintessentially a metaphor of motions and fluids, applied to waters that swell a greater river or freeze as blocks in seas, its many self-contained general and specific uses need to be reinstated not least for its power to map flow, force, currents, divergence and convergence. (93)

In this light, the Proustian 'influence' can be understood as a variety of 'hydraulic forces' that interact with the Chinese intellectual and artistic landscape and its attached cultural system, a process through which these forces themselves undergo unforeseeable transformations.

The three key areas of exploration in the present book—translation, intertext, and transcultural dialogue—signal at once a strict and narrow focus on a particular form of literary relation between Proust and China in each chapter/part of the study, and an interrelated, even theoretically overlapping approach to such a relation in the literary polysystem. In the case of international canonization, such as Proust's work in China, translation is of paramount importance. It is what makes mainland Chinese writers' intertextual engagement with Proust possible. As Susan Bassnett (2007, 143) asserts, 'no discussion of influence or intertextuality can take place without recognition of the role played by translators, and the context in which those translations were produced'. Even more crucial to my comparatist approach to Proust is to see the Chinese translations of his work as a means of understanding the economic, political, and cultural exchange, tension, struggle, and evolution in our current global context.[16] The use of the term 'translation' then gradually shifts from a strict and literal sense and comes to be understood as a 'translational' relation between Proust's and (Franco-)Chinese writers' works, which can be called a form of 'bound intertextuality', in D'Haen's critical vocabulary.[17]

The notions of both 'translation' and 'intertextuality' open up theoretical avenues for 'transcultural dialogue', as in the case of Cheng's thorough and systemic engagement with Proust's work. Although it is beyond the scope of the present study, let us also keep in view Cheng's other career as a literary translator of Baudelaire, Rimbaud, Apollinaire, and Michaux from French to Chinese, as well as of ancient Tang poetry from Chinese to French. As an exophonic migrant writer of the French language from a non-postcolonial background, Cheng has 'un rapport plus décomplexé à la France et au français' ('a more relaxed relation to France and to French') (Mathis-Moser and Mertz-Baumgartner 2012, 43, my English translation) than many French postcolonial writers. However, Mary Pratt's concept of 'autoethnography' can still be transposed and adaptively applied here outside its original postcolonial context. While displacing Proust into the Chinese context, Cheng, as the migrant (instead of the colonized) subject, undertakes to represent his culture of origin in ways that engage with the terms of his adopted culture. His 'autoethnographic writing', which 'involves partial collaboration with and appropriation of the idioms' of his Western readership, is constructed '*in response to* or *in dialogue with* those metropolitan representations' of Europeans themselves as well as Chinese culture.[18] Cheng's transcultural and translingual enterprise aims precisely to rebalance the 'highly asymmetrical relations of domination and subordination' that characterize Pratt's postcolonial conception of the 'contact zone' (informed by linguistic studies on 'contact language'), where 'the relations among colonizers and colonized, or travelers and "travelees"' are treated 'in terms of co-presence, interaction, interlocking understandings and practices' instead of 'separateness' (Pratt 2008, 8). Such radically asymmetrical relations of power are what Cheng's notion of 'dialogue' sets out to 'transcend'. In doing so, Cheng, as he repeatedly acknowledges himself, has effectively created a new *voix/Voie* (voice/way)[19] and invented a new self. As Kellman (2000, 21) rightly points out, translingualism is 'a form of self-begetting' and 'the willed renovation of an individual's own identity'. Therefore, Cheng's transcultural dialogue with Proust is also a personal internal dialogue between his two inextricable identities.

The present book not only follows a geographical progression from mainland China to the Chinese diaspora in France; the discussion of the translations of Proust into Chinese and of Chinese authors' engagement with Proust in their fictional works also largely follows a chronological order. Part I deals with the reception of Proust in mainland China. The first chapter begins with an interpretive account of the ideological trajectory of the reception of Proust in China in the twentieth century. It then compares and contrasts all the available Chinese translations—integral and selective—of *La Recherche* since the late 1980s, and explores their different emphases as well as their negligence of Proustian themes. I extensively comment on the distinctive features of each translation and edition, and, in the case of abridged translations, their selective criteria. I examine how these features have been informed by the development of the two major French editions of *La Recherche* (published by Pléiade and Flammarion). The chapter ends with a close study of various strategies employed to translate passages on homosexuality and sadomasochism in Proust's work, which reflect changing discourses on and attitudes to these subjects in contemporary Chinese society.

Chapter 3 explores the ways in which the three aforementioned mainland Chinese writers' intertextual practices creatively recontextualize and re-energize Proust's text in their respective short stories and novellas (including numerous paratexts). The chapter inspects how the three writers, primarily under the influence of the *First Translation*, cite Proust partly to enhance the cultural prestige of their works, while also creating a horizon of expectation and a favourable climate for the reception of Proust's work in China. Throughout the 1980s and well into the 1990s these writers were, on the one hand, consciously experimenting with Modernist (not just Proust's) styles and techniques, and often prided themselves on being 'avant-gardists'. On the other hand, the ways they took on Proust cannot be innocent of 'kitschifying' the author (i.e. superficially citing Proust and reducing his novel to an easily 'consumable' commodity).[20]

With a shift of focus to the Chinese diaspora in France, Part II thoroughly compares Proust with Cheng. This part explores Cheng's French-language novel *Le Dit* as the author's intellectual and artistic dialogue with Proust's *La Recherche*. The study starts with an intertextual analysis of the various paratexts of Cheng's novel and then proceeds to examine in detail Cheng's conceptual and structural engagement with three key areas of *La Recherche*: the novel as both a *Bildungsroman* and *Künstlerroman*, Proust's novelistic approach to the arts (literature, painting, theatre, and music), and mythological motifs. Cheng's *Le Dit* offers a double perspective on Franco-Chinese literary and cultural interaction which epitomizes a fundamentally different process of literary creation through intertextual practice and transcultural dialogue.

What exactly are the distinctively 'Chinese features' in the Chinese reception and, to a certain extent, recreation of *La Recherche*? How have they evolved along with the shifting ideological tensions in contemporary Chinese society, especially with regard to China's drastically changing relation to the West in the past 30 years? What are the commonalities and qualitative differences between the reception of Proust in China and that of the Chinese diaspora in France? These are the questions that the following study undertakes to illuminate.

NOTES

1. This translation will be referred to as the *First Translation*. Full publication details can be found in the bibliography.
2. One translated by ZHOU Kexi and the other by XU Hejin.

3. Proust was briefly introduced prior to the establishment of the People's Republic of China (PRC) in 1949. Yinde Zhang (2003, 17, 35) observes that Proust's name appeared five times in the influential Shanghai-based literary journal *Xiandai* (subtitled in French 'Les Contemporains') between 1932 and 1935, without however generating much interest. This journal was primarily dedicated to the introduction and reception of foreign literature.

4. As will be examined later in the book, this is also when Freudian and to a lesser extent Foucauldian discourses on sexuality were (re)introduced in China.

5. This is not to suggest that those are the *only* issues explored by the Chinese Proustian community. As Tu Weiqun (2012, 96–99) observes, the 'Chinese Proustian topics' now include philosophy, aesthetics, the arts, and the First World War, in addition to time and memory.

6. The alternative version of the title (with the additional word 'fleeting') is mainly used in the Taiwanese edition.

7. Ironically, one of the most popular Chinese terms for 'homosexual' today, *tongzhi* (同志), is in fact the same word as the Chinese translation of 'comrade' in the communist context. *Tongzhi* was appropriated in 1989 by a Hong Kong gay activist to designate 'homosexual' because of its positive connotation: while *tong* literally means 'same/homo-', *zhi* means 'aspiration'. For a fascinating exploration of the term, see CHOU Wah-shan's (2000, 1–9) introduction.

8. The author's real name is Zhou Weihui, but she mostly uses her pen name Wei Hui instead.

9. Most established contemporary Chinese writers, especially at this time, were affiliated with the official organization under the Communist Party's leadership now known as the China Writers Association. The history of this association dates back to 1949. Even today, it still plays a key role in exercising political and ideological control over writers' and artists' creative activities. Wang's essays demonstrate a very different stance from the dominant and generic views voiced by his contemporaries. For a detailed discussion of the China Writers Association, see Hong Zicheng's (2007, 21–40) chapter, 'Literary Norms and the Literary Environment.'

10. I make this distinction between 'intercultural' and 'transcultural' advisedly, following Alex Hughes's (2007, 9) suggestion: 'both [terms] tend to be employed interchangeably in studies on/of cultural contact, to suggest movement and exchange between divergent cultural organizations and regimes. [...] the former implies the meeting, convergence, and encounter of entities emblematic of cultural difference, while the latter conveys a more active conjunction and blending of differences, of that which epitomizes difference.'

11. '平等对话 [...] 对话是双向的, 收益也是双方的.' See Qian (1999, 12).
12. Dimock is also making a reference to Bakhtin's theory of the 'dialogic' in this context.
13. It is worth mentioning that Zhang was previously involved in the *First Translation* and co-translated the volume *La Prisonnière*. He reiterates many of his points in 'La Traduction de Proust dans le champ littéraire chinois', in *Littérature comparée. Perspectives chinoises* (2008).
14. One should add Luc Fraisse's (2010) rather short and speculative but nevertheless prefigurative book section on Cheng and Proust, '*Le Dit de Tianyi*, palimpseste de *La Recherche?*.'
15. Genette (1997, 5) defines his concept of *hypertextuality* as follows: 'By hypertextuality I mean any relationship uniting a text B (which I shall call the *hypertext*) to an earlier text A (I shall, of course, call it the *hypotext*), upon which it is grafted in a manner that is not that of commentary.'
16. I owe this remark to D'Haen's (2007) article in his reference to Apter's (2006) work.
17. According to D'Haen (2007, 108), bound intertextuality 'posits a stricter link between two (or more) texts than is necessarily the case in an intertextual relation, where the mere mention of an element from another text may suffice to qualify the relation as such. At the same time, the relation here suggested is always less strict than that which we usually associate with a "real" translation.'
18. Pratt's (2008, 9, my italics) original formulation of 'autoethnography' has been largely adapted here to suit my purpose.
19. I will explore Cheng's play on these two French homonyms in detail in Part II.
20. My observation will be built on Margaret Gray's (1992) work on Proust, to which I will return in Part I Chap. 3.

REFERENCES

Apter, Emily. 2006. *The Translation Zone: A New Comparative Literature.* Princeton: Princeton University Press.

Bassnett, Susan. 2007. Influence and Intertextuality: A Reappraisal. *Forum for Modern Language Studies* 43 (2): 134–146.

Beckett, Samuel. 1990. *Proust.* Paris: Editions de Minuit.

Bucknall, Barbara J. 1969. Mysticism. In *The Religion of Art in Proust*, by Barbara J. Bucknall, 173–203. Urbana: University of Illinois Press.

Cattaui, Georges. 1952. *Marcel Proust: Proust et son temps, Proust et le temps.* Paris: R. Julliard.

Cheng, François. 2005. La Double Culture d'un Académicien. In *Débats francophones. Recueil des conférences et actes 2000–2005*, ed. Lise et Paul Sabourin, 357–373. Bruxelles: Bruylant.

CHOU, Wah-shan. 2000. *Tongzhi: Politics of Same-Sex Eroticism in Chinese Societies.* New York: The Haworth Press.

D'Haen, Theo. 2007. Antique Lands, New Worlds? Comparative Literature, Intertextuality, Translation. *Forum for Modern Language Studies* 43 (2): 108–120.

de Botton, Alain. 1997. *How Proust Can Change Your Life.* New York: Pantheon Books.

Deleuze, Gilles. 1964. *Proust et les signes.* Paris: Presses Universitaires de France.

Dimock, Wai Chee. 1997. A Theory of Resonance. *Publications of the Modern Language Association of America* 112 (5): 1060–1071.

Fraisse, Luc. 1997. *Proust et le japonisme.* Strasbourg: Presses Universitaires de Strasbourg.

Fraisse, Luc. 2010. *La Petite Musique du style: Proust et ses sources littéraires.* Paris: Classiques Garnier.

Froula, Christine. 2012. Proust's China. In *Modernism and the Orient*, 74–109. New Orleans: University of New Orleans Press.

Gao, Xingjian. 2004. *Le Témoignage de la littérature.* Paris: Seuil.

Genette, Gérard. 1972. *Figures III.* Paris: Editions du Seuil.

Genette, Gérard. 1997. *Palimpsest: Literature in the Second Degree.* Trans. by Channa Newman and Claude Doubinsky. Lincoln and London: University of Nebraska Press.

Gray, Margaret. 1992. *Postmodern Proust.* Philadelphia: University of Pennsylvania Press.

Hokenson, Jan Walsh. 2004. *Japan, France, and East-West Aesthetics: French Literature, 1867–2000.* Madison: Fairleigh Dickinson University Press.

Hong, Zicheng. 2007. *A History of Contemporary Chinese Literature*, trans. Michael M. Day. Leiden: Brill.

Huang, Hong. 2013. Proust retrouvé. In *D'après Proust*, ed. Philippe Forest and Stéphane Audeguy, 294–304. Paris: Nouvelle Revue Française.

Hughes, Alex. 2007. *France/China: Intercultural Imaginings.* London: Legenda.

Kellman, Steven G. 2000. *Translingual Imagination.* Lincoln: University of Nebraska Press.

Li, Yinhe, and Xiaobo Wang. 1992. *Tamen de shijie (Their World,* 他们的世界*).* Taiyuan: Shanxi People's Press.

Mathis-Moser, Ursula, and Birgit Mertz-Baumgartner. 2012. Introduction. In *Passages et ancrages en France: Dictionnaire des écrivains migrants de langue française (1981–2011)*, 8–51. Paris: Champion.

Orr, Mary. 2003. *Intertextuality: Debates and Contexts.* Cambridge: Polity.

Pereira-Ares, Noemí. 2015. Transculturalism and Cultural Translation in Cauvery Madhaven's Paddy Indian. *Journal of Postcolonial Writing* 51 (4): 476–489.

Pratt, Mary. 2008. *Imperial Eyes: Studies in Travel Writing and Transculturation*, 2nd ed. London: Routledge.

Qian, Linsen. 1999. Zhongxifang zhexue mingyun de lishi yuhe—Cheng Baoyi: Tianyiyan ji qita (The Historical Encounter of Destiny between Chinese and Western Philosophies—François Cheng and Others, 中西方哲学命运的历史遇合—程抱一及其他). *Kua wenhua duihua (Cross-Cultural Dialogue*, 跨文化研究) 3: 2–14.

Suzuki, Junji. 1997. *Proust et le japonisme*. Lille: ANRT.

Tadié, Jean-Yves. 1971. *Proust et le roman. Essai sur les formes et techniques du roman dans 'A la recherche du temps perdu.* Paris: Gallimard.

Tu, Weiqun. 2012. A Review and Analysis of Proust Studies in China Over the Past Sixty Years. *Journal of Peking University (Philosophy and Social Sciences)* 49 (3): 91–100.

Venuti, Lawrence. 1995. *The Translator's Invisibility: A History of Translation.* London: Routledge.

Welsch, Wolfgang. 1999. Transculturality—The Puzzling Form of Cultures Today. In *Spaces of Culture: City, Nation, World*, ed. Mike Featherstone and Scott Lash, 194–213. London: Sage.

Wolf, Maryanne. 2007. *Proust and the Squid: The Story and Science of the Reading Brain.* New York: HarperCollins.

Zhang, Yinde. 2003. *Le Monde romanesque chinois au XXe sècle. Modernité et identité.* Paris: Champion.

Zhang, Yinde. 2008. *Littérature comparée. Perspectives chinoises.* Paris: Harmattan.

PART I

The Reception of Proust in China

CHAPTER 2

Proust and the Chinese Translations

2.1 Proust in China: An Ideological Trajectory

Translation, in the context of late-nineteenth- and early-twentieth-century China, fundamentally shaped the Chinese literary language and precipitated its transformation from 'rigid' classical or literary Chinese to 'free' modern vernacular Chinese. Immediate examples include the use of 'translationese' in creative writing,[1] the implementation of (essentially) Western punctuation,[2] linguistic and literary tools and concepts (such as the linguistic typology developed since Plato) in the 'new' kind of vernacular writing, as well as the reformatting and re-examination of Chinese classic texts.[3] The Chinese translation and reception of Proust has been particularly determined and overdetermined by the changing political and sociological factors behind each of the following key historical stages of twentieth-century China.

Prior to the establishment of the People's Republic of China (PRC) in 1949, Proust was briefly introduced in two or three popular academic journals and reviews—very often through translated articles written by Western writers such as Aldous Huxley and Jean Cocteau—without generating much interest. Only one extract from *Du côté de chez Swann* and one novella from *Les Plaisirs et les jours*, 'La Fin de la jalousie', was translated into Chinese (Huang 2013, 295–296). There was one extensive critical introduction of Proust (around 20,000 Chinese characters) carried out by Zeng Juezhi, published as two journal articles in 1933. But Zeng's work was almost completely overlooked by his contemporary

© The Author(s) 2017
S. Li, *Proust, China and Intertextual Engagement*,
DOI 10.1007/978-981-10-4454-0_2

scholarly community (ibid.; Tu 2012, 92). Modernist writers such as Ezra Pound and T.S. Eliot were met with much more enthusiasm.

Under the Maoist regime (1949–1976), the official slogan 'literature must serve workers-peasants-soldiers and the proletarian cause' constituted the only criterion of selection and judgment for translation projects and critical activities, which naturally excluded Proust, who was considered to be a paragon of bourgeois literature. In fact, almost the entire Western literature of the twentieth century was accused of being 'decadent',[4] except for a few *progressive* writers such as Romain Rolland, Aragon, and Barbusse, accompanied by Roger Vailland and André Stil, who are known for their deep sympathy with the communist cause (Zhang 2003, 88). Proust particularly suffered from Soviet scholars' forceful critique of *La Recherche* as 'an anti-realist, anti-social novel, which especially sums up the decadent tendency of not only France, but the whole of Europe' ('反现实主义、反社会的小说，不仅是法国的、而且也是整个欧洲的颓废倾向的特殊的总结') (Tu 2012, 92, my translation). Due to the contemporaneous political ideological bond, many Soviet scholars' criticisms functioned as a decisive lens through which China saw the West. Then, during the Cultural Revolution (1966–1976), all non-official publications were interrupted.[5]

The immediate period after the economic reform (1978) led by Deng Xiaoping witnessed a major revival of intellectual enthusiasm for translation and the introduction of Western literary and philosophical texts, especially those of the early twentieth century, which directly impacted on what we could perceive as Chinese Modernism.[6] Various fragmentary translations of Proust's works started to emerge and were frequently anthologized in the 1980s.[7] These translation projects were conducive to the eventual publication of the integral translation of *La Recherche* between 1989 and 1991. It must be noted that the intellectual energy of the late 1980s, often discussed under the banner of 'Culture Fever', was characterized by a dynamic tension between the opening up to Western cultural production and a rediscovery of Chinese cultural heritage. Again, this historical specificity will leave its mark on the translation and creative reception of *La Recherche*.

However, the relative intellectual freedom of the 1980s, conducive to the pro-democracy movement, was quickly shattered by the event in Tiananmen Square in 1989, and 'the immediate post-Tiananmen years (1989–1992) saw the collapse of the lively and multi-voiced intellectual space of the late 1980s'.[8] Restrictions on cinematic and literary productions were immediately tightened. And yet, in the same years, the Chinese translation of Proust's *La Recherche* appeared.

The exact year might be coincidental, but the *Zeitgeist* was not. The period between 1989 and 1993 witnessed a crucial ideological battleground emerge in contemporary Chinese intellectual, political, and social history. With the new twist of economic reform known as 'marketization', Chinese society rapidly moved on from the Culture Fever of the 1980s to the Market Fever of the 1990s. Proust was translated in the context of a society where bourgeois values were in the ascendant. Since Proust had been primarily seen as an 'apolitical' writer, with a *typical* 'bourgeois' emphasis on 'aesthetic autonomy', it was politically safe for both Chinese intellectuals to translate and the Communist regime to promote his work, while still staying consistent with the overarching ideology of cultural modernization. Indeed, the Chinese Ministry of Culture officially endorsed this translation project by awarding the first prize for the first National Book Prize for Best Foreign Literature to *La Recherche* as soon as its complete translation was published in 1991. So, interestingly, it seems that the reason that Proust's novel was not translated under Mao—because of its status as 'bourgeois literature'—became the de facto reason that it was translated under Deng, and the official endorsement of such literature in 1991 symbolically announced a new phase of modern China, understood as '*post*-revolutionary'. Jean Milly, the co-founder of the Centre d'Études Proustiennes and the general editor of the Flammarion edition of *La Recherche*, was invited to the Proust conference organized in Beijing in 1991, and he still vividly recalls the formal and in many ways 'novel' procedures with which he was greeted by Communist Party officials.[9]

In sum, we could observe that Proust was translated for the following reasons: first, the Chinese intellectual and artistic enthusiasm for and commitment to introducing the long-awaited Western canon, in an attempt to fill in the blank; second, the text's political safety, or rather ambiguity, in terms of ideological message; and third, the commercial potential in the new social environment under the so-called 'socialist market economy' or, simply, marketization. The last, commercial aspect is confirmed by one translator's report on the Chinese translation to the *Bulletin Marcel Proust* in 1992, in which he was already envisaging a new translation of *La Recherche*.[10] It is worth pointing out that the market also provided a new space for Chinese intellectuals after Tiananmen to 'find their less restrained articulations'.[11] Without the market factor, the rivalry between the two major Chinese publishing houses for their respective launches of the new translation of *Du côté de chez Swann* in 2004 and 2005, along with their massive media promotions, would have been unforeseeable. One of the two individual translators, Zhou Kexi, publicly talked (with established writer Chen Cun) about his concern over the Chinese book market for Proust's work, explaining how this market factor has affected his translation strategy (Zhou 2012, 210–212).[12]

It is important to acknowledge that the Chinese translation and reception of Proust's *La Recherche* as a high Modernist work seriously clashed with the postmodern context in which the translation appeared.[13] The great intensity of China's explosive development from modernity to postmodernity was directly influenced by the West, yet was unparalleled there.[14] The 'profound social anomalies and ideological contradictions'[15] which mark Chinese postmodernity will explain, on a micro level, mainland Chinese writers' rather *equivocal* intertextual engagement with Proust, which will be examined in Chap. 3.

2.2   Proust in Chinese Translations: An Overview

There is only one integral translation of Proust's *La Recherche* into Chinese to date, but there are multiple incomplete translations and editions. The integral translation, a collective work shared by fifteen Chinese scholars, was first published between 1989 and 1991, and was republished thereafter in different formats, sometimes with minor revisions. In 1992, as part of a much wider translation project entitled 'Twentieth-Century French Literature Series', directed by Liu Mingjiu, Shen Zhiming adaptively translated *La Recherche*, condensing it into one single volume subtitled 'Essential Selection' (henceforth referred to as the *Essential Selection*). It is an 'adaptive' translation because the selection of the passages for this translation, as will be examined in detail, is based on Proust's earlier vision of the overall structure of *La Recherche*. Almost a decade later, two influential Chinese publishers for Foreign Studies commissioned two new, competing individual translations of *La Recherche* (which are still works in progress today); Xu Hejin and Zhou Kexi had both previously been involved in the *First Translation*. Zhou's and Xu's translations of *Du côté de chez Swann* appeared in 2004 and 2005 respectively. In addition to *Du côté de chez Swann*, other available volumes from Xu include *A l'ombre des jeunes filles en fleurs* (2010),

Le Côté de Guermantes (2011), and *Sodome et Gomorrhe* (2014); other available volumes from Zhou equally include *A l'ombre des jeunes filles en fleurs* (2010) and then *La Prisonnière* (2012), mainly due to his previous participation in the translation of the same volume. While Xu continues to work on the rest of *La Recherche*, Zhou has publicly expressed his regret for not being able to pursue his ambition any further due to his senility and poor health (Zhou 2006). Meanwhile, Zhou translated the first two volumes of Stéphane Heuet's comic-book adaptation of *La Recherche*. Additionally, in 2009 he published an abridged version of his own translation of *Du côté de chez Swann*.[16]

Whereas discussions on whether *La Recherche* as a whole should be best translated individually or collectively are quite common among readers, translators, and scholars of Proust around the world,[17] the idea of *selectively* translating *La Recherche*, of condensing Proust's work into an 'approachable' size with the good intention of giving the general Chinese reader a quality taster of 'the uniqueness of Proust's literary charm',[18] is indeed quite unique to the Chinese context. Condensation inevitably entails reduction, but, as will be scrutinized, this kind of 'anthological' reduction is fundamentally different from what Margret Gray (1992, 166) terms the 'kitschification' of Proust, whereby Proust's canonical work is reduced to an almost empty signifier, disconnected from its original signified.[19]

2.3   First Translation

The *First Translation* has been most intensely scrutinized by Chinese scholars and writers alike. It exercises the greatest impact on the academic, creative, and popular receptions of Proust in China. Problems with this translation have been well studied by XU Jun (2007), who co-translated the volume *Sodome et Gomorrhe*, and Tu (2010). It would be particularly beneficial for us to recapitulate the following two major critical observations.

First is disparity in translation style. Interestingly, in many ways this major criticism goes against the justification given by Christopher Prendergast—the general editor of *La Recherche*'s new English translation published by Penguin—for the decision to retranslate the novel *collectively*; he comments, 'multiple selves, multiple worlds, multiple styles: this, paradoxically, is the quintessence of Proust' (2002, xviii). While this observation is certainly valid, certain aspects of 'stylistic variation' in the

Chinese translation risk rendering Proust's text gratuitously perplexing. For instance, particular inconsistencies arise when different translators are confronted with the task of translating French proper names *phonetically* with Chinese characters (instead of the Roman alphabet). Given the overwhelmingly large presence of people and places and their (in)frequent (re)appearances in Proust's novel, the *First Translation*, and especially its first edition, is often suspected of somewhat 'irresponsibly' creating an onomastic labyrinth for the Chinese reader that is even more tortuous than in the original.[20] This problem of stylistic inconsistency is exacerbated by the fact that not all of the first translators had finished reading the whole novel at the time of translation.[21]

Second are technical mistranslations, for several reasons. The linguistic difficulty of Proust's work, many translators' rather disparate knowledge of French culture and language,[22] and the lack of collaboration with French or other international Proust scholars all meant that technical mistranslations were quite common. They sometimes included 'basic' errors such as mistaking 'Bretagne' for 'la Grande Bretagne' in the second volume of *A l'ombre des jeunes filles en fleurs*. As Tu (2010, 146) points out, had the translator acquired a better knowledge of even the preceding volume (translated by someone else), this error would have been easily avoided. Unfortunately, as Tu's analysis shows, while correcting many errors found in the *First Translation*, the new translation by Xu also contains mistranslations which do not exist in the *First Translation* (146–147). The coordinator of the *First Translation*, Han Hulin (1990, 62), remarked in a report that quite a few translators were unsatisfied with their own work and kept sending him notes and corrections by post after publication, so that certain inaccurate renditions could be ameliorated in future editions. But there is nothing unique about mistranslating Proust into Chinese. At a recent international conference in Paris entitled 'Comment traduire Proust?' (2013), many scholars and translators alike expressed their common frustration with 'basic'—yet somehow 'unavoidable' (for both cultural and interpretive reasons)—translation errors in different languages, while acknowledging the courage and the overall quality of those translations. In this respect, it seems that the translations of Proust's *La Recherche*, just like the composition of the novel itself, will always remain an *œuvre inachevée*.

The *First Translation* is based on the old French Pléiade edition published in 1954, which is one technical reason why many scholars feel the need to retranslate *La Recherche*, as the novel underwent two major

textual revisions in France, commissioned respectively by two different publishers: Flammarion (1984–1987) and Gallimard (1987–1989).
These two rather competitive revisions in many ways entail the two new,
competing Chinese translations of *La Recherche*, respectively commissioned by Yilin and Yiwen.[23]

Somewhat paradoxically, whereas the Flammarion edition—directed
by Milly and published in 10 volumes in paperback, with limited (but
still quite extensive) notes and references—is the basis for the more
scholarly hardback Chinese translation by Xu, the prestigious new
leather-bound four-volume Pléiade edition—directed by Jean-Yves Tadié
and containing an overwhelming amount of notes and textual variants
from Proust's manuscript and typewritten texts—has turned into the
more 'popular' paperback translation by Zhou, with footnotes being
kept to a minimum.

2.4   Xu's Translation

The first four volumes of *La Recherche* are currently available in Xu's
Translation (i.e. *Du côté de chez Swann, A l'ombre des jeunes filles en
fleurs, Le Côté de Guermantes*, and *Sodome et Gomorrhe*). As mentioned
before, the physical presentation of Xu's Translation based on the
Flammarion edition manifests a scholarly air. This translation is certainly
richer in paratextual materials. Apart from the footnotes, each volume
typically contains 140–300 pages of paratexts, which are generically broken down into the following sections:

Illustrations. Each volume includes 16 pages of illustrations printed
in colour on glossy paper. They are selected from Proust's family photos, photos of Combray and Cabourg, and notable artworks mentioned
in the novel. Where an illustration corresponds to a specific passage in
Proust's text, the page number is given in the caption.

Contents page.

Prefaces. This section is limited to the first volume only. Xu's
Translation still keeps André Maurois's preface, written for the first
Pléiade edition of *La Recherche* in 1954, which already features in the
First Translation. In many ways, this preface is indicative of the main
research interests in Proust Studies in the West in the 1950s. As soon
as it was translated and included in the *First Translation*, it became *the*
point of reference for the Chinese critical, creative, and popular receptions of Proust. In short, Maurois claims that 'time' is the primary theme

of *La Recherche*, and the book begins and ends with it. He continues that the other corresponding and complementary theme is 'memory', and Proust's major contribution is that he has taught us certain ways of remembering the past. Maurois (1954, xiii–xv) also puts considerable emphasis on Proust's health condition in relation to his monumental yet idiosyncratic work, a point which will widely circulate in the Chinese creative imagination of Proust.[24]

The first volume notably includes a second preface written by Milly for the Flammarion edition.[25] This preface is much more extensive (about 30 pages in the French original). In *selectively* recounting the main plots of the entire *Recherche*, Milly effectively outlines most Proustian themes, which significantly extends Maurois's thematic scope of 'time' and 'memory'. As we will discuss in the next chapter, had this preface been included in the *First Translation* (1989–1991), Proust might have inspired those mainland Chinese writers' creative imaginations rather differently.

Chronology. This chronology (also limited to the first volume), which covers Proust's family history and biography and major events in Proust Studies up until 2009, significantly expands the one in the original Flammarion edition. Xu has evidently consulted the chronology included in the Pléiade edition compiled by Tadié, as well as the one included in Tadié's biography of Proust (Tu 2010, 144).

Synoptic summary. The Chinese translation follows the wording in the Flammarion edition.

Indexes of characters' names/place names/artwork names. These three indexes, which do not feature in the Flammarion edition, are variably adapted from the Pléiade edition. The original proper names written in Roman letters are matched by the corresponding names written in Chinese characters phonetically transliterated by this particular translator. This solution could significantly reduce the confusion when readers cross-reference proper names in different translations. These indexes are not included in the *First Translation*.

Postscript. This section takes up pages depending on the volume. It contains a well-researched but succinct critical introduction to a selection of themes in each volume and an account of Xu's strategy for translating certain problematic French expressions, as well as his acknowledgment of the assistance and suggestions he received from colleagues. Xu specifically compares his linguistic solutions to those in the *First Translation*.

Two points of observation need highlighting: one on Milly's new preface written in 2009, and the other on the 'indexes' (especially compared to the English translation published by Penguin).

First, as suggested in our Introduction, the Chinese critical interest in Proust's work is to a certain extent culturally biased. Milly's preface could potentially benefit even the more seasoned Proust critics in China, as he repeatedly puts emphasis on the centrality of issues such as anti-Semitism and homosexuality, which are too often neglected in the Chinese reception of *La Recherche*. For example, this is how Milly (2009, 16) *thematically* summarizes the volume *Sodome et Gomorrhe I* in three sentences:

> Le narrateur fait retour sur sa découverte de l'homosexualité de M. de Charlus et des relations de celui-ci avec l'ancien giletier Jupien. La scène est longuement décrite. Dans un commentaire très oratoire, la condition des homosexuels est rapprochée de celle des Juifs.

> The narrator reverts to the discovery of M. de Charlus's homosexuality and his relations with the ex-waistcoat maker Jupien. The scene is described at length. In a very oratorical commentary, the condition of homosexuals and that of Jews are brought together. (My translation)

This kind of insightful remark fulfils more than a synoptic function, as it points out an entire area of Proustian research with which the Chinese readership is rather unfamiliar. Out of one entire page of 'synopsis' at the back of the original volume, Milly chooses to highlight this salient analogy between Jews and homosexuals, which is, incidentally, missing from the 'synopsis' of the Pléiade edition. The final section of this chapter, as a case study, will partly follow Milly's cue and examine the evolving strategies of translating (homo)sexuality into Chinese by comparing exemplary passages across the available translations.

If Maurois's preface is indicative of the relatively restrictive approaches to Proustian themes of the 1950s, still tinged by a moral sense of modesty or propriety, Milly's preface can be considered suggestive of the more 'liberal' and to some extent more 'honest' pluralistic readings of Proust's work from the 1980s onward. It must be noted that Milly does not accidentally stress the importance of the subject of homosexuality in *La Recherche*. Throughout the 1980s there was a flourishing body of critical work that directly dealt with this subject in Proust: J.E. Rivers's

Proust and the Art of Love (1980), Eva Ahlstedt's *La Pudeur en crise* (1985), and Antoine Compagnon's *Proust entre deux siècles* (1989), to name but a few monographs. In other words, there was an ideological shift between the two phases of Proust Studies. Similarly, as will be explored in the last section of this chapter, there was also a discursive shift in (homo)sexuality from the first to the two new Chinese translations of *La Recherche*. Milly's preface should heighten the translator's sensitivity to Proust's sophisticated sexual discourses and make him aware of his own strategy for translating them into Chinese. In fact, Xu (*XT IV*, 704–750) adds a further 45 page postscript to his translation of *Sodome et Gomorrhe*, largely recapitulating some of the main points on the issue of homosexuality in Proust formulated by Emily Eells-Ogée (1987, 11–51) and Antoine Compagnon (*RTP III*, 1185–1261).

Second, the decision to include the three indexes in the new Chinese translation again goes against the one taken by Prendergast's Penguin translation. It seems that, in order to attenuate the technical problem of the unstable phonetic rendition of proper names into Chinese, one simply has to compromise the quasi-phenomenology-of-reading approach to Proust's text in translation.[26] Roland Barthes sharply articulated the powers of essentialization, citation, and the exploration of Proust's proper nouns in relation to memory. In 'Proust et les noms', Barthes (1972, 124–125) insists, 'le Nom propre est lui aussi un signe, et non bien entendu, un simple indice qui désignerait, sans signifier' (the proper noun is a sign too, it is not, of course, a simple index that would designate a name without giving it meaning'). Both the 'natural' and 'cultural' motivations behind Proust's making of proper names explicated by Barthes—based on Western linguistic theories and the notion of 'Frenchness' (*francité*) respectively (128–131)—are bound to be lost in translation in the Chinese context, which stays outside European cultural referents. Unfortunately, in this case Proust's proper nouns can only be reduced to simple indices (as different from symbols).

Overall, the paratextual material in Xu's Translation aims not only to represent a more 'authentic' Proust, but also to provide Chinese readers, especially academics and students interested in Proust, with lucid guides and useful tools to further their research. In terms of translation philosophy, Xu seems to have adopted a more 'philological' approach to Proust's text (i.e. trying to be morphologically and syntactically 'faithful' to the original),[27] similar to that proposed by the Penguin translation, which inevitably reflects a tendency towards foreignizing conception, especially given the significant linguistic gap between French and

Chinese. In the next section and in the final case study, I will demonstrate how Xu's paratextual features and principles of translation noticeably differ from those adopted by Zhou.

2.5 ZHOU'S TRANSLATION

Zhou has also managed to translate three volumes of *La Recherche* (the first, second, and fifth volumes): *Du côté de chez Swann*, *A l'ombre des jeunes filles en fleurs*, and *La Prisonnière*. Different from the *First Translation* and Xu's Translation, Zhou has decided on a more literal rendition of the title *A la recherche du temps perdu*: *Zhuixun shiqu de shiguang* 追寻逝去的时光 (close to the English title *In Search of Lost Time*). In the translator's preface, Zhou ([2003] 2012, 454) uses examples from *La Recherche*'s English, German, Spanish, Italian, and Japanese translations to justify this decision. Just as in Scott Moncrieff's first English title, *Remembrance of Things Past*, the iconic Chinese title *Pursuing the Memory of Time/Years as Water/River*, in Michael Wood's words, 'actually contradicts one of the major claims of Proust's novel: that what we consciously summon up as remembrance is not memory, only a sort of mummified replacement of what is gone' (2013, 232). Zhou ([2003] 2012, 453) specifically mentions the fact that Proust himself followed his mother's advice on literal translation when translating two of Ruskin's works, although, as Elena Lozinsky (2013, 64, my translation) more recently points out, Proust is also keen to 'soumettre l'œuvre aux lois du français' ('subject work to the rules of French') and, with 'l'intuition raffinée' ('refined intuition'), to 'recréer le texte selon les règles de sa propre langue' ('recreate the text according to the rules of his own language'), thus consciously elaborating his own aesthetic through translation.

Zhou's Translation, published in paperback, offers limited paratextual material. Apart from the synopsis, each volume contains one short introduction written either by Zhou himself or an invited Chinese scholar. Compared to Xu's Translation, Zhou uses footnotes much more sparingly. For instance, on the first page of *Du côté de chez Swann*, Zhou makes no footnote, whereas Xu generously uses two footnotes of eight lines in total, in a rather encyclopaedic manner, to provide information on the French king François I and the Spanish king Charles V. A few pages further on, while Zhou simply footnotes 'kinétoscope' as 'early cinematic projector', Xu further adds that it was invented by Edison and his assistant Dickson in 1891. Xu footnotes so pedantically that he even points out occasional textual differences in the Pléiade edition, although his source is still the Flammarion edition. On Page 9, Xu explicitly states that in the Pléiade edition there is no section break before the paragraph beginning with 'à Combray' (*XT I*). Similarly, when Swann replies to Aunt Céline that people should put something like 'Pensées de Pascal' in the *Figaro* (*RTP I*, 26), in addition to a brief biographical entry on Pascal, Xu notes that the word 'Pensées' is italicized in the Pléiade edition, referring to Pascal's work. Zhou, by contrast, makes no reference to any of these points. Xu clearly demonstrates a scholarly concern over the variants of the source text and endeavours to extract from Proust's work as much factual knowledge of Western cultural heritage as possible for the benefit of the Chinese readership. For Zhou, perhaps, reading a Western canonical novel should be, after all, different from reading a Western cultural encyclopaedia.

Zhou's reformulation of *La Recherche*'s Chinese title may imply that he would advocate a more 'literal', 'foreignizing', and therefore philologically faithful translation of Proust's text. In reality, this observation more often than not goes curiously against his actual translation practice, in which a strong sense of domestication prevails. As we will see in the final case study, in order that the Chinese text flow more naturally, Zhou sometimes lengthens Proust's short sentences by adding or repeating certain adverbial phrases, which in fact changes the staccato rhythm of Proust's original prose. This is partly due to the fact that the Chinese language does not use verbal conjugation to express temporality, and so the translator may feel obliged to adverbially clarify the temporal situation. In modern vernacular Chinese there is a tendency to avoid sentences which are either too short or too long. Sentences should be made long enough to provide a context in which many homonymic characters and words can be rightly understood (especially aurally); if too long, due to the grammatical deficiency of hypotactical structures (e.g. a total lack of relative pronouns), the internal logical relations among different elements of the sentence will become confusing. Incidentally, the appearance and increased use of long sentences in modern and contemporary Chinese is said to ascribe to linguistic Westernization or Europeanization since the beginning of the twentieth century, which has become a source of worry for many contemporary Chinese linguistic purists.[28] But the solution to Proust's long sentences—shared by all three translations of *La Recherche*—has to be a paratactical one, which inevitably loses the grammatical rigour and suggestive chains of reflection in Proust's original.

We have seen Xu's scholarly paratextual efforts to represent an 'authentic' French and essentially foreign Proust in his translation. In a way, Zhou's minimization of paratexts favours domestication, as the Chinese reader is less likely to 'get distracted' by any real photos (of Combray and Cabourg) or encyclopaedic notes, which enhance the exotic appeal of Proust's work. Rather than insisting on a strict philological faithfulness, Zhou puts considerable emphasis on the *literarity* of the translated text. More concretely, Zhou often takes recourse to classical Chinese literary expressions to accommodate Proust's elegant French. In a recent conference on translating Proust, the Chinese Proust scholar Tu Weiqun, using *A l'ombre des jeunes filles en fleurs* as a primary example, meticulously demonstrated how Zhou translates some of Proust's words and expressions in an elegant language appropriated from canonical Chinese literary texts, such as the ancient poem 'The Shadow of Flowers' (花影) by Su Shi (苏轼) and, once again, *Dream of the Red Chamber* (红楼梦), the great classical novel which bears many similarities to Proust's *La Recherche*.[29] It is worth pointing out that, for contemporary Chinese readers, the evocation and appropriation of classical Chinese expressions in modern vernacular writing immediately and significantly increase the unfamiliar yet not exactly 'foreign' literariness of the text, a kind of 'autoexoticism'. Translating the foreign canon becomes an opportunity to rediscover Chinese cultural heritage.[30] As explained at the beginning of this chapter, classical Chinese (*wenyan*) has remained (along with Europeanization and vernacular Chinese) one of the three forces that keep shaping contemporary literary language today.[31] Therefore, what Zhou's translation strategy has announced is a dialogic and reconstructive relationship among translated, classical, and modern vernacular Chinese. Translation, in this light, has been 'enlisted in ambitious cultural projects, notably the development of a domestic language and literature' and 'contributed to the (re)invention of domestic literary discourses' (Venuti 2002 [1998], 76). This translation of Proust could be said to function as a coordinator in the internal debate of national literatures and languages and to '"offer them an image of themselves they could not otherwise have', but which, we may add, they nonetheless desire" (ibid., 77).[32] The recourse to Chinese cultural heritage in Zhou's Translation signals a process of 'mirroring' or self-recognition, as well as misrecognition, and helps shape the formation of modern Chinese domestic subjects (i.e. the reader) (ibid., 76–77). Mary Orr (2003, 160) also utilizes the 'metaphor of transformed articulations [like butterfly from its chrysalis]' to describe 'Chinese and Japanese views of translation', which prioritize the 'enhancement of its own cultural depths by integrating the other'. Chapter 3 will further examine the extent to which such a translation philosophy would help unleash mainland Chinese writers' creative energy.

2.6   ZHOU'S OTHER TRANSLATIONS OF LA RECHERCHE

In addition to the three translated volumes of *La Recherche*, Zhou has published an abridged edition of *Du côté de chez Swann* and translated two volumes of Stephane Heuet's comic-book adaptation of *La Recherche* (published as one volume in China). Indeed, Proust's novel has been frequently adapted to other artistic media. Apart from Heuet's comic-book rendition, the novel—or sometimes certain episodes of it—has been most notably adapted into a play, films, and even ballet (Beugnet and Schmid 2004; Schmid 2013). However, the phenomenon of publishing one novel 'anthologically' (i.e. offering a selection of texts in the same literary medium and, in Zhou's case, from a single volume of the novel) is rare. The selection process is particularly revealing of not only the translator's understanding and intention, but also, to a certain degree, Chinese readers' interests and expectations.

It may be best to start with Zhou's (2009) 'Abridgement Notice', as follows:

《去斯万家那边》, 是七卷本长篇小说《追寻逝去的时光》中的第一卷。

这一卷共分三个部分: 贡布雷; 斯万的爱情; 地方与地名: 地名。

全卷译成中文, 约有36万字。这个节选本, 主要对象是有意阅读这卷小说, 而又苦于抽不出时间, 或者面对这样一卷既不重情节又不分章节的小说, 心里多少有些犹豫的读者。为了尽可能地让读者领略到普鲁斯特独特的文体魅力, 节本采用"大跨度"的节选方式, 即先在全书中选取将近二十个我认为特别精彩的大段, 每个大段的文字一字不易, 完全保留原书中的面貌, 然后用尽可能简洁的文字连缀这些段落, 并作一些必要的交代。

节选后的内容, 就字数而言约为《去斯万家那边》全书的四分之一

Du côté de chez Swann is the first of the seven volumes of the novel *A la recherche du temps perdu*.

This volume contains three parts: Combray; Swann's Love; Place and Place-names: the Names.

The entire volume has been translated into Chinese, about 360 thousand Chinese characters. The main targeted readers of this abridged edition are those who intend to read the novel but bitterly lack the time, or those who feel rather irresolute about venturing into such a 'chapterless' novel which doesn't place emphasis on plots. In order for the Chinese reader to be able to appreciate Proust's unique literary charm as much as possible, this abridged edition has adopted a 'great-leap' selecting method: selecting nearly twenty [eighteen, to be exact] extensive passages, which I consider particularly exciting, from the original translation, and keeping them as they are; then using the most succinct language possible to link these passages together while clarifying a few necessary details [of the plot].

The content after the abridgement, in terms of the number of words, takes up a quarter of the original translation of *Du côté de chez Swann*.

Zhou's fundamental intention to attract more Chinese readers of Proust is clearly expressed in this notice. In many ways, the fact that Zhou *can* so confidently truncate Proust's '"chapterless" novel which doesn't place emphasis on plots' and almost authorially turn *Du côté de chez Swann* into a coherent narrative of 18 sections linked by a kind of theatrical aside, throws light on Zhou's perception of a certain particularity of Proust's literary aesthetic, such as the textual malleability or plasticity that has fascinated genetic critics for many decades. After all, this 'anthological' adaptation has not yet happened to other long and/or difficult Western canonical novels such as *War and Peace* and *Ulysses*.

If we check Zhou's selected passages against the synopsis (provided by the new Pléiade edition), perhaps one of the most striking omissions in Zhou's selection is the famous prologue. It is only summarized in the following words:

有很长一段时间, 叙述者马塞尔睡得挺早。夜间醒来, 在周围的一片黑暗中, 回忆的闸门打开了。他把夜的大部分时间, 用来回想往昔的生活。此刻的思绪回到了巴黎的姑婆家。(Zhou 2009, 1)

For a long time, the narrator Marcel goes to bed quite early. When he wakes up at night, surrounded by darkness, memory opens its door. He spends a large part of the night recalling his past life. At this moment, his thought is directed back to his grand-aunt's house in Paris.

For many Proust scholars, the prologue is indispensable to the understanding of the architectonics of Proust's novel as a whole. It is a crucial point of departure from which to explore Proust's narrative technique, notably the distinction between the narrator's and the protagonist's voices. The fact that Zhou chooses to begin his selection with 'soirée de famille' ('family evenings') (*RTP I*, 1524; *PT I*, 448) almost necessarily implies that the narrative is reconstructed fundamentally from the perspective of the protagonist rather than the narrator.[33] In the 'aside', Zhou clearly blends the identities of the narrator, the protagonist, and the author together, which would irritate many Proust scholars. Zhou may have omitted the prologue out of practical concerns, as the narrator in the prologue makes references to many other 'chambres' ('bedrooms') he has stayed in throughout *La Recherche*, which may not seem immediately relevant to the subsequent content of the first volume. By the same token, passages which contain extensive references to other volumes of *La Recherche*, such as the reverie of Venice, are often omitted. There seems to be a conscientious effort to make this abridged volume as independent as possible from the rest of the novel, so that readers of this volume may be less disturbed by any apparent sense of 'incompleteness'. Incidentally, seasoned Proust readers may be slightly amused to notice how Zhou's omission echoes, at least superficially, Alfred Humblot's candid remark in his correspondence with Louis de Robert (who acted as an intermediary between Proust and the editor at Ollendorff): 'Cher ami, je suis peut-être bouché à l'émeri, mais je ne puis comprendre qu'un monsieur puisse employer trente pages à décrire comment il se tourne et se retourne dans son lit avant de trouver le sommeil' ('Dear friend, I may be thick as a brick, but I really cannot understand how a gentleman could spend 30 pages writing about how he tosses and turns restlessly in bed before falling asleep') (as quoted in Tadié 1996, 689).

In Zhou's selection, there is a general tendency to favour descriptive passages on the external physical world over passages exploring human intimacy and inner psychology. Five out of the eight selected passages from 'Combray' dwell on natural landscapes and physical objects. In comparison, Proust's psychoanalytic-infused episode of 'le drame du coucher à Combray' ('Bedtime at Combray') (*RTP I*, 1523; *PT I*, 448) is kept at a minimum. The complex development of Swann's obsessive love for Odette is largely truncated. The scenario jumps directly from Swann's first hearing of 'la petite phrase' ('the little phrase') (*RTP I*, 1526; *PT I*, 449) to 'La soirée Saint-Euverte' ('An evening at the Marquise de Saint-Euverte') (*RTP I*, 1527; *PT I*, 450), at the end of which Swann hears the last movement of the sonata. The nearly 50 pages of Swann's psychological struggle, especially in relation to his jealousy, are summarized in two sentences: '得知奥黛特是个靠情人供养的女人，斯万感到痛苦、忧郁。威尔迪兰夫人的沙龙，现在成了斯万和奥黛特约会的障碍' ('informed that Odette is a kept woman, Swann feels unwell and sad. The Verdurins' salon now becomes an obstacle for Swann and Odette's meeting' (Zhou 2009, 116–117). Given such a selection preference, it is not surprising that the Montjouvain passage which features the first description of a homosexual act in the novel has been largely ignored by Zhou. As mentioned before, the importance of homo- and bisexuality in Proust's work is poorly received in China.

Zhou's selection necessarily rearranges the narrative movement and temporality of Proust's original work, which is most systematically elaborated by Gérard Genette in *Narrative Discourse: An Essay in Method*. Genette duly observes four narrative movements in *La Recherche*: ellipsis, descriptive pause, scene, and summary (1980, 94–112). Zhou's selection principles evidently favour those Proustian moments of descriptive pause which reflect 'a narrative and analysis of the perceptual activity of the character contemplating: of his impressions, progressive discoveries, shifts in distance and perspective, errors and corrections, enthusiasms or disappointments, etc.' (ibid., 102) Different from dramatic scenes in traditional narratives, Genette characterizes Proustian scenes as the ones in which 'action […] is almost completely obliterated in favor of psychological and social characterization' (ibid., 111). The dominance of the scene in the novel's internal organization has been further examined in detail by Jean-Yves Tadié (2003, 372–383). Zhou, by contrast, frequently cuts out extensive details in the already very limited number of selected scenes. Given the role of the Proustian scene as 'temporal hearth' or 'magnetic pole for all sorts of supplementary information and incidents' (Genette 1980, 111), the narrative movement affected by the Proustian scene arguably registers the greatest temporal change in Zhou's selection. Instead, much of the volume's internal organization has to rely on Zhou's added 'asides' to push the narrative forward, as they are used to both sustain a clear temporal frame—Genette's 'explicit ellipses' (e.g. 'long years', 'many years') (ibid., 206)—and provide an acceleration from one section to another—Genette's summary. Thus Zhou's interventions inevitably render Proust's narrative technique much less original. In comparison, as we will soon see, these kinds of 'asides' are completely absent in Shen's *Essential Selection*.

Although Zhou states in the Abridgement Notice that his 'asides' are meant to ensure smooth transitions between sections, 'clarifying a few necessary details [of the plot]', they frequently serve as a 'reader's guide' to, in Zhou's words, 'Proust's unique literary charm'—far more than a mere synopsis. Consider his clarification ahead of 'Lecture de George Sand' ('A reading of George Sand') (*RTP I*, 1524; *PT I*, 448):

有一天晚上，妈妈留在小马塞尔的卧室里陪他，这个温馨的夜晚留在了记忆之中。

但叙述者知道，理性的回忆是无法保存往事的。往事隐匿在智力范围之外，在某个我们意想不到的物质对象之中。只有不由自主的回忆，才能让往事从记忆中清晰地浮现出来。小玛德莱娜唤起的无意识联想，就是这样一种不由自主的回忆。(Zhou 2009, 13–14)

One evening, Maman stays with little Marcel in his bedroom. This warm and sweet evening stays in his memory.

But the narrator understands that it's impossible to preserve the past through rational recollection. The past is hidden outside the realm of intelligence, in some material object that we cannot anticipate. Only involuntary remembering can enable the past to emerge vividly from the memory. The unconscious associations evoked by the little Madeleine are this kind of involuntary memory.

Zhou briefly introduces a central Proustian concept in this passage, namely the distinction that the narrator makes between voluntary and involuntary memories. This effectively makes the following section— from the reading of George Sand up to the tasting of the madeleine—a detailed demonstration of the point Zhou makes in the preceding 'aside'. Such introductions give the selected passage a clear *purpose*, which many 'confused' readers of *La Recherche* perhaps often wonder about.

Does Zhou's strategy help Chinese readers 'appreciate Proust's unique literary charm'? On the one hand, readers are indeed spared the frequent anxiety of getting lost in the textual labyrinth of Proust's seemingly banal plot, and we can consequently rechannel that energy to Proust's minute textual details. This kind of literary appreciation, on the other hand, can only stay superficial. A much deeper or more *affective* appreciation of *La Recherche* will have to precisely involve the unsettling experience of reading the novel, which is, to return to Prendergast's (2002, x) remark, 'co-extensive with the experience of his narrator-hero *in* the novel, namely the repeated pattern of forgetting and remembering, getting lost and refinding one's way, and that detailed "guides" sit uneasily with this important dimension of the work'.

As mentioned before, Zhou also translated the first two volumes of Stéphane Heuet's comic-book adaption of *La Recherche*, published in China as one single volume.[34] Heuet's adaption is a highly condensed visualization of Proust's work. Rather than selecting *passages* from *Du côté de chez Swann* like Zhou, Heuet selects Proust's original *sentences and phrases* as the text appearing in balloons and captions.[35] Heuet's seventy-page illustration actually covers more plots than Zhou's two-hundred-page selection. Interestingly, Zhou's translation of Heuet's comic-book adaptation—published 3 years before Zhou's own abridged edition—does not seem to have influenced Zhou's choice of passages. Heuet tries to include as many plots as possible, which is, of course, very different from Zhou's intention. However, Zhou would have been aware of the *proportion* that Heuet gives to certain scenes in his adaptation. In many ways, the disparity between Zhou's selection of what he considers to be 'particularly exciting' passages and Heuet's illustrative emphases indirectly reflects a broader cultural and *temporal* difference in the reception of Proust's work, especially in terms of socio-political ideologies, which I briefly touched upon in the Introduction. The Montjouvain passage is an excellent example: whereas Zhou completely cuts it out, Heuet devotes three out of 70 pages—proportionally even more significant than Proust's original—to this first homosexual scene in *La Recherche*. Our final case study of the Montjouvain passage will focus precisely on the gradually evolving translation strategy and reception of Proust's representation of sadomasochism and homosexuality in China.

2.7   SHEN'S ESSENTIAL SELECTION

Zhou is neither the first nor the only Chinese scholar to decide on an abridged version of Proust's work. Shen selectively translated *La Recherche* back in 1992, *seemingly* condensing the entire novel (around 2300 pages according to one edition of the *First Translation*) into a single volume of nearly 550 pages. Shen's *Essential Selection* was published under a rather different framework: it is only one out of seventy contributions to a much wider translation project entitled 'Twentieth-Century French Literature Series', directed by Liu Mingjiu. The publisher's statement on the cover makes the purpose of this series crystal clear:

本译丛以系统地介绍20世纪法国文学为任务，选择各种倾向、各种流派、各种艺术风格，有影响、有特色的作品，以期为中国读者勾勒出20世纪文学的一个比较清晰的轮廓。

The present series undertakes the task of systemically introducing twentieth-century French literature, selecting influential and distinctive works that cover a wide variety of tendencies, schools, and artistic styles. We hope to be able to offer Chinese readers a relatively clear overview of twentieth-century French literature.

This statement is further elaborated in the general preface of the series by Liu (newly written in 2010), in which he surveys the various developments of twentieth-century French literature (and their associated writers): naturalism, psychological realism, psychological modernism, the *nouveau roman*, resistance and left-wing progressive literatures, philosophical literatures (e.g. absurdism, existentialism), and so on. Liu also reveals that this ambitious translation project was in many ways born out of public demand. Numerous established Chinese writers sent in queries regarding the progress of the project, and the series has been 'particularly beloved of creative writing circles' ('特别得到了文学创作界的青睐') (Liu [1992] 2013, 1). This latter observation will become increasingly important when we discuss the ideological implications of contemporary Chinese writers' intertextual practices in Chap. 3.

The second preface, written in 1990 by the same author, is dedicated to Proust's work alone, which once again manifests strong influences from André Maurois's preface to the 1954 Pléiade edition of *La Recherche*, as well as his critical work *De Proust à Camus* (1963). While dedicating 15 pages to introducing many artistic particularities of *La Recherche*, Liu as the general editor of the book series ostensibly tries to tone down any excessive glorification of Proust's work: 'to say that the literature of our century still hasn't got out of Proust's shadow is obviously an exaggeration, but it would not indeed be exaggerating if we say that Proust invented something new for the art of the novel' ('如果认为我们这个世纪的文学还没有走出普鲁斯特所投射的身影，那显然是夸大其词，但如果说普鲁斯特在小说艺术中发明了一些新的东西，　那确实并不言之过分') (ibid.). Liu's main intention is to critically introduce the 'grand narrative' of twentieth-century French literary history; rather than tending to idolize the writer, readers are encouraged to perceive Proust fundamentally in relation to many *other* writers before, around, and after his time—a kind of 'Proust among the stars', to borrow the title of Malcolm Bowie's book.

However, despite the general editor's references to Maurois's preface, the translator of the *Essential Selection*, Shen, specifies that the present translation is based on the new 1987 Pléiade edition of *La Recherche*:

> [...] 各章标题除部分采用原著卷目，其余是选译者参照《七星文库》编者编写的提要段落标题所加的。为了尊重原著，各段编排、句号分布都未作变动(除了极个别的地方)，另外，为了不改变句号，不得不在冗长的句子中扩大分号的用途，尚希见谅。(*ES*, 2)

> [...] some of the chapter titles are derived from the original volume titles, others are adapted from the synopsis provided by the editor of the Pléiade edition. In order to respect the original, no change has been made about the arrangements of paragraphs and full stops (with only a few exceptions). Furthermore, to avoid changing the full stops [in the original], the translator has to increase the use ofsemicolon for long sentences [in the translation], and hopes that readers can understand [this decision].

Therefore, an important difference between Shen's *Essential Selection* and the *First Translation* (despite the former's being published only 1 year after the latter) is that of the source text. Moreover, Shen proposes a solution to Proust's long sentences, which may render his Chinese translation syntactically unidiomatic to the degree that he feels obliged to apologize in advance. It is interesting that Shen should show such keen awareness of Proust's original punctuation. As we know, one remarkable difference between the old and new Pléiade editions is the latter's editorial decision to get rid of the commas added by the former editors in their attempt to increase the readability of Proust's complex syntax and unconventional use of French punctuation. But in any case, Shen still has to add more commas and semicolons in his Chinese translation, even though he claims to be 'faithful' to the number of full stops in the original.

However, to say that Shen's *Essential Selection* condenses the *entire Recherche* is actually quite misleading. In reality, the selection is informed by Proust's tripartite vision of the novel in 1913, namely *Du côté de chez Swann*, *Le Côté de Guermantes*, and *Le Temps retrouvé*. Shen's volume comprises seven chapters, which somehow gives Chinese readers an illusion that each chapter may correspond to one volume of the entire *Recherche*: 'Combray' (Shen's translation literally reads 'Combray Night'), 'Du côté de chez Swann' ('The Way by Swann's'), 'Du côté de Guermantes' ('The Guermantes Way'),[36] 'Un Amour de Swann'

('A Love of Swann's'), 'La Soirée chez les Guermantes' ('Dinner with the Guermantes'), 'Le Temps retrouvé I' ('Finding Time Again I') (largely covering 'Adoration Perpétuelle' ['Perpetual Adoration'] and 'Le Bal de tête' ['Masked Ball']), and 'Le Temps retrouvé II' ('Finding Time Again II') (the very end of the novel where the narrator decides to write *the* book).

Finally, to pave the way for our following case study, it must be pointed out that, unlike Zhou's selection, Shen does not omit the Montjouvain passage. But Shen does omit certain details of Mlle. Vinteuil and her lesbian lover's sexual act, and shows a tendency to tone down or even evade Proust's sexual vocabulary, which will form interesting comparisons and contrasts with other Chinese translations. Meanwhile, the passages portraying explicit male homosexual acts, notably involving Saint-Loup, Charlus, Jupien, and Morel, which feature prominently in the published volume *Le Temps retrouvé*, are entirely cut out in *Essential Selection*. These passages, much like Proust's posthumously published volumes from *Sodome et Gomorrhe* to *La Fugitive*, are excised perhaps for technical rather than ideological reasons, since these male homosexual characters (as well as other lesbian characters) do not saliently figure in Proust's tripartite vision of the novel.

2.8   TRANSLATING MONTJOUVAIN: A SHOWCASE

The Montjouvain scene is an ideal point of departure from which to broach the subject of Chinese sexual discourses for two main reasons: first, its thematic particularity in Proust's work and its thematic singularity in *Du côté de chez Swann*, notably sadism and homosexuality; second, its wide availability across all major Chinese translations of *La Recherche* (except for Zhou's abridged translation of *Du côté de chez Swann*), which cover a time span from the late 1980s until now. But before venturing into the area of evolving Chinese sexual discourses, let us take the opportunity to substantiate some of the observations on the different Chinese translations outlined in previous sections, with examples from the passage in question.[37]

First, all available translations demonstrate a consistent reliance on a *paratactic* approach to Proust's long and essentially *hypotactic* sentences. In practice, the translators either resolutely break them into shorter and independent sentences, which would seem more natural to the Chinese reading habit, or they significantly increase the use of commas or semicolons in the translated text, which creates a superficial semblance of Proust's notoriously long sentences. Of course, whether the latter option is syntactically more 'faithful' to Proust's original is very much debatable. Even with an increased use of commas or semicolons, the syntactical structure of the translated text remains essentially paratactic as the various syntactical elements within one sentence do not necessarily bear any *subordinate relations* with each other. Consider the following sentence:

C'était par un temps très chaud; mes parents, qui avaient dû s'absenter pour toute la journée, m'avaient dit de rentrer aussi tard que je voudrais; et étant allé jusqu'à la mare de Montjouvain où j'aimais revoir les reflets du toit de tuile, je m'étais étendu à l'ombre et endormi dans les buissons du talus qui domine la maison, là où j'avais attendu mon père autrefois, un jour qu'il était allé voir M. Vinteuil. (*RTP I*, 157)

It was during a spell of very hot weather; my parents, who had had to leave for the whole day, had told me to return home as late as I pleased; and having gone as far as the Montjouvain pond, where I liked to look at the reflections of the tile of roof again, I had lain down in the shade and fallen asleep among the bushes of the hillock that overlooks the house, in the same spot where I had once waited for my father on a day when he had gone to see M. Vinteuil. (*PT I*, 160)

Proust employs four commas, two semicolons, and one full stop. Let's compare it to Shen's translation in the *Essential Selection*:

这一天, 天气非常热, 我的父母要出门一整天, 对我讲, 我随便多晚回家都行; 我一直走到蒙菇万的池塘边, 我喜欢观看池中瓦屋顶的倒影, 我爬到俯瞰万特伊先生那栋房子的山坡上,   以前有一天我父亲来看望他时我就在这里等候的, 我躺在山坡灌木丛的阴凉处, 居然睡着了。(*ES*, 75)

Ce jour, il fait très chaud, mes parents sont dehors pendant toute la journée, me disant, que je peux rentrer aussi tard que je voudrais; je marche jusqu'à la mare de Montjouvain, j'aime revoir les reflets du toit de tuile, je monte dans la colline dominant la maison de M. Vinteuil, auparavant un jour [que] mon père lui rend visite j'attends ici, je m'étends à l'ombre dans les buissons du talus dans la colline, en fait m'endors.

This day, it is very hot, my parents are outside for the whole day, saying to me, that I can come back as late as I'd like; I walk as far as the Montjouvain pond, I like to look at the reflections of the tile of roof again, I climb up to the hill dominating M. Vinteuil's house, previously on a day my father visits him I wait here, I lie down in the shadow of the bushes of the embankment on the hill, actually fall asleep.[38]

As we know, Shen claims to be most 'faithful' to Proust's use of full stops—but full stops *only*—and he also apologizes for his overuse of semicolons (in this sentence he actually uses fewer semicolons than Proust's original). So, in his translation there are nine commas (as opposed to four in Proust's original) and one semicolon (instead of two). Parataxis often implies a greater flexibility to rearrange syntactical elements, which is shown in the reordering of the second half of the sentence. Other translations demonstrate similar rearrangements. However, it is quite intriguing as to why Shen so absolutely prioritizes full stops over other punctuation such as commas and semicolons in his 'respect' for the original. Reading the translated text, one would hardly perceive any change of prosaic rhythm if we replaced at least one or two of the commas with full stops, since Proust's original rhythm—heavily dependent on hypotactical constructions—is already broken once the relative pronouns have been removed.

In sharp contrast to Shen's 'full-stop fidelity' is Zhou's sinicized repunctuation:

那天挺热, 家里的大人有事外出, 整天不在家, 所以对我说爱玩多久都行。我一路来到蒙舒凡的那个池塘, 我爱看那小乌瓦顶的倒影。看着看着, 我躺在灌木的阴影里, 不知不觉睡着了; 这个斜坡正对着凡特伊先生的屋子, 我跟父亲一起去看凡特伊先生那回, 我曾经在这儿等过父亲。(*ZT I*, 160)

Ce jour-là [il] fait assez chaud, les grandes personnes de la famille sont engagées dans des affaires dehors, pendant toute la journée absentes, donc me disant de jouer aussi longtemps que je voudrais. Je marche jusqu'à la mare de Montjouvain, j'aime revoir les reflets du toit de tuile. En regardant, je m'étends à l'ombre de buissons du talus, m'endors à mon insu; cette colline fait face à la maison de M. Vinteuil, j'accompagne mon père pour voir M. Vinteuil autrefois, un jour [que] j'attends ici mon père.

That day is quite hot, the big people of the family are out on some business, for the whole day not at home, so telling me that I can play for as long as I like. I walk as far as the Montjouvain pond, I like to look at the reflections of the tile of roof. While looking at them, I lie down in the shadow of the bushes of embankment, fall asleep without my knowing it; the hill faces M. Vinteuil's house, that time when I and father visit M. Vinteuil together, I wait for father here then.

Zhou breaks Proust's original sentence into three, with eight commas in total and one semicolon which does not correspond to either of the two semicolons found in Proust's original. If we compare the above two translations, a similar paratactic rhythm—whether marked by commas, semicolons, or full stops—is perceivable. The distinctive grammatical and semantic values ascribed to each of these punctuation marks are less rigid in Chinese than in most of their European counterparts. And Zhou's repunctuation of the translated text clearly reflects Chinese reading habits. In his discussion with the established writer Chen Cun on Proust, Zhou suggested that he would seriously consider breaking up sentences which contain more than twenty-four Chinese characters as he would try to be more 'considerate' to the reader.[39] In fact, Zhou not only breaks up Proust's long sentences, he also takes the liberty of breaking up Proust's long paragraphs. Elsewhere in his translation, Zhou notably turns all the long conversations within one paragraph into independent paragraphs according to the speaker. Zhou's emphasis on the notion of *fluency* in the target language, which aims to facilitate the Chinese reader's cognitive processing of the text, is further reflected in his frequent utilization of Chinese idiomatic expressions: 'the big people of the family' ('家里的大人') for 'mes parents' ('my parents'), 'out on some business' ('有事外出') for 's'absenter' ('go out'), 'jouer' (玩, 'play') instead of 'rentrer' ('get back'), and the added Chinese adverbial expression 不知不觉 ('without my knowing it', or more literally, 'without either knowing or sensing').

Meanwhile, in translations other than Shen's *Essential Selection*, there are infrequent cases in which Proust's short paratactical sentences are technically *lengthened* by a change of punctuation from full stop to comma or semicolon. For example, the sentence 'bientôt son amie entra' may have been considered 'too short and simple' or 'too plain' as an independent sentence in Chinese. Both Zhou and the translators of the *First Translation* take the liberty of changing Proust's full stop to a comma, so that the sentence as one element can paratactically flow into the next sentence, forming a chain of actions: 'bientôt son amie entra[,] Mlle Vinteuil l'accueillit sans se lever, ses deux mains derrière la tête et se recula sur le bord opposé du sofa comme pour lui faire une place' ('Soon her friend came in[,] Mlle Vinteuil greeted her without standing up, both hands behind her head, and moved to the end of the sofa as though to make room for her') (*RTP I*, 158; *PT I*, 161; *FT I*, 118; *ZT I*, 161).

Another syntactic feature worthy of our attention is the translator's frequent insertion of additional adverbial phrases as well as conjunctions. This is particularly the case in Zhou's Translation. For example, as he translates Proust's sentence 'elle était en grand deuil, car son père était mort depuis peu. Nous n'étions pas allés la voir [...]' ('she was in mourning, because her father had died a short time before. We had not gone to see her') (*RTP I*, 157; *PT I*, 160), Zhou specifically repeats the phrase 'during the period of mourning' ('丧父期间') at the beginning of the second sentence. Presumably, the added adverbial phrase approximately reflects Proust's use of the pluperfect tense in the original, as the Chinese language does not use verbal conjugations to express temporality. Another example is found in the paragraph beginning with 'dans l'échancrure de son corsage de crêpe Mlle Vinteuil sentit que son amie piquait un baiser' ('Mlle Vinteuil felt her friend plant a kiss in the opening of her crêpe blouse') (*RTP I*, 160; *PT I*, 162), before which Zhou adds the expression 'as soon as the phrase ends' ('话音刚落') (*ZT I*, 163), repeating the word 'phrase' from the last sentence of the precedent paragraph. This 'phrase', which refers to 'Mademoiselle me semble avoir des pensées bien lubriques, ce soir' ('Mademoiselle seems to have rather libidinous thoughts this evening') (ibid.), is already a repetition from their previous experience, 'qu'elle [Mlle. Vinteuil] avait entendue autrefois dans la bouche de son amie' ('[which] she [Mlle. Vinteuil] had heard before on her friend's lips') (ibid.). By linking the two paragraphs with an added expression, Zhou effectively enhances the logical progression of Mlle. Vinteuil and her girlfriend's erotic foreplay from words to actions, from a 'phrase' to a 'kiss'. Such adverbial (temporal, spatial, and sequential) additions are consistently applied in Zhou's Translation. To a certain extent, they also contribute to the elongation of Proust's sentences in translation.[40]

However, despite all the scholarly and collaborative efforts, technical mistranslations persist in all the available translations. We do not even have to look beyond the Montjouvain passage for examples.

Errors in the *First Translation* have not necessarily been corrected in the new translations. For example, when Mlle. Vinteuil tries to seduce her girlfriend to join her on the sofa, she seems to 'lui [her girlfriend] imposer une *attitude* qui lui était peut-être importune. Elle pensa que son amie aimerait peut-être mieux être loin d'elle sur une chaise' ('be forcing her friend into a *position* that might be annoying to her. She thought her friend might prefer to be some distance away from her on a chair') (*RTP I*, 158, *PT I*, 161, my italics). 'Attitude' in this context leans towards the meaning of 'bodily position or posture' rather than 'a settled way of thinking or feeling', although the former *could* potentially reflect the latter. Nevertheless, the Chinese word used in both the *First Translation* and Xu's Translation, *taidu* (态度), only refers to the latter, which appears strange in the translated text. *Zitai* (姿态), literally 'posture and attitude', would be a near equivalent of 'attitude' in this case. When translating the sentence 'elle [the narrator's mother] éprouvait un veritable chagrin et songeait avec effroi à celui *autrement amer que* devait éprouver Mlle Vinteuil tout mêlé du remords d'avoir à peu près tué son père' ('she was moved by real sorrow and thought with horror of the *far more bitter* sorrow that Mlle Vinteuil must be feeling, mingled as it was with remorse at having more or less killed her father') (*RTP I*, 158; *PT I*, 161, my italics), both Xu and the translators of the *First Translation* misunderstand the construction 'autrement + adjective + que' as '(utterly) different from', which almost reverses the meaning of the original text.[41]

Meanwhile, both Xu's and Zhou's individual translations also contain mistakes which do not feature in the *First Translation*. For instance, when the narrator spots Mlle. Vinteuil's room after waking up from an afternoon slumber, he remarks, 'en face de moi, à quelques centimètres de moi, dans cette chambre où son père avait reçu le mien et dont elle avait fait son petit salon à elle' ('opposite me, a few centimetres from me, in the room in which her father had entertained mine and which she had made into her own little drawing-room') (*RTP I*, 157; *PT I*, 160). Zhou mistranslates 'le mien' ('mine', i.e. the narrator's father) as the protagonist-narrator himself, and throws in extra information on the nature of Mlle. Vinteuil's room by rendering 'son petit salon à elle' ('her own little drawing-room') as 'the little drawing room she now uses to receive her secret friend' ('这个房间她现在改作接待密友的小客厅了') (*ZT I*, 160), hence being more explicit about Mlle. Vinteuil's lesbian relationship with her friend. Likewise, the narrator observes the family trait of blue eyes passing on from the grandmother to the father and to Mlle. Vinteuil as follows: 'c'était la ressemblance de son visage, les yeux bleus de *sa mère à lui qu'il lui* avait transmis comme un bijou de famille' ('[it] was the resemblance between her face and his, *his own mother's* blue eyes which he had handed down to her like a family jewel') (*RTP I*, 162; *PT I*, 165, my italics). Proust's use of pronouns can indeed appear rather confusing. The first 'lui', which is the stressed pronoun for the masculine third-person singular, in fact refers to the father, and so does the 'il' after the relative pronoun 'que'; the second 'lui', which is the indirect object that can be either masculine or feminine, should refer to the daughter in this context. Xu mistranslates this family heritage as 'the blue eyes of *her* mother' ('她的母亲的蓝眼睛') (*XT I*, 164) rather than the grandmother on her father's side, which misses Proust's subtle portrayal of Mlle. Vinteuil's complex sadist psychology in relation to her antagonism to the father, concretized in her spitting on the father's portrait as part of the 'profanations rituelles' ('ritual profanations') (*RTP I*, 160; *PT I*, 163) to gain sexual pleasure with her girlfriend. In Douglas B. Saylor's (1993, 93) words,

> [...] spitting on the replication of her father's appearance is like spitting on herself [due to the resemblance of their faces and blue eyes]. The father's portrait serves as an image of the father, but also an exteriorization of the ego. Through identification with the father, spitting on the portrait becomes a rejection of her own self.

As mentioned before, both errors are absent from the *First Translation*.

Of course, lesbianism or homosexuality in general is not necessarily a comfortable subject. It is one of the areas of *La Recherche* which frequently received vehement criticism in Proust's lifetime, and certain translations of the novel are still censored for that reason today. A concrete example is found in the passage we have already touched upon:

> Mademoiselle me semble avoir des pensées bien lubriques, ce soir', finit-elle par dire, répétant sans doute une phrase qu'elle avait entendue autrefois dans la bouche de son amie.
>
> *Dans l'échancrure de son corsage de crêpe Mlle Vinteuil sentit que son amie piquait un baiser, elle poussa un petit cri, s'échappa, et elles se poursuivirent en sautant, faisant voleter leurs larges manches comme des ailes et gloussant et piaillant comme des oiseaux amoureux.* (*RTP I*, 159–160, my italics)
>
> —Mademoiselle seems to have rather libidinous thoughts this evening, she said at last, probably repeating a phrase she had heard before on her friend's lips.
>
> *Mlle Vinteuil felt her friend plant a kiss in the opening of her crêpe blouse, she gave a little cry, broke free, and they began chasing each other, leaping, fluttering their wide sleeves like wings, and clucking and cheeping like two amorous birds.* (*PT I*, 162, my italics)

2 PROUST AND THE CHINESE TRANSLATIONS 47

The translator of the *Essential Selection*, Shen, notably cuts out the sentence in italics and combines the two paragraphs together:

"我觉得小姐今晚春情大发," 她终于进出这么一句, 大概是重复以前从她女友口中听来的一声,赶紧躲开, 于是两人跳跳蹦蹦追逐起来, 宽大的衣袖像翅膀似的飞舞, 她们格格地笑着, 喳喳叫着, 活像两只调情的小鸟。[42]
(*Essential Selection*, 77–78)

For someone who claims to be faithful to Proust's use of full stops, this change of paragraph and punctuation has to be an exception. Shen is evidently not being entirely honest when he affirms in the translator's note that the selected passages or paragraphs are 'absolutely complete, without any expurgation' ('所选章节或段落全是完整的, 没有任何删节') (*ES*, 2, my translation). As can be seen, the concrete action of the 'lesbian kiss' is left out, leaving only the more figurative part of the 'foreplay'. How the Proustian themes of homosexuality and sadism are translated into Chinese is our next investigation.

2.9   DE-PATHOLOGIZING PERVERSION: PROUST'S SEXUAL DISCOURSES AND THEIR CHINESE TRANSLATIONS

As has been argued at the beginning of this chapter, since the 1980s, which marks the proper beginning of Proust Studies in China, Chinese critical interests in Proust's works have revolved almost exclusively around traditional Proustian themes such as time and memory, and the Modernist literary style commonly known as 'stream of consciousness'. These aspects of Proust's work seem to resonate particularly well with the long line of Chinese aesthetic and philosophical traditions, as emblematized by the Chinese title for *À la recherche* as, literally, *Pursuing the Memory of Time/Years as (Flowing) Water* (追忆似[逝]水年华). In the West, in comparison, perhaps partly reflecting the wider political and cultural movement of sexual liberation since the 1960s, a rich body of critical works that directly deal with the subject of 'deviant sexuality' in Proust's works have flourished since the 1980s: J. E. Rivers's *Proust and the Art of Love* (1980), Eva Ahlstedt's *La Pudeur en crise* (1985), and Antoine Compagnon's *Proust entre deux siècles* (1989), to name but a few monographs. In the next decade, Proust became a major point of reference in the writings of literary scholars working in queer theory and studies of gender and sexuality. Notable examples include Eve Sedgwick's *Epistemology of the Closet* (1990), Douglas B. Saylor's *The Sadomasochistic Homotext: Readings in Sade, Balzac and Proust* (1993), and Leo Bersani's *Homos* (1995). Indeed, the sexological aspect of Proust's work has been so thoroughly explored that *À la recherche* is nowadays recognized as the 'first major literary work in France to take on the issue of same-sex sexual relations directly and in an apparently objective manner' (Ladenson 2014, 115), and 'has remained into the present the most vital centre of the energies of gay literary high culture, as well as of many manifestations of modern literary high culture in general' (Sedgwick 2008, 213).

Since the Policy of Economic Reform and Opening Up in 1978, 2 years after Mao's death, Chinese society has undergone drastic changes, not least in its perception of sexuality. However, despite the influx of Western cultural productions and the intensity of translation activities, the Chinese translators of the *First Translation* were hardly sensitized to Proust's complex sexual discourses. In fact, while Proust's depiction of 'deviant sexuality' is morally ambiguous, early Chinese translations of *La Recherche* manifest strong moral condemnation and pathological treatment of the subject, and they additionally indicate a lack of lexical variety and conceptual understanding to accommodate Proust's different use of a wide range of vocabulary regarding 'homosexual(ity)' and his nuanced formulation of 'sadisme/sadique'. However, the de-pathologization of Proust's sexual discourses is evident in later Chinese translations, and it takes place along with the exponential increase in the translation and (re)introduction of influential Western sexological texts in post-Mao China. By comparing and contrasting exemplary passages (from *Du côté de chez Swann, Sodome et Gomorrhe, La Prisonnière*, and *Le Temps retrouvé*) across the available Chinese translations, this section aims to demonstrate the evolving strategies of translating (homo)sexuality and sadomasochism into Chinese, and the extent to which such an evolution refracts changing and largely de-pathologizing discourses on, and attitudes to, these subjects in China from the late 1980s until now.[43]

In the PRC, it was only in the 1980s that modern and contemporary Chinese sociological works on homosexuality started to emerge, and the social practices of homosexuality—such as the formation of homosexual group identity and the occurrence of cruising venues, as well as the development of a certain codified common language—appeared only towards the end of this period.[44] The Chinese intellectual landscape of the 1980s, under the banner of 'Culture Fever', was marked by a revived enthusiasm for translating Western texts, including many Western discourses of sexuality—'revived' because Western discourses of sexuality *were* briefly introduced in Republican China (1912–1949). However, their development—appropriation and recontextualization—came to a premature end with the establishment of the PRC in 1949, as the Communist regime under Mao consistently imposed sexual puritanism, and an overt display of sexuality would have been seen as Western contamination and corruption. That is to say, modern sexology did not properly commence until the 1980s in the PRC, and the Chinese translation of modern Western sexual discourses was and has been an essential component of that development. The *People's Daily*, the official newspaper of the Chinese Communist Party which wields special authority over the voicing of official government policy, published its first formal article with a positive take on the issue of sexuality in 1986. In the same year, the newspaper reported the establishment of the first Chinese sexological organization in Shanghai. In 1988, sexology as a discipline was formally introduced in Chinese universities. By the end of the 1980s, official as well as popular attitudes to Freudian theory, for example, were said to have evolved from total negation to general recognition (Li 2014, under '性行为规范的变迁'/'The Evolution of the Norms of Sexual Behaviour' and '性研究'/'Research in Sexology'). One of the initial tasks of this section is to reveal how the translators of the *First Translation* in the mid-1980s responded to the significant lexical as well as epistemic challenges they faced when unravelling Western sexual idioms and concepts in Proust's work. An extensive list of sexual vocabulary needed to be (re)invented and adapted into modern vernacular Chinese to accommodate Proust's sexual discourses. It should be further stressed that, as far as sexology is concerned, it was those Western theories popular in the first half of the twentieth century that received primary attention, and the list of translated and/or (re)introduced authors (other than Freud) included Magnus Hirschfeld, Havelock Ellis, Richard von Krafft-Ebing, and Edward Carpenter.[45] Many intellectuals working in translation in the 1980s regarded their project as both a recapitulation and continuation of their predecessors' work from the early twentieth century, which was brutally interrupted under the Communist regime. The more revolutionary or radical Western discourses of sexuality from the 1960s and 1970s, perhaps most importantly those advocated by Foucault, were not properly introduced in China until the 1990s.[46]

For instance, the first book-length study of male homosexuality in mainland China, titled *Tamen de shijie* (他们的世界, *Their World*) and co-authored by Wang Xiaobo and Li Yinhe, only came out in 1992, after 3 years of research, which coincided exactly with the first Chinese publication date of *La Recherche*. The sociologist Li subsequently went on to publish one book-length study on sadomasochism (1998a) and another on the (homo)sexuality of Chinese women (1998c). In terms of explicitly and often sadomasochistically gay-themed Chinese cultural productions, notable early cinematic works include *East Palace, West Palace* (*Donggong xigong*, 东宫西宫) (Zhang 1996) and *Happy Together* (Wang 1997), both of which appeared in the second half of the 1990s.

It should be noted that, in China, although the social phenomenon of same-sex eroticism has been well documented since ancient times,[47] systematic scholarly works on homosexuality in mainland China, as mentioned before, did not take off until the late 1980s. In mainland China, although homosexuality is not a criminal act, in a Chinese Classification of Mental Disorder passed as late as 1994 by the Chinese Psychiatric Association, homosexuality was still considered a mental disorder (Chou 2000, 111). This pathological designation of homosexuality was finally removed from the official list in 2001.

Those sociological enquiries and artistic productions emerging in the 1990s meant that, by the time the first volumes of the two new translations came out in 2004 and 2005, the Chinese scholarly and popular discourses on and social attitudes to the subjects of sadomasochism and homosexuality had significantly evolved.

2.9.1   *Proust's Sexual Discourses*

Proust's conceptualization of homosexuality, as has been widely acknowledged, reflects the dominant theory of homosexuality of his time—the *Zwischenstufen* or man-woman theory formulated by the German sexologist Karl Heinrich Ulrichs in *Memnon* (1868) (Rivers 1980, 262–278)—and is, in Lucille Cairns's words, 'flawed by the limitations of this theory' (1997, 43). This theory is 'predicated not on the idea of same-sex attraction per se but rather on the *anima muliebris in corpore virili inclusa* (the soul of a woman trapped in the body of a man)' (Ladenson 2014, 118), which explains Proust's preference of the designation 'invert' or 'inversion' to 'homosexual' or 'homosexuality'. Homosexuality in Proust, states Leo Bersani, is 'nothing but disguised or mistaken heterosexuality'

(1995, 134), although Eve Sedgwick's close analysis of Proust's 'metaphorical models' does suggest how Ulrichs's doctrine of sexual inversion is also constantly destabilized in the novel ([1990] 2008, 219–223). Proust himself clarifies the conceptual differences he makes between 'inversion' and 'homosexuality':

> D'ailleurs il y a une nuance. Les homosexuels mettent leur point d'honneur à n'être pas des invertis. D'après la théorie, toute fragmentaire du reste que j'ébauche ici, il n'y aurait pas en réalité d'homosexuels. Si masculine que puisse être l'apparence de la tante, son goût de virilité proviendrait d'une féminité foncière, fût-elle dissimulée. Un homosexuel ça serait ce que prétend être, ce que de bonne foi s'imagine être, un inverti. (*RTP III*, 955)

> Moreover, there is a nuance. As a point of honour, homosexuals do not consider themselves to be inverts. According to the theory, which I'm still sketching out here, there wouldn't be any homosexuals in reality. However masculine the appearance of the 'auntie' can be, the taste for virility would derive from a fundamental femininity, even if it's disguised. A homosexual, as it is thought to be in good faith, would just be what an invert claims to be. (My translation)

Interestingly, Proust also seems to consider the word 'homosexual' to be too German and pedantic, linking it to the notorious Eulenberg affair[48]:

> Mais le lecteur français veut être respecté' et n'étant pas Balzac je suis obligé de me contenter d'inverti. Homosexuel est trop germanique et pédant, n'ayant guère paru en France [...] et traduit sans doute des journaux berlinois, qu'après le procès Eulenbourg. (*RTP III*, 955)

> But the French readership want to be respected and, without being Balzac, I'm obliged to be content with 'invert'. 'Homosexual' is too Germanic and pedantic. The word has hardly appeared in France [...] and probably translated from the newspapers in Berlin, and it's appeared only after the Eulenberg trial. (My translation)

However, these unambiguous and unguarded lines apropos of homosexuality, rather uncharacteristic of Proustian digression, come from Proust's notebook (*Cahier 49*) which contains draft material for *Sodome et Gomorrhe*. This passage is marked as an extensive note that Proust is ostensibly making to himself where he outlines his theory of sexuality.

But it is largely obliterated in the published text. And when the 'traces' of this theory appear in the novel, they are not articulated through the narrator but rather the character Charlus (*RTP III*, 810). There would seem to be a certain epistemic danger, were we to uncritically accept this theory as Proust's view. The infrequent insertion of an indeterminable 'je' ('I')—the author? The narrator? Charlus?—in this passage, and the deliberate obliteration of this material could suggest that 'queer textual practices in Proust have precisely to do with certain kinds of objectivity being in crisis, with a contingent need claiming a right to expression, with a nearly intentional metaleptic failure to respect distinctions between the real world and literary characters, a failure that produces borrowings and sharings among characters as well as between real people and characters' (Lucey 2006, 208). For Michael Lucey, the development of the novel from its avant-texts itself reflects a complicated negotiation among the ambient ideological currents concerning homosexuality in Proust's time (240–241).

In addition to 'homosexual' and 'invert', Proust employs 'man-woman' ('homme-femme'), 'sodomite', 'auntie' ('tante'), and 'hermaphrodite', to name but a few other terms, with specific implications and emphases in their different contexts. As will be explored later in detail, translators have struggled to find terminological variants in modern vernacular Chinese to accommodate Proust's wide range of vocabulary regarding 'homosexual(ity)'.

It is worth reiterating that, even in France, the issue of 'deviant sexuality' in Proust's work was largely neglected, or perhaps deliberately ignored, by critics up until the 1980s. André Maurois (1954, xiii–xv), in his preface to the old Pléiade edition of *La Recherche*, claims that time and memory are the only two central themes of Proust's novel. Indeed, it is almost inconceivable nowadays for anyone to ignore the thematic centrality of time and memory, which is even reflected in Proust's initial—up until 1913—tripartite structural envisioning of the novel, revolving around a time 'lost', 'sought', and 'regained' in and through memory. However, as his novelistic conception evolved, Proust spent the rest of his life expanding the inner volumes of the novel, which comprise a separate volume of *À l'ombre des jeunes filles en fleurs* and what is known as the *Sodome et Gomorrhe* cycle (including *La Prisonnière* and *La Fugitive*), covering Charlus's homosexuality and Albertine's lesbianism (Schmid 2006, 67). In fact, in several crucial avant-texts of *La Recherche* from as early as 1909—notably *Cahiers 6* and *7* of what we know as the

Sainte-Beuve series—the homosexual theme was already emphasized, especially in the fragment 'La Race des tantes' (literally, 'the race of aunties', or in Schmid's translation, 'the queer race') where the author 'classifies' different types of male homosexuals (61–62). After the publication of *Du côté de chez Swann* in 1913, Proust, facing strong criticism from influential readers such as Paul Souday, defended his decision to keep the Montjouvain passage in this first volume, where the protagonist first witnesses sadism and same-sex acts, as it both thematically and structurally echoes later volumes of the novel (i.e. *Sodome et Gomorrhe* and *La Prisonnière*, as well as the sadomasochistic scene of flagellation involving Charlus in the last volume) (Proust 1990, 464). Therefore, as Ladenson highlights, the Montjouvain scene 'bridges the perceived structural binarism between the serious outer volumes addressing the nature of time and memory and the trivia-infused inner volumes that deal with deviant sexuality' in *La Recherche* (1999, 62). What follows then is some concrete analysis of this discursive evolution across the available Chinese translations of *La Recherche*.

2.9.2   *Translating Sadomasochism*

As we know, the vocabulary of sexuality was in great flux during Proust's time. Sadism and masochism, as medical terms and concepts, had only recently been proposed by the German psychiatrist Richard von Krafft-Ebing around 1900, especially in his *Psychopathia Sexualis*, and sadomasochism was understood as essentially a manifest form of sexual perversion. Although Proust might have been aware of Krafft-Ebing's influential theory, the word 'sadisme' or 'sadique' is employed hardly in its clinical sense. In fact, Proust's use of the word seems rather out of line with Krafft-Ebing's clinical categorization as it overlaps with what we now usually understand as masochism. With references to Georges Bataille's essays on Sade and Proust (1957a, 108–157), Hendrika Freud (2013, 108) describes both Sade and Mlle Vinteuil as 'bogus sadists' because 'the true sadist is cruel and does not explain his actions', or, in Bataille's words, 'les méchants ne connaissent du Mal que le bénéfice matériel' ('the wicked know only the material benefits of Evil') (1957b, 154, 154, my translation). As H. Freud further demonstrates, in the Montjouvain passage, Proust 'tries to clarify the difference between sadism as sexual perversion and actual cruelty' (101) by characterizing the sadists of Mlle. Vinteuil's kind as 'purement sentimentaux' ('purely sentimental') and 'naturellement vertueux' ('naturally virtuous'), 'ce qu'une créature entièrement mauvaise ne pourrait pas être' ('something that an entirely bad creature could not be') (*RTP I*, 161–162; *PT I*, 164–165). In Proust's example, as H. Freud continues:

> Mlle Vinteuil can only reach an erotic climax by transgressing the impediment of the social conventions that are so restrictive to her. She is a straitlaced girl who is able to experience pleasure and lust only when she furtively succumbs to sadistic excesses. [...] the proclivity for sadistic phantasies originates in its opposite: an oversensitivity that prevents excitement. (2013, 99)

Instead of establishing a clinical diagnosis, Proust repeatedly highlights the theatricalized expression of human intimacy while considerably deflating the abnormality of sadistic acts by comparing the scenario to commonplace 'théâtres du boulevard' ('popular theatre') with 'l'esthétique du mélodrame' ('aesthetics of melodrama') (*RTP I*, 161; *PT* 164).

In early translations (i.e. the *First Translation* [1991] and the *Essential Translation* [1992]), it is the Chinese word *shi-nüe-kuang* (施虐狂) that is consistently used. It can refer to both the concept of sadism and the person who practices sadism. *Shi-nüe-kuang*, literally meaning 'abuse craze', sounds far too colloquial, judgmental, and emotional to be an accurate conceptual term for sadism or sadists, but it has largely remained in use today and can still be frequently found in many contemporary retranslations of, for example, Freud's or Ellis's works, in predominantly clinical contexts.[49] The character *kuang* clearly denotes a form of mental disorder or pathological disease, which was subject to modification when the word and the concept of 'sadism' was gradually transposed from medical to sociological and literary frameworks in the 1990s. Y. Li in *The Subculture of Sadomasochism* (1998a, 174) clarifies that the Freudian premise of sadomasochism being pathological is rather outdated, especially in comparison with Foucault's pioneering view, according to which sadomasochism is an 'un-pathological' form of pleasure, and no pleasure is abnormal.[50] The pathological elements in sadomasochism formulated by some of the early- and mid-twentieth-century Western sexologists find distinct echoes in Chinese sexological works coming out in the 1980s. Probably due to the still relatively rigorous sexual morality of the time,[51] some of the newly trained Chinese sexologists' writings demonstrate a prejudicially crude and morally simplistic understanding of 'sexual perversions' like sadomasochism, rhetorically inviting moral condemnation. Despite the author's formal acknowledgement of Ellis's (1933) work,[52] one of the most popular books, *Sexual Sociology* (*Xing shehuixue*) by Dalin Liu (1988), defines *shi-nüe-kuang* and *shou-nüe-kuang* (for 'masochism') as the urge to 'reach sexual satisfaction through violence committed between the two sexes', and the example he cites is Hitler, who is said to be 'both a sadist and a masochist' because he 'sometimes maltreated his lovers very cruelly and sometimes asked them to flagellate him soundly' (83, my translation), further highlighting the monstrous qualities associated with sadomasochism. By the end of the 1980s, sex psychology clinics had appeared in the PRC, offering help to 'patients' suffering from 'sexual perversions' such as 'exhibitionism', 'voyeurism', and 'transvestism' (Y. Li 2014, under '性生活'/'Sex Life').

In the context of the Montjouvain passage, 'abuse craze' would sound too strong to most Chinese readers to describe an act of spitting on M. Vinteuil's portrait. However, both the *First Translation* and the *Essential Selection* explicitly refer to Proust's 'sadisme' as a 'mental illness' and 'sadiste' as a 'patient' or 'sufferer' (*RTP I*, 161; *FT*, 120; *ES*, 79),[53] which is, of course, a significant addition to the source text. Spitting on the deceased father's portrait while still in mourning may be severely condemnable according to the fundamental Confucian teaching of filial piety, which is deeply rooted in traditional as well as contemporary Chinese thought, but it is highly unlikely that an ordinary Chinese reader—or indeed any reader—would automatically connect this particular act to mental illness. The translators' decision to deliberately pathologize the concept of sadism is most likely to have been affected by contemporaneous popular medical opinions in China, or at least the clinical use of the term in Chinese. Therefore, there seems to be a reapplication of dominant medical discourses on sexuality from Proust's era which were not necessarily in line with Proust's own conception, to the translation of Proust's work in the Chinese context.

In the sadomasochistic passage from the end of the novel, often considered to structurally mirror the Montjouvain passage, where the narrator witnesses Charlus being chained and whipped in a male brothel, the word 'sadique' appears again and is translated (by different translators) as *xing-nüe-dai-kuang-(zhe)* ([the person of] sexual abuse craze, 性虐待狂[者]). Although my literal English translation of the term seems to have only added the adjective 'sexual' to the previous term used in the Montjouvain passage, their corresponding Chinese characters are actually quite different in terms of specificity. Whereas the previous term, *shi-nüe-kuang* (abuse craze), clearly indicates the active role of the agent and may not be specifically related to sex, *xing-nüe-dai-kuang* (sexual abuse craze) is explicitly sexual but rather vague about the roles of the abuser and the abused. In fact, when the word 'sadique' reappears in other volumes of *La Recherche* (with different translators), it almost always has a slightly different wording in Chinese. Given the number of translators involved in the *First Translation*, such terminological inconsistencies are somewhat expected. More significantly, it suggests that there is a lack of a coherent 'theory' or common acknowledgement of sadism or masochism in Chinese (until today). But this lack of a uniform lexical and epistemic approach to Proust's sexual discourses and other Western as well as indigenous literary and sociological works also means that the translators could potentially enjoy a special 'freedom to cite and appropriate certain materials rather than others', in the process of which 'we witness the possibility of cross-cultural understanding and coalition'.[54] Whereas an English or German translator is able to systematically translate 'sadique' as 'sadist' or 'Sadist(in)' due to their common etymology, a Chinese translator finds no equivalent of the term and has to translate it according to the context. The words 'sadism' and 'masochism', which respectively derive from two literary figures (i.e. Sade and Sacher-Masoch), are not translated etymologically or phonetically.[55] The closest Chinese 'conceptual equivalents' are *shi-nüe(-zhe)* (sexual abuse[r], 施虐[者]) and *shou-nüe(-zhe)* (the sexually abused, 受虐[者]). Unlike in the West where sadism and masochism could be seen first as *literary* phenomena which were then developed as medical and pathological discourses through Krafft-Ebing, and perhaps even more influentially through Freud and Ellis, their Chinese translation recognizes only the latter development. In the passage, Charlus is called 'un sadique' (*RTP IV*, 403) but is actually the abused (i.e. more of a masochist), which seems to contradict our current usual understanding of the term, hence the vague Chinese variation *xing-nüe-dai-kuang* instead of *shi-nüe-kuang* (which unequivocally refers to the active agent).

At any rate, the translators of the two new translations of *La Recherche*, Xu and Zhou, have both tried to modify the Chinese rendition of 'sadism' and, crucially, both Xu's and Zhou's translations remove the decidedly negative reference of sadism as a pathological disease, which features in earlier translations. Accordingly, Xu changes the pathologically inflected character *kuang* (狂) to *yin* (淫), so *shi-nüe-kuang* (abuse craze) becomes *shi-nüe-yin* (literally 'abuse excess'). This term is more literary as the character *yin* carries multiple meanings: (1) excessive; (2) wanton; and (3) illicit sexual relations. This choice of word seems to be able to capture at once different aspects of Mlle. Vinteuil's relationship with her girlfriend, and indeed most other lesbian relationships portrayed in the novel. The language of pathological condition is thus transferred to that of sexual desire. However, the rather negative value judgment is still evident.

Zhou's terminological proposal also comes out of careful research: *nüe-lian-pi* (虐恋癖). *Nüe-lian*, literally 'abusive love', is currently one of the most commonly accepted Chinese terms for 'sadomasochism'.[56] The word is accorded privilege due to its relatively positive connotation; 'love' is less judgmental than 'craze' or 'excess/wantonness/illicitness'. More importantly, as Y. Li points out: 'the word has a specific implication: this [sadomasochistic] tendency is relevant to human love behaviour, much more than to abuse or to be abused' ('表达一层特殊含义: 这种倾向与人类的恋爱行为有关, 而不仅仅是施虐和受虐的活动') (1998a, 1, my translation). The term was already coined and consistently employed by Pan (1987 [1946]) in his translation of Ellis's *Psychology of Sex* (1933). Accordingly, 'sadism' is rendered as *shi-nüe-lian* (execution of abusive love) and 'masochism' as *shou-nüe-lian* (reception of abusive love). But the term *nüe-lian* for 'sadomasochism' was recovered and popularized only in the 1990s, strongly advocated by pioneering sociologists such as Y. Li. Perhaps in an attempt to make *shi-nüe-lian* and *shou-nüe-lian* sound more objectively descriptive, Li changes the *lian* (love) in these two terms into *qingxiang* (倾向, tendency), and *nüe-lian* is also frequently extended to *nüe-lian-qingxiang*.

Informed by Y. Li's sociological works, Zhou further modifies these terms and opts for a more literary and morphologically concise synonym for *qingxiang*: pi (癖). In modern Chinese, *pi* is predominantly used to mean 'addiction', 'hobby', or 'natural inclination'.[57] Both the etymology and the concept of *pi* have a very rich history in classical Chinese culture. For one thing, the character does have a rather pathological origin, as implied by the character component 疒 (nè) meaning 'illness'. In classical Chinese, 癖 is frequently interchangeable with its homonym 痞, referring to a kind of lump in the abdomen which may cause serious indigestion in Chinese medicine. For another, the 'sense of pathological blockage' has also subsequently been extended to mean 'obsession or addiction', as Judith Zeitlin explains: 'something that sticks in the gut and cannot be evacuated, hence becoming habitual' (1993, 62–63). As Zeitlin duly observes, the concept of *pi*, or what she chooses to translate as 'obsession' (but free from the technical psychiatric sense), was 'mated with connoisseurship and collecting' from the late Tang dynasty, and reached its height in the Ming dynasty, during which 'obsession had become a *sine qua non*, something the gentlemen could not afford to do without' (69), and 'the objects of obsessions became increasingly standardized as indexes of certain virtues and personalities' (71). In the sixteenth-century *Pidian xiaoshi* 癖癫小史 (*Brief History of Obsession and Lunacy*) by HUA Shu, homosexuality is actually listed as one of the 'highly conventionalized obsessions', along with 'books, painting, epigraphy, calligraphy, or rocks; a particular musical instrument, plant, animal, or game; tea or wine; cleanliness' (71). In modern Chinese, pi is utilized in a variety of character combinations to signify human proclivities for certain specific things or activities. It is a near equivalent of the suffix '-philia', which, depending on the word combination and its context, can be negative, positive, or non-judgmentally descriptive. In this respect, the intrinsic semantic ambiguity of *pi* seems to suitably capture Chinese social attitudes to sadomasochism. This use of pi in the context of sadomasochism seems to have gained further currency in philosophical and literary discourses.[58]

2.9.3   Translating Homosexuality

Earlier translations expose a distinct lack of Chinese terminological variety for 'homosexual(ity) '. In the vast majority of cases, *tongxinglian*—literally 'same-sex love', designating both the concept and the person—is consistently applied throughout the novel, regardless of the local terminological variations in the source text. The word was one of the many 'medical neologisms'—such as *yichang* (abnormality) and *biantai* (perversion)—propagated by Chinese intellectuals in the Republican period in their translation and introduction of contemporary Western 'modern science' (Sang 2003, 24). It has nowadays become the standard and arguably the least ambiguous Chinese translation of 'homosexual(ity)'. 'Inversion (sexuelle)' is rendered as *xingyü daocuo* (性欲倒错 or 性欲倒置, literally 'sexual desire reversal'), and, if we cut out 'sexual desire' in the Chinese expression, 'inversion' is also understood as a Proustian aesthetic concept (Tu 1999, 114–115).[59] However, 'invert' as the person is indiscriminately translated as *tongxinglian* (same-sex love [person]) rather than *xingyü daocuo zhe* (性欲倒错者, sexually inverted person), which happens to be *the* term endorsed by Proust. According to Étienne Brunet's *Le Vocabulaire de Proust*, the word 'inverti(e,s)' appears forty-two times in *La Recherche*, whereas such words as 'homosexualité', 'homosexuel(s)', and 'lesbiennes' appear altogether only 25 times (qtd. in Fladenmuller 2015, 83). *Tongxinglian* sometimes also covers 'sodomie', as in the phrase 'incriminer la sodomie' ('incriminate sodomy') (*RTP III*, 33; *FT II*, 1142; *PT IV*, 35).

The dominant Chinese scholarly view on homosexuality in the 1980s (and well into the 1990s) was, to cite one sexologist's comment, that it was 'a psychological illness [...] an abnormal behaviour that should be penalized' (Zhang 1994, 17).[60] Some translators of the *First Translation* seem to have been strongly influenced by such a dominant view and choose to explicitly pathologize Proust's description of homosexual characters in the novel. In *Sodome et Gomohrre II*, at one of the Verdurins' dinners where Charlus's *ladylike* femininity is discussed, the gradual feminine 'transformation' of Charlus's body is translated as *biantai* (perversion), and the 'origine spirituelle' ('spiritual origin') of this transformation is translated as *jingshen de binggen* (having a psychopathological root) (*RTP III*, 300; *FT II*, 1340). As expected, in his new translation of the volume, Xu replaces these pathological expressions with more neutral ones (*XT IV*, 326).

In both old and new translations, we also occasionally discover examples of Chinese appropriation of Proust's homosexual vocabulary. For instance, Proust's 'homme-femme' ('man-woman') is rendered as *yin-yang-ren* (阴阳人, yin-yang person) (*RTP III*, 23; *FT II*, 1136; *XT*, 3; *PT IV*, 25), a term which evidently derives from traditional Chinese cosmology, notably found in Daoism. Nevertheless, it must be stressed that *yin-yang*, which refers to two primordial, mutually complementing, and generative forces, is by no means a discourse specifically *on/of* sexuality per se, although it is often reductively and abusively applied to Gender and Sexuality Studies in modern and contemporary China and becomes at times indistinguishable from Western biological, medical, and sociological discourses. The concept of *yin-yang*, which can be traced back to one of the oldest classic Chinese texts, *Yijing* or the *Book of Changes* (around the first millennium BCE), encompasses a much wider cosmological vision than merely sexual acts. Another related example is the

Chinese translation of 'viril(ité)' ('virile' or 'virility') as *yang-gang* (阳刚)—*yang* as in *yin-yang*, and *gang* meaning 'hard' as opposed to *rou* (soft) in *yinrou* (阴柔).[61] The character *qi* (气, air), signalling the primordial energy and active principle forming all things in classical Chinese thought, is often used to complement *yang-gang* (as *yanggang zhi qi*) to form a more elaborate translation for 'viril', which further indigenizes Proust's homosexual vocabulary.[62]

Moreover, the translators of the *First Translation* extend their terminological application of *yin-yang* to the translation of the adjective 'androgyne' ('androgynous'), which appears only twice in Proust's novel (*RTP III*, 313, 370; *FT II*, 1349, 1391). What is even more interesting is that the translators feel the need to add supplementary qualifiers in their rendition of 'androgyne', which points to the modern Chinese bio-scientific categorization of sex and sexuality (imported from the West in the early twentieth century). Thus 'Vénus androgyne' is translated as *yinyang Weinasi liangxing zhuanbian* (阴阳维纳斯, yin-yang Venus capable of changing between the two sexes) (*RTP III*, 313; *FT II*, 1349); the 'androgyne' race is *yinyang erxing(zi)* (阴阳二性子, yin-yang with two sexes) (*RTP III*, 370; *FT II*, 1391).[63] Most English- and French-Chinese dictionaries do list the two entries, *yin-yang-ren* and *liang-xing-ren* (two-sex person), side by side for the translation of 'androgyne' (as a noun referring to the person). The juxtaposition between traditional Chinese and Western-imported contemporary Chinese bio-scientific terms in this example reflects, in fact, the translators' lingering epistemic uncertainty over Proust's sexual discourses more generally in the 1980s. However, Xu in his new translation chooses to stick with a decidedly bio-medical designation, *liangxing jixing* (两性畸形, two-sex abnormality), for 'androgyne'. Not only does the term sound incongruous in the mythological and metaphorical context in which it appears, its usage also intriguingly goes against Xu's otherwise largely de-pathologizing (re) translation of *La Recherche*.

We could perhaps further advance this observation on the tentative employment of *yin-yang* discourse in the Chinese translation of Proust's sexual vocabulary. In the context of sex and sexuality, *yin* is predominantly woman and *yang* is man. But as Charlotte Furth (1988, 3) stresses:

> There was nothing fixed and immutable about male and female as aspects of yin and yang. [...] They are interdependent, mutually reinforcing and

capable of turning into their opposites. This natural philosophy would seem to lend itself to a broad and tolerant view of variation in sexual behavior and gender roles.

Chou (2000, 18) further clarifies: 'yin and yang are not ontologically binary, as what they produce are not generic women and men, but persons in specific relations such as mother and father, husband and wife, brother and sister, emperor and favorite'. In other words, *yin* and *yang* are fundamentally relativistic and conceptually distinguished from Western biological determinism, through which gender differences are naturalized and, quite literally, embodied.

Proust in *Sodome et Gomorrhe I* may have demonstrated a keen interest in appropriating contemporary bio-scientific vocabulary to 'naturalize' homosexuality, but this naturalization is also profoundly metaphorical. As Marcel Muller (1971, 472, my translation) remarks: 'êtres composites, Charlus et Jupien sont les produits d'une biologie métaphorique qui est à la vie ce qu'est à l'art la vision d'un Elstir' ('as composite beings, Charlus and Jupien are the products of a metaphorical biology for life as much as Elstir's vision for art'). Far from essentializing gender identities, the conceptual richness of 'Proustian *inversion*' lies precisely in its ability to '[blur] the boundaries of male and female, and encompasses bisexuality, male homosexuality and lesbianism'.[64] In this light, the *yin-yang* discourse tentatively articulated in the Chinese translation constitutes a refreshing cross-cultural prism through which the linguistic and philosophical locus of the target text can potentially reaffirm, reshape, and reconfigure the source text, encouraging more lateral thinking about the source text.

It is worth pointing out that there is, indeed, a long list of classical Chinese words and expressions that describe the phenomenon of same-sex eroticism. But they are mostly metaphors or contain explicit references to specific classical tales and anecdotes and have almost never been formulated in a rigorous conceptual or analytical language, which would have been required to accommodate Proust's text.[65]

Compared to the early translations, the new translations of *La Recherche* demonstrate an epistemic effort to adopt more varied and theoretically informed expressions of homosexuality in Chinese.[66] The most obvious evidence is Xu's aforementioned extensive postscript to his translation of *Sodome et Gomorrhe*. Informed by Eells's and Compagnon's critical works, Xu synthetically explains a wide range of issues concerning homosexuality in Proust's *œuvre*: the biblical background of Sodom and Gomorrha; the expression 'la race maudite' ('the cursed race') that Proust employs to link homosexuals' conditions to those of Jews; Proust's appreciation of Balzac's designation of homosexuals as 'tante' ('auntie', translated as *guma*, 姑妈 in Chinese); the botanic sexual metaphors; the codified and secret language circulated among homosexual characters such as Charlus; the mythological origin of 'androgyne' and hermaphrodite (described in Plato's *The Symposium*); and finally *the* theoretical observation of Proust's conceptual discrimination between 'homosexuality' (*tongxinglian*) and 'inversion' (*xingyu daocuo*)—which has led the translator to make systemic terminological changes to the *First Translation*. Xu (*XT IV*, 747) additionally acknowledges his consultation of certain Chinese sexological works, as well as the Chinese translation of the works that Proust himself consulted while composing the novel, such as Maurice Maeterlink's *L'Intelligence des fleurs* (1907), Jules Michelet's *La Mer* (1861), and Titus Lucretius Carus's *De rerum natura*.

The other translator, Kexi Zhou, is one of the three collaborators who translated *La Prisonnière* for the *First Translation*, and he then translated the same volume independently. We are thus able to gain a very concrete and specific perspective on the evolving Chinese homosexual discourse by examining how this translator's intellectual development over a decade has shaped his perception of a similar text.[67]

Two most striking examples are found in the passage where guests at the Verdurins' are openly discussing homosexuality. First, the Latin chant which Brichot recites to please Charlus contains the line 'Sumus enim Sodomitae' ('Because we are Sodomites', my translation) (*RTP III*, 807; *FT III*, 1719; *PT V*, 280). In the *First Translation*, the word 'Sodomitae' is directly translated as *jijian* (鸡奸), a rather pejorative term for a homosexual act. It literally means 'chicken lewdness', referring to 'the belief that domesticated fowls commonly engage in same-sex acts' (Chou 2000, 23). Although most dictionaries consider *jijian* to be the standard translation of 'sodomy', the image of lewd chickens seems quite incompatible with the biblical reference to Sodom. There is no Chinese word that can express the biblical city of sin *and* the homosexual act at the same time. Proper nouns such as 'Sodom' and 'Gomorrah' can be rendered phonetically as *suo-duo-mu* (索多姆) and *ge-mo-er* (戈摩尔), but these nouns have not developed any sexual sense in Chinese.

A person of 'suo-duo-mu' is literally understood as an inhabitant of this biblical place, without any sexual overtone. One simply cannot use 'inhabitant of Sodom' to mean 'homosexual' in Chinese. When translating the word 'Sodomite', the Chinese translator has to choose either a *literal* rendition of the term, which is biblical but not homosexual, or an *explicit* rendition of the term, which is homosexual but not biblical. The context of the chant clearly refers to the burning of Sodom: 'Sumus enim Sodomitae/Igne tantum perituri' ('Because we are Sodomites/ And must perish by fire', my translation) (*RTP III*, 807; *FT III*, 1719; *PT V*, 280).[68] In the new translation, Zhou replaces *jijian* with a contemporary Chinese slang word, *jilao* (基佬), a term of Cantonese origin which has gained huge popularity in recent years, especially with the new meaning and use of *ji* (基) in contemporary Chinese to indicate homoeroticism among men. This second *ji* corresponds to a different Chinese character and bears no relation to 'chicken'. Interestingly, due to the relative novelty of the Chinese term, the translator feels obliged to explain what *jilao* means in the footnotes: '[contemporary Chinese] slang for male homosexual, which comes from the pronunciation of the English word "gay", See Yinhe Li's *The Subculture of Homosexuality*' (*ZT V*, 314). Additionally, *lao* is a slightly pejorative word for 'man', so *jilao* is really the equivalent of 'gay man'. In this case, the translator explicitly takes recourse to an indigenous sociological source and applies contemporary new knowledge of gender and sexuality to the translation of *La Recherche*, ascribing—perhaps unintentionally—a new 'gay' identity to the text in its Chinese context. However, translating 'Sodomitae' as 'gay man' still does not settle the issue of the biblical reference. This fundamental cultural and theological dissociation of homosexuality from resonances of 'sin' and 'divine punishment' that it holds in the biblical tradition will always cause problems when we translate Proust's homosexual discourse into Chinese.[69]

The second example, which is found two pages later, confirms once again Proust's view of 'homosexuality' (as distinguished from 'inversion') as a German conception, as Charlus remarks: 'mais j'avoue que ce qui a encore le plus changé, c'est ce que les Allemands appellent l'homosexualité' ('But I will admit that the thing that has changed most of all is what the Germans call homosexuality') (*RTP III*, 810; *PT V*, 282). Rather surprisingly, Zhou renders 'homosexualité' as *deguobing* (德国病, German disease) in italics and provides the following footnote:

二十世纪初, 德国同性恋人数众多, 一说柏林当时有二万名男妓。因此法国人称同性恋为"德国病"。此处原文, 直译应为"德国人所说的同性恋"。但因原文中前后多处, 各以不同的词来指同性恋, 为避免行文过于费解, 译文稍作了变通. (*ZT V*, 317)

At the beginning of the twentieth century, Germany had a great number of homosexuals [*tongxinglian*] ; one source states there were 20,000 male prostitutes in Berlin. Therefore, the French called homosexuality the 'German disease'. The original text here should be more literally translated as 'what the Germans call homosexuality'. But because different words for homosexual are used before and after the passage, in order to avoid making the text too difficult to understand, the translated text has made some changes. (My translation)

What the translator forgets to mention is that this piece of information is also adapted from his anecdotal reading of Y. Li's work (2009, 15). Zhou clearly feels uncomfortable about repetitively using the same word, *tongxinglian*, for Proust's 'different words for homosexual' and makes a scholarly attempt to adopt a new term with justification from a Chinese source text, which reinforces—but also medicalizes—Proust's view of 'homosexuality' as a German phenomenon.

However, what needs to be further clarified is that Proust himself does not hesitate to employ the analogy of physician and patient to depict many of his characters' considerations of homosexuality. But, as Eve Sedgwick acutely points out, the figure of the physician under the medical discursive system appears only 'metaphorically' in this context, rather than being there to assume pathological jurisdiction over the homosexual characters in the novel, because 'since the late nineteenth century it was by medicine that the work of taxonomy, etiology, diagnosis, *certification* of the phenomenon of sexual inversion was most credibly accomplished' and 'even the vestibular attendance of the medical consultant ratifies a startling, irreversible expropriation' (2008, 225). In fact, it was the very existence of medical and popular 'expertise' that allowed *anyone* to articulate the issue of homosexuality whilst being 'momentarily insulated from the edginess of "It takes one to know one"' (225). When Proust was given Hirschfeld's book by his friend Paul Morand in 1921, he was reportedly dismayed by this medical approach to homosexuality: 'c'est épouvantable. [...] Toute la poésie de la damnation disparaît. Le vice est devenu une science exacte!' ('it's appalling. [...] All of the poetry of damnation disappears. Vice has become an exact science!') (Morand 1954, 54).

Zhou's reading of Y. Li's work on homosexuality is worthy of further attention as it plays a crucial role in the evolution of the Chinese
homosexual discourse reflected across Zhou's translations. Li is known
to be sympathetic to issues of gay rights and gender equality. In *The
Subculture of Homosexuality*, Li notably dedicates her last chapter to the
right and appropriate ways in which one should treat the phenomenon
of homosexuality in China. In fact, after homosexuality was removed
from the official list of mental illnesses in China in 2001, Li has vowed
to propose the same-sex marriage act to the National People's Congress
almost annually since 2003. Li's influence may well be one of the main
reasons why Zhou has shown a palpable attempt to tone down a number of negative references to homosexuality in Proust's text and to *de*-
pathologize its perception. The word 'vice' is most frequently associated
with homosexual acts in *La Recherche*. In both early translations and Xu's
Translation, 'vice' is consistently translated as *exi* (恶习, evil habit) or
chou'e (丑恶, ugly evil) (*FT I*, 121; *FT II*, 1720; *ES*, 80; *XT IV*, 17),
which clearly expresses a firm moral condemnation.[70] Notwithstanding
this perception of homosexuality as something inherently evil, as earlier
translations imply, Zhou consistently changes all the 'vices' of homosexuality into *pi-xi* (癖习). *Pi*, as explained earlier, means 'proclivity' and
xi 'habit'. In many ways, this is not necessarily a deliberate softening of
tone purely based on Zhou's 'learned sympathy' towards homosexuality (i.e. the cultural change brought about by, for instance, Li's works).
Proust's narrator himself states on several occasions that the word 'vice'
is only used for the sake of convenience: 'le vice (on parle ainsi pour la
commodité du langage)' ('vice [I put it thus for the sake of linguistic
convenience]'), and he questions the validity of this conventional designation of homosexual acts: 'leur vice, ou ce que l'on nomme impropre-
ment ainsi' ('their vice, or what is improperly so called') (*RTP III*, 15,
19; *PT IV*, 17, 21).

Rather different from the Chinese context, Proust's English translators seem to have been well aware of Proust's subtle homosexual vocabulary since the beginning. Scott Moncrieff, who carried out the first—but
incomplete—English translation of *La Recherche* (1922–1930), is said
to champion the adroit use of homosexual slang in English. As Terence
Kilmartin, who 'revised' Moncrieff's translation in 1981, points out,
Moncrieff's rendition of Proust's expression 'ce "chichi" voulu' (*RTP
III*, 717) as 'this deliberate "camping"' (*Moncrieff and Hudson II* 2006,
619) to describe Charlus's affected habit of homosexual chatter may well

be the 'earliest appearance of this word in print, preceding the lexicographer Eric Partridge's tentative date of 1935 by 6 years' (1981, 144). This expression is subsequently changed to 'this purposely "camp" manner' (*PT V*, 195) by Clark. In fact, Moncrieff seems to have grasped the subtlety of Proust's homosexual discourse better than Clark in this case. For example, for Proust's 'invertis qui s'interpellent en s'appelant "ma chère"', Clark directly renders it as 'homosexuals [...] [who] call out to each other—"darling!"' (*PT V*, 194), while Moncrieff translates it as 'inverts who refer to one another as "she"' (*Moncrieff and Hudson II* 2006, 619). By highlighting the feminine gender in the appellation (i.e. 'she' for 'ma chère'), Moncrieff's version clearly suggests the man-woman theory behind Proust's preference for 'invert' over 'homosexual' as discussed earlier in this section.[71] In contrast, the *First Translation* almost completely misses Proust's homosexual slang, very vaguely translating 'ce "chichi" voulu' as *niuni zuotai* (忸怩作态) (*FT III*, 1651), a rather literary expression meaning 'to behave coyly' or 'to be affectedly shy'. In his new translation of the same volume, Zhou, while keeping *niuni zuotai* somewhere else in the passage, finally adds the expression *zhe guzi niangniangqiang* (这股子娘娘腔), literally 'this blast of effeminate tune' (*ZT V*, 213). In contemporary Chinese, the word *niangniang qiang* strongly implies the idea of homosexuality. Although not translating the same passage, Xu's footnotes and postscript of *Sodome et Gomorrhe* also inform the reader of his gender-sensitive translation. For instance, the translator specifically stresses homosexual characters' tendency to change the gender of the adjectives they use and their preference for feminine nouns in the novel, such as Charlus's ostensibly grammatical insistence on 'la petite personne' and 'Son Altesse' (*XT IV*, 714; *RTP III*, 12, 19).

In sum, this evolution of the Chinese sexual discourse from the early to new translations of *La Recherche* not only reflects an enhanced understanding of Proust's work, but more significantly signals an *epistemic* shift in the way contemporary Chinese society perceives gender and sexuality from the 1980s to now. For one thing, as we have seen in the discussions of prefaces and postscripts, attention to the theme of homosexuality and to Proust's sexual vocabulary is vehemently encouraged by authoritative Western Proust scholars such as Milly, Compagnon, and Eells-Ogée. For another, translations and introductions of Western sexological texts, which largely determine and overdetermine the development of modern and contemporary Chinese sexual discourses, evidently find their literary reincarnations in the translations of Proust's text. The different translation strategies adopted by Xu and Zhou, and their respective resorting to Western and Chinese epistemic resources, should be best regarded as mutually complementary.

However, despite the strong implication of the 'improved' new Chinese translations of Proust's sexual discourses, the empirical findings outlined in this section do not primarily aim to provide a general affirmation of the well-known Retranslation Hypothesis in Translation Studies: the assumption that 'reiterative (and therefore progressively accomplished) force of retranslation will bring about a recovery of the source text and its specificities, be they linguistic or cultural' (Deane-Cox 2014, 4). Not only is my critical angle very specific, but my more important emphasis is on the increasingly varied Chinese expressions and differential (e.g. paratextual, extra-textual, and intertextual) strategies employed to accommodate, (re)interpret, and (re)translate Proust's sexual discourses, which mark a sociological evolution in mainland China. As the two new translations are still works in progress, the evaluation of their general translation qualities compared to the *First Translation* must still wait. But perhaps contrary to our expectations of a retranslation, both Tu (2010, 146) and I have spotted technical mistranslations in the available volumes of the new translations, which do not exist in the *First Translation*. In fact, the continuous re-editions of the *First Translation*, which should serve as 'a good index of public demand' (Pym 1998, 83), show that this collaborative work still wields considerable authority. It has never been Xu's or Zhou's ultimate goal to challenge the extant translations. Their respective individual translations may be 'motivated by no more than the retranslator's personal appreciation and understanding of the foreign text, regardless of transindividual factors' (Venuti 2004, 30). And this discursive evolution regarding sadomasochism and homosexuality across the Chinese translations of *La Recherche* has demonstrated the (re)translators' changed 'appreciation and understanding' of the sexological aspect of Proust's work.

To better conceptualize discourses of sadomasochism and homosexuality in certain French texts, Douglas Saylor in his study strongly advocates the term 'sadomasochistic homotextuality'. The concept of 'homotextuality', more precisely, suggests 'the way in which homosexuality is interwoven in a text', and 'it is not', Saylor continues, 'the transference of an actual sociological phenomenon into the literary plane. Rather, it is the creation of a discourse, as all written discussions of sexuality invent, rather than mimic actual realities' (1993, 2–3). The Latin suffix '-textus' further points out the problematics of language in literary representations of 'deviant sexuality'. In his chapter on Proust, Saylor convincingly argues:

> Homosexuality itself is unnameable, natural yet secretive, and has a peculiar relationship with language. The 'vice' of homosexuals is not their sexuality, but the perversion of language. [...] the only real perversion is linguistic. [...] Special languages, lies and distinct signs: these are the elements of homotextuality within the text. It is not the actions of the characters which are important, rather, it is the rerendering of words. (101)

Such homotextuality *in translation*, however, requires a shift of critical focus. It is no longer so much about the textual fabrication and, indeed, complication (especially given the instability of Proust's manuscript and narrative technique) around the unnameability and secrecy of homosexuality. In my analysis, I have demonstrated the Chinese translators' evolving reliance on dominant social and cultural discourses, as well as their personal epistemic efforts to describe and understand homosexuality and other 'sexual perversions', and to illuminate the sexual secrecy by ways of paratexts and intertexts, and by supplementing and even overcompensating the source text. In a way, the translators are effectively undoing what homosexual characters in the novel are trying to do—the former are textually outing the latter.

Nevertheless, 'the perversion of language' doggedly persists in the Chinese translations of *La Recherche*, but in this case it is the Chinese socio-historical conditioning of ironclad clinical opinions from the 1980s that has linguistically 'perverted' Proust's sexual discourses in translation. It must be noted that, although in theory both the judicial system and psychiatric establishments have officially relinquished their regulatory power over homosexuality in mainland China since the end of the 1990s (Sang 2003, 169), pathologically inflected discourses on homosexuality and other 'sexual perversions' are still widespread in clinical circles, and even in the sphere of higher education.[72] In this light, Xu's and Zhou's decision to move away from medical discourses and to resort to, and actively participate in, alternative sociological and literary discourses on/of sexuality in their respective translations signals a de facto political stance, indirectly challenging pathological views of sadomasochism and homosexuality. Their palpable epistemic exertion has brought the active agency of the translator to the forefront, as they are seen to 'use language as cultural intervention, as part of an effort to alter expressions of domination, whether at the level of concepts, of syntax or of terminology' (Simon 1996, 9). In a way, this engaging translation process is not fundamentally different from Proust's own linguistic appropriation and conceptual refashioning of the dominant sexological theories of his time, as the sexologist Ellis (1936, 174–175) acknowledges in his chapter on Proust that literary masters 'often possessed within themselves a plastic force by which, for good or for evil, they were impelled to mould language afresh, to invent new words, to spell old words afresh, to bend language into new constructions, and to make it possible to express what had never been expressed before'. If 'linguistic perversion' essentially defines Saylor's 'sadomasochistic homotexuality', this concept in Proust's Chinese translations must then be further characterized by the translators' 'rerendering of words' to de-pathologize perversion.

Notes

1. 'Translationese' designates the deliberate use of unidiomatic language in a translated text, as Venuti adds: 'what is unidiomatic in one cultural formation can be aesthetically effective in another' (Venuti 1995, 98). For a recent discussion of the role of 'translationese' in modern and contemporary Chinese creative writings, see J. Wang (2013).
2. Interestingly, as will be discussed, when translating Proust's long sentences into Chinese, due to the grammatical absence of relative clauses, one of the solutions is a significantly increased use of commas—their usage being far less strict than in English, French, or German (Xu 1993, 13–14). For a comparative study of Chinese and English punctuation, see also K. Sun (2006).
3. This advocacy of a new modern vernacular Chinese (*baihua*) to replace classical Chinese (*wenyan*) as the legitimate literary medium is at the heart of the so-called 'Chinese Literary Revolution', which was formally proclaimed in 1917. It was an essential component of the broader New Culture Movement (1915–1921), which aimed to renew Chinese culture based on Western (and Japanese) cultural standards and values. Classical or literary Chinese is a traditional style of *written* Chinese which had developed very rigid rules of composition by this time. Written vernacular Chinese, on the other hand, had already existed since the Ming dynasty (1368–1644), but 'literature written in the vernacular or even in mixed styles was held in low esteem and considered incapable of conveying morality and higher principles' (Kaske 2004, 269). What the Chinese

language reformers then endeavoured to achieve was not only to respond to the modern demands for the 'unification of the written and spoken language' (Kaske 2004, 272), but also to improve and reinvent a modern vernacular written style which could be made sophisticated enough to challenge and even replace classical Chinese as the dominant literary language. Against this background, translation of foreign works into vernacular Chinese became an indispensable way to raise the literary prestige of the 'new' language. Translation itself became a field of linguistic, aesthetic, and stylistic experimentation for writers of modern vernacular Chinese (Wang 2008, 124–127), and the relationship between translated texts and literary creations in vernacular Chinese became almost inextricable (Min 1997, 32). In fact, classical Chinese, vernacular Chinese, and the Westernized/Europeanized language (*ouhuayu*, 欧化语) are the three forces that continue to shape modern Chinese today.

4. In the context of modern and contemporary Chinese literature, the most widely accepted word for 'decadent' is *tuifei* (颓废), which is not unrelated to the European literary and artistic movement of the late nineteenth century. But *tuifei* as an adjective is loosely used to describe the artistic and literary mood that conveys pessimism or indulgence in physical desire—much broader a notion than *tuifei zhuyi*, literally 'decadentism', which specifically refers to an artistic and literary movement both in Europe and China. See H. Wang's (2012) doctoral thesis on twentieth-century Chinese decadent literature.

5. In terms of Chinese literary production in general during this period, Julia Lovell observes that there was an average of eight increasingly socialist realist novels being published each year between 1949 and 1966, and that figure shrank during the Cultural Revolution. She further adds that an independent relationship between a mainland Chinese writer and a Western translator (or vice versa) was virtually impossible (Lovell 2012).

6. This is sometimes referred to as 'residual modernism' (Tang 2000, 198–200) because Western Modernism *was* extensively introduced and developed in China at the beginning of the twentieth century—but Proust did not receive much attention—and was only severely interrupted after the establishment of the PRC in 1949.

7. For a list of extracts and novellas selected for translation, see Huang (2013, 297).

8. It is difficult to assess the general impact of this event on ordinary Chinese people throughout China. Western and Chinese media, both calling on witnesses, tend to offer polarized views on the subject. But the Chinese intelligentsia was certainly hurt most deeply, and the event decidedly changed their relation with the state. See X. Zhang (2001, 14–15).

9. Personal communication effectuated on 16 November 2012, on the Proust Study Day organized by Mireille Naturel, entitled 'Le Centre de Recherches Proustiennes de la Sorbonne nouvelle: historique et perspectives'. See also Milly (1991). Milly is still in close collaboration with the translator Xu Hejin, who is responsible for one of the two new translations of *La Recherche*. Milly's new extensive preface interestingly mentions the theme of homosexuality several times, in sharp contrast to André Maurois's preface included in the first translation of *La Recherche*. The importance of *La Recherche*'s Chinese prefaces will be fully explored later in this chapter.

10. 'Je crois que, avec le développement de cette recherche et compte tenu de la multiplicité des éditions de *la Recherche* en France, il apparaîtra dans quelques années une nouvelle traduction chinoise, moins commerciale, plus littéraire et de meilleure qualité' (Xu 1992, 180).

11. For an insightful account of Chinese intellectuals' position after Tiananmen, see X. Zhang (2001, 14–24).

12. I will return to Zhou's remark in Sect. 2.5.

13. There have been important scholarly works that explore the 'postmodern elements' in Proust's work, perceiving Proust as a proto-postmodern writer. However, this is not the way Proust was received in China. My focus here and later in Chap. 3 is on certain 'postmodern characteristics' reflected in mainland Chinese writers' *use* of Proust. See Gray (1992).

14. The theoretical legitimacy of discoursing on Chinese postmodernism was most famously initiated by Frederic Jameson's guest lecture at Peking University in 1985. It was later published in Chinese as 'Postmodernism and Cultural Theory', which exercised a profound influence on many Chinese intellectuals far into the 1990s.

15. The quotation continues: 'Chinese *postmodernism* is the most forceful expression of these anomalies and contradictions in the realm of art and culture' (Lu 2001, 66).

16. Full publication details of all the above-mentioned editions are given in the bibliography.

17. For an example, see Christopher Prendergast's (2002) preface to the Penguin translation of *La Recherche*.

18. The quoted phrase is taken from Zhou's 'Abridgement Notice' (2009). In Shen's *Essential Selection*, similar remarks are made by the general director of the book series, Liu, in the preface. In the Western context, however, such a 'taster' approach to Proust in translation tends to appear in the audiobook version, but the choices of the passages are often made by the producer (rather than the translator) from the available translation in print. See, for example, Wimmer (2010).

19. The tendency to 'kitschify' Proust's work in the Chinese *creative* reception of *La Recherche* will be examined in the next chapter.

20. However, the editor of the *First Translation* does specify that there were indeed attempts before and during the translation process to unify proper nouns.

21. This is an important anecdote recounted by the translator Zhou himself. See K. Zhou (2012, 193).

22. It is worth reminding ourselves that the reform and opening up policy of China was in place for barely 10 years by then and the field of Proust Studies was still in its embryonic stage.

23. The Yilin translation carried out by Xu Hejin will be referred to as 'Xu's Translation', abbreviated as *XT I-IV* in the in-text citations. The Yiwen translation undertaken by Zhou Kexi will be referred to as 'Zhou's Translation'. Note that the publisher Yiwen bought the copyright of only the first volume of *La Recherche*, and Zhou subsequently published his translation of *À l'ombre des jeunes filles en fleurs* with People's Literature Publishing House, and then all three volumes he has translated so far (including *La Prisonnière*) with East China Normal University Press. All these translations are based on the new French Pléiade edition published in 1987 and will be referred to as 'Zhou's Translation', abbreviated as *ZT I, II, V* in the in-text citations. To avoid referential confusions, I will stick to those editions published by East China Normal University Press.

24. I will examine the 'exact' influence of this preface on mainland Chinese writers in the next chapter.

25. This preface was originally written in 1987 but rewritten for the new Flammarion edition in 2009. I use the new edition of Xu's Translation, published in 2010, which includes Milly's revised preface. Milly's central points do not change, but certain paragraphs, especially those at the beginning of the preface, are considerably reformulated. Instead of using section breaks as in the original preface, Milly gives a new subtitle to each section in the revised preface, which helps clarify his analysis.

26. Prendergast justifies the editorial decision not to include the indexes as follows: 'the experience of reading Proust's novel is co-extensive with the experience of his narrator-hero *in* the novel, namely the repeated pattern of forgetting and remembering, getting lost and refinding one's way, and that detailed "guides" sit uneasily with this important dimension of the work' (2002, x).

27. This point will be illustrated in our case-study section 'Translating Montjouvain'.

28. See F. Wang's (2008, 126) remark on the 'bad example' of Europeanized Chinese syntaxes. For a discussion on the linguistic 'normality' and 'abnormality' of modern and contemporary Chinese, see G. Yu (2002, 151–168).

29. Tu Weiqun, 'Les possibilités du chinois contemporain face à la richesse langagière proustienne', presented at the conference entitled 'Comment traduire Proust? Problématiques traductologiques et réflexions théoriques', which took place in Paris on 28–29 November 2013. The conference proceedings have not been published.

30. I will notably examine Zhou's lexical adoption of the modern, classically informed character *pi* 癖 (proclivity) in his translation of 'sadomasochism' in Sect. 2.9.

31. See Note 3.

32. Venuti was quoting Berman's (1992, 65) remark of Goethe's thinking. I have largely adapted both Venuti's and Berman's words to my discussion of Proust's translation in the Chinese context.

33. Zhou's final section does, however, include the last few pages of *Du côté de chez Swann*, where the narrator's voice re-enters.

34. Four volumes of Heuet's adaption are currently available, but only two volumes were available in 2006.

35. In a recent interview, Heuet frankly admits that there were cases in which he was obliged to 'correct' Proust's text in order to make it more comprehensible. 'Stéphane Heuet et Daniel Mesguich' on *Radio Française Internationale* (RIF) broadcasted on 5 February 2014. http://www.rfi.fr/emission/20140205-2-stephane-heuet-daniel-mesguich. [Accessed on 3 December 2014].

36. It refers to the section included in the first volume, *Du côté de chez Swann*, as different from the title of the fourth volume, *Le Côté de Guermantes*, which appears later.

37. In this section, I will adopt a more conventional *prescriptive* approach to the various Chinese translations of Proust's passage, which may appear to be 'an invariably source-oriented exercise' that 'constantly [holds] the original up as an absolute standard and touchstone' with 'the implicit norm being a transcendental and utopian conception of translation as reproducing the original, the whole original and nothing but the original' (Hermans [1985] 2014, 9). But it *is* my purpose in this short section—and in the interests of many readers' expectation of some kind of 'translation quality assessment'—to illustrate what exactly happens syntactically and lexically in the Chinese translations of *La Recherche* in *practice*. A much more theoretically informed *descriptive* approach to the translation of Proust's sexual discourses will be adopted in the next section, which aims to uncover the evolving ambient ideological current behind translation choices and to link them with broader socio-political discourses on sexuality in the Chinese context.

38. I have retranslated this sentence—and hereafter—from Chinese back to French and English to help clarify my points, especially for the benefits of

those readers whose knowledge of the Chinese language is limited. The retranslation tries to be as 'literal' as possible—lexically and syntactically as close as possible to Proust's translated text in Chinese. However, in terms of verbal conjugation, only the present tense is consistently used, as the Chinese language does not employ this grammatical feature to indicate temporality. Likewise, relative pronouns are added only out of grammatical necessity and are indicated accordingly. Finally, the use of punctuation in the retranslation corresponds exactly to that in the Chinese translation, which may not at all conform to its usual French and English usage.

39. This is Zhou's original remark: 'I'm being a bit considerate, because I hope that the book I've been translating will still have readers. I translate for the reader' ('我是有点仁，因为觉得我翻译出来的书还是希望有读者读的。我是为读者翻译的') (Zhou 2012, 196, 198).

40. Remarkably, a few details of this erotic foreplay appear to have been taken out in Shen's *Essential Selection*. I will soon return to this observation.

41. '当然苦涩之情完全不同' (*FT I*, 117); '只是痛苦得并不相同' (*XT I*, 160).

42. I have underlined the change of punctuation from full stop to comma.

43. In many ways, my critical approach is quite similar to Siobhan Brownlie's (2006) take on the five British (re)translations of Zola's *Nana*, where the comparison of the treatment of sensual material is used to map the changing ideologies in British society since Victorian times.

44. See Sang (2003, 166–169) for a more detailed bibliographic survey on this topic.

45. Among them, Freud's and Ellis's writings have arguably exerted the longest-lasting impact on contemporary Chinese sexual discourses until today. I will therefore mainly cite the Chinese translation of these two authors' works while making links to the evolving sexual vocabulary used by Proust's Chinese translators.

46. The Chinese translation of Foucault's *Histoire de la sexualité* first appeared in 1988, followed by *Folie et déraison: Histoire de la folie à l'âge classique* in 1990, but they proved to be intellectually inaccessible for the Chinese public then.

47. Major works of reference include Gulik (1961), Xiong (1984), and Hinsch (1992).

48. Philippe, Prince of Eulenburg-Hertefeld, was accused of homosexual conduct which would have potentially involved the emperor Kaiser Wilhelm II himself. This scandal is often seen to have provoked the first major public discussion of homosexuality in Germany (Schmid 2004, 363–364).

49. Freud's *Three Essays on the Theory of Sexuality* (1905) and *Introductory Lectures on Psycho-analysis* (1916–1917) and Ellis's *Psychology of Sex* (1933) are among the most frequently retranslated sexological works.

For Freud, see Gao (1985), Lin (1986), L. Zhou (2014), Liao (2015), and Y. Xu (2015); for Ellis, see Pan ([1946] 1987), Chen et al. (2011), and Jia (2015). *Shi-nüe-kuang* is consistently used in all these translations except for Pan's and Jia's. Some translators such as Lin (1986, 36) frequently replace *kuang* with an even more explicitly pathological term, *zheng* (症), meaning 'disease' or 'illness'.

50. Ellis (1933, 113, 147), too, considers sadomasochism to be a 'sexual deviation' and advocates 'the scientific and medical approach' to 'sexual anomalies, and if necessary to treat them, but not to condemn them'.

51. For a detailed discussion of the ambient ideological currents in the 1980s, based on official discourses on sexuality in the PRC, see Y. Li (2014, under '性行为规范的变迁').

52. Ellis (1954 [1933], 112–113) specifically disqualifies the suitability of the word 'perversion' (*xing biantai*)—hence his suggestion of 'sexual deviation'—to designate 'sexual activities entirely and by preference outside the range in which procreation is possible'. Ellis's most celebrated Chinese translator, PAN Guangdan (1987, 182), is also explicit about Ellis's advocacy of the term, which he translates as *xing de qibian* (sexual divergence and change). Pan's translation was originally published in 1946 and was reprinted many times in the 1980s. In fact, it continues to be reprinted today, especially due to the epistemic values manifested in Pan's notes that prompted the revaluation and reinvention of traditional Chinese scholarship on sexuality (Guo 2016, 48). In this light, Liu appears to have deliberately *chosen* to clinically pathologize and morally condemn non-procreative sexual activities.

53. The original expression from the *First Translation* is 施虐狂患者 (the patient of abuse craze), and the one from the *Essential Selection* is 施虐狂的病例 (the clinical case of abuse craze).

54. As we will see, this particularly holds true for Xu's and Zhou's new translations. The quotation is borrowed from Sang (2003, 101), although the author is engaging with the Chinese translation of Western sexological discourses in the Republican period.

55. Some translators and sociologists do explain the etymologies of 'sadism' and 'masochism' and have attempted to translate them phonetically, but only in passing. Pan (1987) and Jia (2015) employ *sa-de xianxiang* (Sade phenomenon) and *ma-suo-ke xianxiang* (Masoch phenomenon); Chen et al. (2011) even coin the terms *sa-de-kuang* (Sade craze) and *ma-suo-ke kuang* (Masoch craze). These phonetic renditions have never gained popularity even within professional circles. Incidentally, Sade's and Sacher-Masoch's works still remain largely untranslated in Chinese today.

56. Both *nüelian* and the acronym 'SM' have gained huge popularity in China thanks to sensationalist Internet media. But they are generally used to

describe the kind of mental—rather than physical—sadomasochism frequently found in Chinese and Korean TV drama series.

57. In order to mark the literary register of *pi* for the purpose of comparison with *qingxiang* (tendency), I have chosen to translate it as 'proclivity'.
58. For an example, see MAI Yongxiong's (2013, 69–70) recent discussion of Deleuze's essay on masochism.
59. For a recent book-length study of Proustian inversion as a literary aesthetic, see Fladenmuller (2015).
60. For an extensive list of similar pathological remarks on homosexuality made by mainland Chinese sexologists and psychiatrists in the 1980s and 1990s, see Chou (2000, 111–113).
61. Interestingly, *yinrou* is one of Wei's perceptions of Proust's work as a whole. See Chap. 3.
62. Main homosexual characters such as Charlus and Saint-Loup in *A la recherche* are portrayed as victims of the 'ideal of virility'. See Proust (*RTP IV*, 323–325) for his explicit discussion of homosexuality and virilism.
63. For a short discussion of the emergence of the new bio-scientific meaning of *xing* (originally meaning 'nature' or 'human nature') for 'sex' or 'sexuality' in the early twentieth century, see Sang (2003, 103). A more extensive exploration of this semantic transformation can be found in Rocha (2010).
64. See Eells (2002, 24–26) for a more detailed illustration of this point.
65. For example, *fen/yu tao* (分/余桃, split peach), *duan xiu* (断袖, cut sleeve), *long yang* (龙阳, proper name of a ruler), and *qi xiongdi* (契兄弟, contract brothers) for (different kinds of) male homosexuals; words for female homosexuals are fewer but far from non-existent: *jinlan* (金兰) and *zishu nü* (自梳女, self-combing girl) are two examples. For a fascinating account of these terms and their contexts, see Chou (2000, 26–42) and Li (2009, 9–20).
66. At this stage, it is technically impossible to gain a global view of the evolving discourse on homosexuality across translations because both new translations are still works in progress. The following observations are based on the (re)translated volumes of *Sodome et Gomorrhe* (by Xu) and *La Prisonnière* (by Zhou).
67. As mentioned before, whereas Zhou's new translation is based on the new Pléiade edition published between 1987 and 1989, the *First Translation* is based on the old Pléiade published in 1954.
68. This verse in the *Chinese Translation* is rather forcedly translated as '就为我们是鸡奸, /要毁只有被火毁'.
69. The nonetheless sizeable Christian community in China is very diverse. They do not, however, share a common discourse on homosexuality, and the subject of homosexuality has rarely topped the priority list of their

theological teaching. Christian discourses have seldom been explicitly used to condemn homosexuality in China.

70. Xu does elucidate the ambiguity of Proust's use of the word 'vice' in his postscript (*XT IV*, 736).

71. Conversely, as Eells (2002, 190) remarks, Proust himself often 'appropriates English words, encoding them with meaning and placing them almost systematically in a context relating to homosexuality'. See also Hayes (1995). The kind of interpenetration between English and French with regards to homosexual characters' codified language in Proust's novel poses further challenges for Chinese translators.

72. The legal action recently taken by a lesbian student from Sun Yat-sen University in Guangzhou, demanding the removal and correction of the pathological reference to homosexuality in one of the national psychology textbooks, has again sparked off public debates and attracted international media attention. 'Fighting the views of homosexuality in China's textbooks', Stephen McDonell, BBC News, last modified 12 September 2016, http://www.bbc.com/news/world-asia-china-37335802.

REFERENCES

Ahlstedt, Eva. 1985. *La Pudeur en crise: un aspect de l'accueil d'A la recherche du temps perdu de Marcel Proust*. Paris: J. Touzot.

Barthes, Roland. 1972. *Le Degré zéro de l'écriture suivi de noueaux éssais critiques*. Paris: Seuil.

Bataille, Georges. 1957a. *La Littérature et le mal*. Paris: Gallimard.

Bataille, Georges. 1957b. *L'Érotisme*. Paris: Éditions de Minuit.

Berman, Antoine. 1992. *The Experience of the Foreign: Culture and Translation in Romantic Germany*, trans. S. Heyvaert. Albany: State University of New York Press.

Bersani, Leo. 1995. *Homos*. Cambridge: Havard University Press.

Beugnet, Martine, and Marion Schmid. 2004. *Proust at the Movies*. Aldershot: Ashgate.

Brownlie, Siobhan. 2006. Narrative Theory and Retranslation Theory. *Across Languages and Cultures* 7 (2): 147–170.

Cairns, Lucille. 1997. Homosexuality and Lesbianism in Proust's Sodome et Gomorrhe. *French Studies* 51 (1): 43–57.

Chen, Weizheng, Decheng Yuan, Kui Long, Zuohong Wang, and Bangxian Zhou, trans. 2011. *Xing xinlixue* 性心理学 (Psychology of Sex), by Havelock Ellis. Nanjing: Yilin chubanshe.

Chou, Wah-shan. 2000. *Tongzhi: Politics of Same-Sex Eroticism in Chinese Societies*. New York: The Haworth Press.

Compagnon, Antoine. 1989. *Proust entre deux siècles*. Paris: Gallimard.

Deane-Cox, Sharon. 2014. *Retranslation: Translation, Literature and Reinterpretation*. London: Bloomsbury Academic.

Douglas, Saylor B. 1993. *The Sadomasochistic Homotext: Readings in Sade, Balzac and Proust*. New York: Peter Lang.

Eells, Emily. 2002. *Proust's Cup of Tea: Homoeroticism and Victorian Culture*. Aldershot: Ashgate.

Eells-Ogée, Emily. 1987. *Introduction to Sodome et Gomorrhe I*, by Marcel Proust, 11–51. Paris: Flammarion.

Ellis, Havelock. 1954 [1933]. *Psychology of Sex*. New York: The New American Library of World Literature.

Ellis, Havelock. 1936. *From Rousseau to Proust*. London: Constable and Company Ltd.

Fladenmuller, Frédéric. 2015. *Proust, ou, L'Écriture inversive: du temps perdu au temps retrouvé*. New York: Peter Lang.

Freud, Hendrika C. 2013. *Men and Mothers: The Lifelong Struggle of Sons and Their Mothers*. London: Karnac Books.

Furth, Charlotte. 1988. Androgynous Males and Deficient Females: Biology and Gender Boundaries in Sixteenth- and Seventeenth-Century China. *Late Imperial China* 9 (2): 1–30.

Gao, Juefu, trans. 1985. *Jingshen fenxi yinlun* 精神分析引论 (Introductory Lectures on Psycho-analysis), by Sigmund Freud. Beijing: Commercial Press.

Genette, Gérard. 1980. *Narrative Discourse: An Essay in Method*, trans. Jane E. Lewin. Ithaca: Cornell University Press.

Gray, Margaret. 1992. *Postmodern Proust*. Philadelphia: University of Pennsylvania Press.

Guo, Ting. 2016. Translating Homosexuality into Chinese: A Case Study of Pan Guangdan's Translation of Havelock Ellis' Pyschology of Sex: A Manual for Students (1933). *Asia Pacific Translation and Intercultural Studies* 3 (1): 47–61.

Han, Hulin. 1990. Zheli you yipian pinghe de jingtu-ji zhuiyi sishui nianhua de yizhemen 这里有一遍平和的净土–记《追忆似水年华》的译者们 (Here is a peaceful land: A note on the translators of La Recherche). *China Publishing Journal* 4: 60–65.

Hayes, Jarrod. 1995. Proust in the Tearoom. *PMLA* 110 (5): 992–1005.

Hermans, Theo. 2014 [1985]. Introduction: Translation Studies and a New Paradigm. In *The Manipulation of Literature*. Studies in Literary Translation, ed. Theo Hermans. New York: Routledge.

Hinsch, Bret. 1992. *Passions of the Cut Sleeve: The Male Homosexual Tradition in China*. Berkeley: University of California Press.

Huang, Hong. 2013. Proust retrouvé. In *D'après Proust*, ed. Philippe Forest and Stéphane Audeguy, 294–304. Paris: Nouvelle Revue Française.

Kaske, Elizabeth. 2004. Mandarin, Vernacular Chinese and National Language–China's Emerging Concept of a National Language in the Early Twentieth Century. In *Mapping Meanings: The Field of New Learning in Late Qing China*, ed. Michael Lackner and Natascha Vittinghoff, 265–314. Leiden: Brill.

Ladenson, Elizabeth. 1999. *Proust's Lesbianism*. Ithaca, NY: Cornell University Press.

Ladenson, Elizabeth. 2014. Sexuality. In *Proust in Context*, ed. Adam Watt, 115–122. Cambridge: Cambridge University Press.

Li, Hengji, Jizeng Xu, Yufang Gui, Shuren Yuan, Lizhen Pan, Yuanchong Xu, Jun Xu, et al., trans. 2008 [1989–1991]. *Zhuiyi sishui nianhua* 追忆似水年华 (In Search of Lost Time), by Marcel Proust, 3 vols. Nanjing: Yilin chubanshe.

Li, Yinhe. 1998a. *Nüelian yawenhua* 虐恋亚文化 (The Subculture of Sadomasochism). Beijing: Jinri zhongguo chubanshe.

Li, Yinhe. 2009 [1998b]. *Tongxinglian yawenhua* 同性恋亚文化 (The Subculture of Homosexuality). Hohhot: Inner Mongolia University Press.

Li, Yinhe. 1998c. *Zhongguo nüxing de ganqing yu xing* 中国女性的感情与性 (Love and Sexuality of Chinese Women). Beijing: Jinri zhongguo chubanshe.

Li, Yinhe. 2014. *Xinzhongguo xinghuayu yanjiu* 新中国性话语研究 (Studies in Sexual Discourses in the PRC). Dangdang eBook. Shanghai: Shanghai Academy of Social Sciences Press.

Liao, Yudi, trans. 2015. *Xingxue yu aiqing xinlixue* 性学与爱情心理学 (Sex and Love Psychology), by Sigmund Freud. Nanchang: Jiangxi renmin chubanshe.

Lin, Keming, trans. 1986. *Aiqing xinli xue* 爱情心理学 (Psychology of Love), by Sigmund Freud. Beijing: Zuojia chubanshe.

Liu, Dalin. 1988. *Xing shehuixue* 性社会学 (Sexual Sociology). Jinan: Shandong renmin chubanshe.

Liu, Mingjiu. 2013 [1992]. Pulusite chuanqi 普鲁斯特传奇 (Proust's Legend). In *Zhuiyi sishui nianhua. Jinghuaben*. 追忆似水年华 (精华本) (In Search of Lost Time. Essential Selection), by Masai'er Pulusite, trans. Zhiming Shen, 1–15. Shanghai: Yiwen.

Lovell, Julia. 2012. The Key to China. *Prospect*. http://www.prospectmagazine.co.uk/magazine/the-key-to-china-literary-magazines-new-chinese-fiction-pathlight-chutzpah. Accessed 7 Nov 2016.

Lozinsky, Elena. 2013. *L'Intertexte fin-de-siècle dans À la recherche du temps perdu de Marcel Proust: Les Carafes dans la Vivonne*. Paris: Champion.

Lu, Sheldon H. 2001. *Transnational Visuality, Global Postmodernity*. Stanford: Stanford University Press.

Lucey, Michael. 2006. *Never Say I: Sexuality and The First Person in Colette, Gide, and Proust*. Durham: Duke University Press.

Mai, Yongxiong. 2013. *Delezi zhexing shixue: kua yujing lilun yiyi* 德勒兹折性诗学: 跨语境理论意义 (Deleuze's Philosophical Poetics: Cross-Contextual Theory and Meaning). Guilin: Guangxi Normal University Press.

Maurois, André. 1954. Préface. In *A la recherche du temps perdu I*, by Marcel Proust, ed. Pierre Clarac and André Ferré, xiii–xv. Paris: Gallimard.

Milly, Jean. 1991. La Chine rattrape le temps perdu. *Libération*, December 26.

Milly, Jean. 2009 [1987]. Préface. In *Du côté de chez Swann*, by Proust Marcel, 3–39. Paris: Flammarion.

Min, Le. 1997. Hanyu de ouhua 汉语的欧化 (The Europeanization of Chinese). *Baijia zhengyan* 百家诤言 12: 29–33.

Moncrieff, C. K. Scott and Stephen Hudson, trans. 2006. Remembrance of Things Past by Marcel Proust. 2 vols. Hertfordshire: Wordsworth Editions.

Morand, Paul. 1954. *L'Eau sous les ponts*. Paris: Grasset.

Muller, Marcel. 1971. Sodome I ou la naturalisation de Charlus. *Poétique* 8: 470–478.

Ning, Jia, trans. 2015. *Xing xinlixue* 性心理学 (Psychology of Sex), by Havelock Ellis. Nanjing: Yilin chubanshe.

Orr, Mary. 2003. *Intertextuality: Debates and Contexts*. Cambridge: Polity.

Pan, Guangdan, trans. 1987 [1946]. *Xing xinlixue* 性心理学 [Psychology of Sex], by Havelock Ellis. Beijing: Sanlian shudian chubanshe.

Prendergast, Christopher. 2002. General Editor's Preface. In *The Way by Swann's*, by Marcel Proust, trans. Lydia Davis, vii–xxi. London: Penguin.

Proust, Marcel. 1987–1989. *À la recherche du temps perdu*, ed. J.-Y. Tadié, 4 vols. Paris: Pléiade.

Proust, Marcel. 2002. *In Search of Lost Time*, trans. Lydia Davies, James Grieve, Mark Treharne, John Sturrock, Carol Clark, and Ian Patterson, 6 vols. London: Penguin.

Proust, Marcel. 1990. Lettre à Paul Souday [10 novembre 1919]. In *Correspondance XVIII*, ed. Philip Kolb, 464. Paris: Plon.

Pym, Anthony. 1998. *Method for Translation History*. Manchester: St Jerome.

Rivers, J.E. 1980. *Proust and the Art of Love: The Aesthetics of Sexuality in the Life, Times, and Art of Marcel Proust*. New York: Columbia University Press.

Rocha, Leon Antonio. 2010. Xing: The Discourse of Sex and Human Nature in Modern China. *Gender and History* 22 (3): 603–608.

Sang, Tze-lan. 2003. *The Emerging Lesbian: Female Same-Sex Desire in Modern China*. Chicago: University of Chicago Press.

Schmid, Marion. 2004. Eulenbourg (Philippe, prince de) [1847–1921]. In *Dictionnaire Marcel Proust*, ed. Annick Bouillaguet and Bryan Rogers, 363–364. Paris: Champion.

Schmid, Marion. 2013. Proust at the Ballet: Literature and Dance in Dialogue. *French Studies* 2: 184–198.

Schmid, Marion. 2006. The Birth and Development of À la recherche du temps perdu. In *The Cambridge Companion to Proust*, ed. Richard Bales, 58–73. Cambridge: Cambridge University Press.

Sedgwick, Eve Kosofsky. 2008 [1990]. *Epistemology of the Closet.* Berkeley: University of California Press.

Shen, Zhiming, trans. 2012 [1992]. *Zhuiyi sishui nianhua. Jinghuaben.* 追忆 似水年华. 精华本. (In Search of Lost Time. Essential Selection.), by Marcel Proust. Shanghai: Yiwen.

Simon, Sherry. 1996. *Gender in Translation: Cultural Identity and the Politics of Transmission.* London: Routledge.

Sun, Kun. 2006. Yinghanyu fanyi yu biaodianfuhao yanjiu 英汉语翻译与标点符号研究 (The Study on C-E & E-C Translation and Punctuation). In *Zhongguo yinghanyu bijiao yanjiuhui diqici quanguo xueshu yantao lunwenji* 中国英汉语比较研究会第七次全国学术研讨会论文集 (Collected Essays from the Seventh National Conference of the Society for English-Chinese Comparative Studies), 1–10. Yantai.

Tadié, Jean-Yves. 1996. *Marcel Proust.* Paris: Gallimard.

Tadié, Jean-Yves. 2003. *Proust et le roman.* Paris: Gallimard.

Tang, Xiaobing. 2000. *Chinese Modern: The Heroic and the Quotidian.* Duke: Duke University Press.

Terence, Kilmartin. 1981. Translating Proust. *Grand Street* 1 (1): 134–146.

Tu, Weiqun. 1999. *Pulusite pingzhuan* 普鲁斯特评传 (A Critical Biography of Proust). Hangzhou: Zhejiang wenyi chubanshe.

Tu, Weiqun. 2010. Wenxue jiezuo de yongheng shengming: Guanyu Zhuiyi sishui nianhua de langge zhongyiben 文学杰作的永恒生命: 关于《追忆》的两个中译本 (The Eternal Life of Great Literary Work: About the Two Chinese Translations of In Search of Lost Time). *Wenyi yanjiu* 文艺研究 12: 138–148.

Tu, Weiqun. 2012. Xinzhongguo 60 nian pulusite xiaoshuo yanjiu zhi kaocha yu fenxi 新中国60年普鲁斯特小说研究之考察与分析 (A Review and Analysis of Proust Studies in China Over the Past 60 Years). *Journal of Peking University (Philosophy and Social Sciences)* 49 (3): 91–100.

Van Gulik, Robert Hans. 1961. *Sexual Life in Ancient China.* Leiden: Brill.

Venuti, Lawrence. 1995. *The Translator's Invisibility: A History of Translation.* London: Routledge.

Venuti, Lawrence. 2002 [1998]. *The Scandals of Translation: Towards an Ethics of Difference.* New York: Routledge.

Venuti, Lawrence. 2004. Retranslation: The Creation of Value. In *Translation and Culture*, ed. Katherine M. Faull, 25–38. Lewisburg: Bucknell University Press.

Wang, Fei. 2008. Fanyi yu xiandai baihuawen de xingcheng 翻译与现代白话文的形成 (On the Role of Translation in the Formation of Modern Vernacular

Chinese). *Journal of Anqing Teachers College (Social Science Edition)* 27 (1): 124–127.

Wang, Hongjian. 2012. Performing Perversion: Decadence in Twentieth-Century Chinese Literature. PhD dissertation, University of Chicago, ProQuest LLC.

Wang, Jiaxin. 1997. *Happy Together.* Directed by Kar-wai Wang. Kino International.

Wang, Jiaxin. 2013. Fanyi wenxue, fanyi, fanyiti 翻译文学,翻译,翻译体 (Literature in Translation, Translation, Translationese). *Contemporary Chinese Writers Criticism* 当代中国作家批评 2: 129–137.

Wang, Xiaobo, and Yinhe Li. 1992. *Tamen de shijie* 他们的世界 (Their World). Taiyuan: Shanxi renmin chubanshe.

Wimmer, Maria. 2010. *Auf der Suche nach der verlorenen Zeit (Audio-CD).*

Wood, Michael. 2013. Translations. In *Marcel Proust in Context*, 230–240. Cambridge: Cambridge University Press.

Xiong, Xiaoming. 1984. *Zhongguo tongxing'ai shilu* 中国同性爱史录 (The History of Chinese Homosexual Love). Hong Kong: Fenhong Sanjiao Chubanshe.

Xu, Hejin. 1992. La Traduction de La Recherche en chinois. *Bulletin Marcel Proust* 42: 179–180.

Xu, Hejin, trans. 2005–2014. *Zhuiyi sishui nianhua* 追忆似水年华 (In Search of Lost Time), by Marcel Proust, Vols. I–IV. 4 vols. Nanjing: Yilin chubanshe.

Xu, Jun. 1993. Juzi yu fanyi—ping zhuiyi sishui nianhua hanyi chanju de chuli 句子与翻译–评《追忆似水年华》汉译长句的处理 (Sentence and Translation: Accessing the Chinese Translation of Long Sentences in In Search of Lost Time). *Waiyu Yanjiu* 外语研究 *(Foreign Studies)* 1: 9–16.

XU, Jun. 2007. Pulusite zai zhongguo de yijie licheng 普鲁斯特在中国的译介历程 (Translating Proust into Chinese: Retrospection and Reflection). *Chinese Translators Journal* (1): 27–31.

Xu, Yin, trans. 2015. *Xingxue sanlun* 性学三论 (Three Essays on the Theory of Sexuality), by Sigmund Freud. Hangzhou: Zhejiang wenyi chubanshe.

Yu, Guangzhong. 2002. *Yu Guangzhong tan fanyi* 余光中谈翻译 (Yu Guangzhong Discussing Translation). Beijing: China Translation & Publishing Corporation.

Zeitlin, Judith. 1993. *Historian of the Strange: Pu Songling and the Chinese Classical Tale.* Stanford: Stanford University Press.

Zhang, Beichuan. 1994. *Tongxing'ai* 同性爱 [Homosexual Love]. Shandong: Shandong Science and Technology Press.

Zhang, Xudong. 2001. *Wither China: Intellectual Politics in Contemporary China.* Duke: Duke University Press.

Zhang, Yinde. 2003. *Le Monde romanesque chinois au XXe siècle. Modernité et identité.* Paris: Champion.

Zhang, Yuan. 1996. *East Palace, West Palace*. Directed by Yuan Zhang. Fortissimo Films.

Zhou, Kexi. 2006. Yixu 译序 (Preface to the Translation). In *A la recherche du temps perdu (comic book adaptation)*, by Stéphane Heuet, trans. Kexi Zhou. Beijing: People's Literature Publishing House.

Zhou, Kexi, Trans. 2009. *Qu siwanjia nabian. Jieben* 去斯万家那边. 节本 (The Way by Swanns. Abridged trans.), by Marcel Proust. Shanghai: Sanlian shudian.

Zhou, Kexi. 2012. *Yi Bian Cao* 译边草. Shanghai: East China Normal University Press.

Zhou, Kexi. 2012 [2003]. Yixu 译序 (Preface to the Translation). In *Zhuixun shiqu de shiguang* 追寻逝去的时光 (In Search of Lost Time), by Ma'saier Pulusite, 453–459. Shanghai: East China Normal University Press.

Zhou, Kexi. 2012 [2004–2012]. *Zhuixun shiqu de shiguang* 追寻逝去的时光 (In Search of Lost Time), by Marcel Proust, vols. I, II, V. 3 vols. Shanghai: East China Normal University Press.

Zhou, Li, trans. 2014. *Jingshen fenxi yinlun* 精神分析引论 (Introductory Lectures on Psycho-analysis), by Sigmund Freud. Wuhan: Wuhan Publishing House.

CHAPTER 3

Proust and Mainland Chinese Writers: *La Recherche* and Its Postmodern Hypertexts

3.1 INTRODUCTION

In Chap. 2, I examined certain discursive and epistemic shifts reflected in the old and new translations of *La Recherche*, but the impact of the ongoing new translations of the work on the younger generations of writers and their reception of Proust's work will have to wait for at least another decade to be properly assessed. The present chapter will focus on three mainland Chinese writers' creative reception and intertextual engagement with just one particular translation of *La Recherche*—the *First Translation*—in their respective novellas and short stories.

The three writers chosen for our corpus, Wang Xiaobo (1952–1997), Yu Hua (1960–), and Wei Hui (1973–), represent three successive generations and different literary schools of contemporary Chinese writers. Whilst they share a number of common intertextual and appropriative strategies, their respective engagements with Proust are greatly influenced by, and at the same time interact with, the *First Translation*. This corpus has been informed largely by the existing scholarship on the subject. For example, Huang Hong (2013, 294–304) and Yinde Zhang (2003, 109–132) have, albeit briefly, studied the intertextual references to Proust in the three writers' works. However, both of them attempt to offer a general overview and tend to treat those references as 'empirical findings' without necessarily investigating textual details and their particular contexts. Huang does not propose any conceptualization of the intertextual phenomenon, let alone examine its cross-cultural

© The Author(s) 2017
S. Li, *Proust, China and Intertextual Engagement*,
DOI 10.1007/978-981-10-4454-0_3

implications. On the other hand, grounded in the context of the entire Chinese literary landscape of the twentieth century, Zhang's seminal work, which deals with Proust and contemporary Chinese intellectual history almost separately, has a much broader scope than mine.

Much like the previous discussion of translation, the present approach firmly embeds the creative reception of Proust's work in China's troubled history of the twentieth century, examining how these literary activities refract not only the internal ideological tensions and transformations of modern and especially post-Mao China, but also the exponential cultural exchange between China and France and the West at large. Against the backdrop of China's explosive development from modernity to postmodernity at the beginning of the 1990s, the 'profound social anomalies and ideological contradictions' (Lu 2001, 66), outlined at the beginning of the last chapter will explain and characterize some of my observations on the three contemporary mainland Chinese writers' equivocal intertextual engagement with Proust. As Lu continues, 'Chinese *postmodernism* is the most forceful expression of these anomalies and contradictions in the realm of art and culture' (ibid.). These writers were, on the one hand, consciously experimenting with Modernist (not just Proust's) styles and techniques, and often prided themselves on being 'avant-gardists'. On the other hand, the ways they took on Proust cannot be innocent of 'kitschifying' him (i.e. reducing Proust's canonical work to an easily 'consumable' level),[1] and of rather superficially citing Proust in order to enhance the cultural prestige of their own works.

The novellas and short stories that I will examine were all written and published in the 1990s.[2] On the surface, their respective uses of Proust appear to be eclectic and do not bespeak any ostensible common ground. But this is precisely one of the reasons why these writers were chosen in the first place: they reflect a representative variety of literary and cultural appropriations of Proust in contemporary Chinese fiction. What will gradually unfold in the course of our study is that these writers' diverse approaches to Proust often illuminate different aspects of the same socio-historical context of a drastically changing China from the 1980s to the 1990s. In this respect, Franco Moretti's (1983, 8) theoretical observation seems particularly relevant to our demonstrative purpose:

> Knowledge of the socio-historical context of a literary work or genre is not therefore an 'extra' to be kept in the margins of rhetorical analysis. In general, whether one is aware of it or not, such knowledge furnishes

the starting point for interpretation itself, providing it with those initial hypotheses without which rhetorical mechanisms would be hard to understand, or would tell us very little indeed.

3.2 WANG XIAOBO'S *SI SHUI LIU NIAN* 似水流年 (FLEETING YEARS AS WATER) (1992)

Wang is a scholar, essayist, and creative writer. He is actively involved in Chinese social and ethical debates on such miscellaneous topics as homosexuality, feminism, Chinese cinema, and the environment, to name but a few. His collection of essays entitled *Wo de jingshen jiayuan* (我的精神家园, *My Spiritual Home*) is representative of the range of cultural and sociological topics with which his writings engage. He is famous for his inclination to play intellectual games and to 'use the language of logic for parody' (Zhang and Sommer 2007, viii) in his creative works.

Although it is not immediately relevant to the present novella, it is worth pointing out that Wang is the husband of the leading Chinese sociologist on gender and sexuality, Li Yinhe, whose influence on the development of the Chinese sexological discourse was noted in Chap. 2. Together, the couple co-authored the first book-length study of predominantly male homosexuality in contemporary mainland China, *Their World*, which came out in 1992 after 3 years of research (coinciding exactly with the first Chinese publication dates of *La Recherche*).[3] Wang's ethical engagement with the topic of homosexuality can be found in his essays, such as 'About the Issue of Homosexuality' ([1994] 2011) and 'About the Ethical Issue of Homosexuality' ([1993] 2011). Furthermore, his other novella, 'Si shui rou qing' (似水柔情, 'Tender Feelings Like Water', 2011), later adapted into the film *East Palace, West Palace* (1996), explicitly deals with homosexuality and sadomasochism.[4] This title strongly echoes 'Si shui liu nian' ('Fleeting Years as Water') because of the shared water analogy, although the two stories are unrelated, and the former does not contain any references to Proust either. Meanwhile, as we will see, although Proust features in 'Fleeting Years as Water', Wang does not engage at all with the themes of homosexuality or sadomasochism in Proust's work. From the critical angle of the present book, this fact reaffirms our observation in Chap. 2 that certain important aspects of *La Recherche*, such as homosexuality, were simply absent in the Chinese reception of Proust's work in the early 1990s, even for those readers and writers who are generally interested in the topic(s) and courageous enough to tackle taboo subjects.

The storyline of 'Fleeting Years as Water' has almost nothing to do with *La Recherche*. It follows a narrator who, through a consistently sarcastic tone, self-referentially recounts the somewhat absurd and grotesque stories and anecdotes of those people of his generation who lived through the hardship of the Cultural Revolution. Yet allusions and references to *La Recherche* suddenly become omnipresent once the narrator has revealed to the reader, in the following 'pivotal' passage which features Proust, why he adopted the title 'Fleeting Year as Water' for this novella:

> 在似水流年里，　有件事叫我日夜不安。在此之前首先要解释一下什么叫似水流年。普鲁斯特写了一本书，谈到自己身上发生过的事。这些事看起来就如一个人中了邪躺在河底，眼看潺潺流水，粼粼流光，落叶，浮木，空玻璃瓶，一样一样从身上流过去。这个书名怎么译，翻译家大费周章。最近的译法是追忆似水年华。听上去普鲁斯特写书时已经死了多时，又诈了尸。而且这也不好念。

> 照我看普鲁斯特的书, 译作似水流年就对了。[...]

> 似水流年是一个人所有的一切，只有这个东西，才真正归你所有。其余的一切，都是片刻的欢愉和不幸，转眼间就跑到那似水流年里去了。我所认识的人，都不珍视自己的似水流年。他们甚至不知道，自己还有这么一件东西，所以一个个像丢了魂一样。(Wang 2011, 169)

In 'Fleeting Years as Water', one thing left me unsettled. But before all that, I need to explain what 'fleeting years as water' is. Proust has written a book about all that happened in his life. It's like a possessed person lying on the riverbed, observing dead leaves, driftwood, and empty bottles, flowing by and being carried away by running water. How to translate the title? It has given the translators a hard time. The most recent translation is 'Pursuing the Memory of Time/Years as Water/River'. It sounds as though Proust was already long since dead when he was writing the book, and then his dead body suddenly stood erect. It is also too much of a mouthful to pronounce.

In my view, it would be just right to translate Proust's book as 'Fleeting Years as Water'. [...]

Time as water is all that we have and it's the only thing that really belongs to us. Everything else is just momentary pleasure and misfortune, which joins the time as water like a flash. The people that I know do not cherish their own fleeting years as water. They don't even know they actually possess such a thing, and so they are all living as if they had lost their souls.

Manifestly, Wang's refutation of the official Chinese title for *La Recherche* derives from the somewhat morbid Chinese expression 'to pursue the memory of' as it is often used in a funereal or obituary context. Interestingly enough, forgetting and remembering actually represent the core dynamics in Proust's conception of death and resurrection. There are vital similitudes between the mourning process and the creation of writing. In Aude le Roux-Kieken's (2005, 156) words, 'les êtres face au deuil (au sens littéral ou au sens amoureux) et dans leur relation à l'art font l'objet d'une même évaluation, quasi axiologique chez Proust' ('people in mourning [whether in the literal sense or after a separation] and in their relation to art are subjected to the same quasi-axiological evaluation in Proust).[5] Wang is probably unaware of Proust's rather positive sentiment about death.[6] In any case, he expects his version of the title, which contains the reference to water but without the implication of death, to be more appealing to the Chinese readership.

Furthermore, Wang's four-character version *si shui liu nian* (hence my four-word translation) serves well as a typical Chinese collocation which conforms to the classical formation of the vast majority of Chinese locutions (known as *chengyu*, 成语). In other words, Wang's title is more catchy and indeed less 'of a mouthful to pronounce'. In the passage quoted, Wang clearly attempts to nuance different modes of temporality: momentary, universal, and individual. They are not conceptually irrelevant to Proust's notions of everything being transformed 'in Time' and writing a book 'about' yet 'outside Time' based on the individual experience 'of time', as well as on Proust's idea of 'temps perdu' understood as 'wasted time'.

The added water element in both the official and Wang's titles is likely to strike Western readers of Proust. This is due to the strong, rich, and recurrent association between time and water/river found in classical Chinese literary texts. In fact, in classical Chinese thought, the perception of the movement of water/river sometimes *is* the definition of 'time' (which is of course different from our modern understanding of it).[7] *The Analects*, a founding text of Confucianism, for example, describes Confucius, standing by the river—rather than lying in or beneath the river as in Wang's case—saying, 'what passes away is, perhaps, like this.

Day and night it never lets up' ('子在川上曰: '逝者如斯夫, 不舍昼夜')
(Lau 1979, 98). On the conceptual level, it is also interesting to see how
Wang's narrator's imagist perception of time and water/river itself signals an ontological *repositioning* from the classical Confucian teaching of
time.

Like *La Recherche*'s famous incipit 'longtemps' ('for a long time')
and ending phrase 'dans le Temps' ('in Time'), Wang begins the novella
with 'years flow (like water)' (*sui yue ru liu*, 岁月如流) and ends with
'(needing a little) more time' (*hai xuyao yidian shijian*, 还需要一点时间)
([1992] 2011, 124, 198). The expression 'fleeting years as water' is
repeated at least 12 times throughout the novella, with slight variations
in terms of word order and substitution with synonyms, which effectively
function as a Proustian leitmotif that holds miscellaneous narrative frag-
ments together while ostensibly trying to bring these very concrete plots
to an abstract and conceptual level concerning time. The following are
some further examples of this structural device, often used at the beginning or towards the end of a section to either introduce or recall a different narrative focus:

流年似水, 转眼就到了不惑之年。好多事情起了变化。(ibid., 130)

Fleeting years as water, in the twinkling of an eye, I've turned forty. Many
things have changed.

流年似水, 有的事情一下子过去了, 有的事情很久也过不去。(ibid., 131)

Fleeting years as water, certain things quickly become past, certain things
stay for a long time.

流年似水, 转眼到了不惑之年。我和大家一样, 对周围的事逐渐司空见惯。
过去的事过去了, 未过去的事也不能叫我惊讶。(ibid., 142)

Fleeting years as water, in the twinkling of an eye, I've turned forty. Like
everyone else, I've gradually become used to things around us. What's past
is past, what has not yet passed will no longer surprise me either.

虽然岁月如流, 什么都会过去, 但总有些东西发生了就不能抹杀。(ibid., 166)

Although as water time flows, everything will pass, but there are always
things which, once they've happened, cannot be effaced.

我说过, 在似水流年里, 有一些事情叫我日夜不安。(ibid., 186)

As I said, in the fleeting years as water, certain things make me uneasy day and night.

For a novella of about 70 pages (in the Chinese edition used), there are 22 divisions, some sections being much longer than others. Indeed, this fragmentary and scattered narrative structure formally embodies what Wang understands by Proust's 'fleeting years as water': 'It's like a possessed person lying on the riverbed, observing dead leaves, driftwood, and empty bottles, flowing by and being carried away by running water' (ibid., 169). Perhaps Wang's various formulations of 'fleeting years as water' are most reminiscent of the final line of Proust's *Du côté de chez Swann*: 'le souvenir d'une certaine image n'est que le regret d'un certain instant; et les maisons, les routes, les avenues, sont fugitives, hélas, comme les années' ('the memory of a certain image is only regret for a certain moment; and houses, roads, avenues are as fleeting, alas, as the years') (*RTP I*, 420; *PT I*, 430). Everything in time passes away like flowing water.

Finally, just as towards the end of his novel Proust's narrator debates what should and should not be included 'in Time' as 'la matière de [son] livre' ('the material of [his] book'), Wang's narrator self-consciously selects and adapts material from his 'fleeting years as water', tentatively making a certain distinction between memory and history: 'if I wrote down all these details, it would be a historical method. For now, I don't know how to employ such a method yet. So I recount my fleeting years as water [...]' ('如果我要把这一切写出来, 就要用史笔。我现在还没有这种笔。所以我叙述我的似水流年') (ibid., 142). Wang's emphasis on the 'fictional' writings of amusing and grotesque anecdotes against the atrocious backdrop of the Cultural Revolution enhances the bitter irony of the novella. The only fictional things are the names of the characters and places, as the narrator concludes:

写小说不可以用真名, [...] 所以在本书里,没有一个名字是真的。[...] 人名不真, 地点不真,唯一真实的是我写到的事。不管是龟头血肿还是贺先生跳楼, 都是真的。(ibid., 143)

We can't use real names when writing novels [...] Therefore in this book, none of the names are real. [...] The names of the characters are unreal, the names of the places are unreal, only the things I write about are real. Whether it's Swelling Glans or the jump-out-of-the-building Mr. He, it's all real [...].

Thus, in addition to the Proustian themes of time and memory, Wang seems also to have picked up the characteristic of *La Recherche* as *autofiction*, in which the author deliberately takes a fictional diversion from real autobiographical events. Just like Proust's somewhat apocryphal revelation of his protagonist-narrator's name as 'Marcel', who 'évolue pourtant dans un univers en grande partie imaginaire' ('evolves nevertheless in a largely imaginary universe') (Colonna 1989, 16, 24), Wang's protagonist-narrator is named 'Wang Er', literally Wang Number Two, which points to the author's status as the second son of the family, following the traditional methods of ranking sons.[8]

3.3   Yu Hua's *Zai Xiyu Zhong Huhan* 在细雨中呼喊 (*Cries in the Drizzle*) (1991)[9]

3.3.1   *Prefaces*

Yu is a key member of the Chinese literary movement known as Chinese Avant-garde Literature (*Zhongguo xianfengpai wenxue*, 中国先锋派文学) which briefly flourished in the 1980s. *Cries*, Yu's first novel, was published in 1991, the same year as the complete Chinese publication of *La Recherche* appeared. The novel is often said to mark the writer's intellectual and artistic transformation from the Kafkaesque world of absurdity and brevity to, in Yu's own words, 'real [or realistic] things' (*xianshi de dongxi*, 现实的东西) (Wang 2005, 159). The critic Isabelle Rabut speaks of 'une métamorphose indiscutable' ('an indisputable metamorphosis') (Rabut 2004, 60).

The author offers two explanations for his change of literary direction: first, 'people change, ideas change, times change' ('人在变, 想法在变, 时代在变') (cited in Wang 2005, 158); second, 'while composing, [the writer] must look for the most appropriate way to represent [the particular subject of] the novel' ('写着写着肯定会寻找一种最适合这篇小说的表达方式') (ibid.). Concerning the first reason, we can see that Yu was living up to his self-proclaimed avant-gardist status. His turn from Kafka to Proust as a source of literary inspiration while he was writing *Cries* was largely affected by the major translation projects in China in the 1980s.

Like many other Chinese avant-gardist writers, Yu had no knowledge of any foreign language. The discovery of foreign literatures *in translation* played an essential role in making those writers' works avant-garde, as Yu (2002, 4) confesses: 'only in foreign literature can I really understand writing techniques; and then through my own writing practice, I learn the richness of literary expression' ('只有在外国文学里，我才真正了解写作的技巧，　然后通过自己的写作去认识文学有着多么丰富的表达'). As WU Liang (2000, 124–125) duly observes, the 'common background for Chinese avant-garde literature and its promoters' is 'rapid shifts among styles', 'knowledge and imitation', 'disconnected, fragmented, shallow, and abstruse styles of expression', and 'the borrowing of imported subjects, modes of consciousness, and sentence structure'.[10] As far as the particular subject or the central theme of *Cries* is concerned, Yu (*Huhan*, 4) remarks in one of the prefaces that it is 'a book about memory' ('一本关于时间的书') and especially the 'time in memory' ('记忆中的时间'). Due to the major thematic resonance, as well as Yu's explicit references to Proust in the new prefaces to later editions of the novel, Yu has often been asked if this novel was directly inspired by Proust's *La Recherche*. Yu's answer is rather equivocal: 'I hope so' ('我希望如此') (Lin 1998, 166). As the following analysis will demonstrate, we have legitimate reasons to believe that Yu did indeed come across at least the first volume of *La Recherche* at the time he was writing *Cries*.[11] Given the publication year of *Cries* (1991), Yu did not perhaps manage to read *La Recherche* in its entirety until much later, which, in turn, could explain his equivocal and in many ways diplomatic answer. It could also explain why Proust was explicitly mentioned only in the prefaces of the much later editions of the novel.

Secondly, Yu's firm intention to look for the right novelistic form to represent time and memory makes Proust's *La Recherche* an ideal aesthetic inspiration—rather than an exact aesthetic model—for Yu to follow; Yu had, after all, probably read and understood only part, and not the whole, of *La Recherche* when he was composing *Cries*. In this respect, as mentioned in the Introduction and Chap. 2, Maurois's preface must have played an important role in generally informing Yu about the Proustian aesthetics of time and memory. Maurois's preface is further complemented by Luo's (*FT I*, 19–30) Chinese preface entitled 'An Attempted Critical Introduction to *La Recherche*', written in 1988. While elaborating on Maurois's points on Proust's poor health and the central themes of *La Recherche*, Luo tries to offer an overview of Proust's place in French literary history since Montaigne and Balzac. For the benefit of the Chinese readership, he also frequently makes references to the Chinese classic novel *Dream of the Red Chamber* (mid-eighteenth century). Some of Luo's formulations find distinct echoes in Yu's prefaces to *Cries*.

For instance, Luo remarks: 'the innovation of *La Recherche* lies in the fact that it is the content which determines the form. As the author was mulling over new content, a new form has naturally emerged' ('《似水年华》的创新是内容决定形式, 由于作者心中酝酿新的内容, 所以自然而然用新的形式来表现') (*FT I*, 26). Literary avant-gardists like Yu were particularly sensitive to formal innovations. In the preface, the author retrospectively justifies the structure of *Cries* as follows: 'I think this should be a book about memory. Its structure originates from our feeling and experience of time, and more precisely, those of the time known to us, that is, time in memory' ('我想, 这应该是一本关于记忆的书。他的结构来自于对时间的感受, 确切的说是对已知时间的感受, 也就是记忆中的之间') (*Huhan*, 4), a structure that follows what he calls 'the logic of memory' ('记忆的逻辑') (ibid., 5).

Another important remark is Luo's reiteration of the Proustian 'real life', highlighted previously by Maurois:

> 他认为人的真正的生命是回忆中的生活, 或者说, 人的生活只有在回忆中方形成"真实的生活", 回忆中的生活比当时当地的现实生活更为现实。《似水流年》整部小说就是建筑在回忆是人生的精华这个概念之上的。(*FT I*, 21)

> He [Proust] considers that real life is life in memory, or, our life can be 'real life' only in memory. Life in memory is more 'real' than the reality of the present time and place. The entire novel of *La Recherche* is constructed on the idea that memory is the essence of life.

The Franco-Chinese writer François Cheng (2009 [2003], 2) makes a very similar observation in his 'Proustian quotation' cited in the Chinese preface of *Le Dit de Tianyi*: 'real life is a relived life, and that relived life is obtained through the recreation by memory and language' ('真正的生命是再活过的生命。而那再活过的生命是由记忆语言之再创造而获得的').[12]

In comparison, although Yu does not appear to have such a quasi-metaphysical take on the notion of 'real life', he is nevertheless convinced of the idea that a new life can be 'relived' through and in memory: 'the moving part of remembering is that you could make new choices, reconnect and recombine those unrelated past things, in order to obtain a brand-new past' ('回忆的动人之处就在于可以重新选择, 可以将那些毫无关联的往事重新组合起来, 从而获得了全新的过去') (*Huhan*, 5).

In another preface, prior to the explicit discussion of Proust, Yu's reformulation of 'memory' is drawn all the closer to Proust's involuntary memory crystalized in the madeleine episode:

> 我想这应该就是记忆。当慢慢的人生长途走向尾声的时候, 财富荣耀也成身外之物, 记忆却显得极其珍贵。一个偶然被唤醒的记忆, 就像是小小的牡丹花一样, 可以覆盖浩浩荡荡的天下事。(*Huhan*, 7)

> I think this must be memory. As the long, slow journey of life is coming to an end, wealth and glory have become external worldly possessions, but memory has become extremely precious. An accidentally revived recollection, just like that little peony, could majestically cover all the matters of the world.

The 'little peony' is a continued reference to the lines of verse by the classical poet LU You (陆游) (1125–1209) cited at the beginning of this preface: 'forgetting all matters of the world as I grow old, but still seeing the peony in my dreams' ('老去已忘天下事, 梦中犹见牡丹花') (ibid.). Yu's elaboration of an 'accidentally revived recollection' through the 'little peony' is a palpable analogy to Proust's involuntary memory through the 'little madeleine'. Furthermore, as the national flower of China, as well as a topos in traditional Chinese literature and art, Yu's evocation of the peony can be seen as his first creative attempt to appropriate *La Recherche* and to readapt Proust to the Chinese context.

As already mentioned, in terms of the exact structure of *Cries*, it is difficult to assess the extent to which Yu's alleged 'logic of memory'—in so far as it informs the structure of *Cries*—may be based on his close study of the structure of *La Recherche*. For example, Yu's *Cries* bears no mark of Proust's signature narrative technique of the 'double internal focalization' embodied by the dual identity of a protagonist and narrator.[13] But what must have been inspirational for Yu is the idea of an almost 'organic' connection between a fragmented narrative structure and the thematic representations of time and memory. Yu (*Huhan*, 5) explains his 'logic of memory' as follows: 'I considered it to be my structure then. Time, broken into pieces, reappears at the speed of light, because throughout the narrative there is always the "standpoint of today", which governs the rearrangements of memory' ("'记忆的逻辑", 我当时这样认为自己的结构, 时间成为了碎片, 并且以光的速度来回闪现, 因为在全部的叙述里, 始终贯穿着"今天的立场", 也就是重新排列记忆的统治者').[14] Yu wrote only short stories in the 1980s and his favourite themes were violence and death, so the length of a novel and the thematic novelty of time and memory presented a great aesthetic challenge to Yu in the late 1980s. In one of his interviews, Yu suggests that he struggled to find a clear overall structure and adopted a heuristic approach, rather like Proust's own creative method, to the writing of the novel. Yu actually describes the birth of the novel as a 'misunderstanding' ('误会') (Lin 1998, 60). His suggestion indicates that the final structural unity of the novel following the 'logic of memory' is in many ways perceived in retrospect by the writer, through self-analysis. Such a phenomenon is reminiscent of Proust's narrator's characterization of the aesthetic achievement of Balzac and Wagner: '[...] se regardant travailler comme s'ils étaient à la fois l'ouvrier et le juge, [ils] ont tiré de cette auto-contemplation une beauté nouvelle, extérieure et supérieure à l'œuvre, lui imposant rétroactivement une unité, une grandeur qu'elle n'a pas' ('watching themselves at work as if they were both worker and judge, [they] drew from this self-contemplation a new beauty, separate from and superior to their work, conferring on it retrospectively a unity, a grandeur which it does not have in reality') (*RTP III*, 666; *PT V*, 143).

Yu's prefaces have shown an intuitive understanding of time and memory in relation to *La Recherche*. Hans Robert Jauss, in *Zeit und Erinnerung in Marcel Prousts 'A la recherche du temps perdu'* (1955), generally regarded as the first formal analysis of the temporal system in *La Recherche*, acknowledges Proust's aesthetic achievement as the innovation of a 'forme narrative des mémoires' ('a narrative form of memories'), a 'distance intérieure du souvenir' ('an internal distance of memory') and a 'poétique du souvenir' ('a poetics of memory') (Fravalo-Tane 2008, 380). Additionally, Jauss recognizes that the questions of the genesis and genre of *La Recherche*, which have formerly been examined separately, essentially relate back to one single problem of narrative and structural order (ibid.). He further demonstrates how time itself, as the principle of composition, founds the ultimate unity of the novel (ibid., 388). Of course, it is highly unlikely that Yu would have come across Jauss's work on Proust, even through second-hand knowledge. But the apparent affinity between Jauss's and Yu's perceptions of Proust's aesthetic innovation could indicate a more specific direction in which Yu intuitively and creatively engages with Proust.

Moreover, Yu notably approaches Proust's work through the angle of a 'roman d'enfance' or 'novel of childhood', with a certain self-identification: 'I need to clarify that [*Cries*] is not an autobiography, but it gathers a lot of feelings and understandings from my childhood and adolescence. Of course, such feelings and understandings are revisited through memory' ('我要说明的是, 这虽然不是一部自传, 里面却是云集了我童年和少年时期的感受和理解, 当然这样的感受和理解是以记忆的方式得到了重温') (*Huhan*, 7). This remark is then followed by Yu's elaboration on a scene found in the very first pages of *La Recherche*:

马塞尔·普鲁斯特在他那部像人生一样漫长的《追忆似水年华》里, 有一段精美的描述。当他深夜在床上躺下来的时候, 他的脸放到了枕头上, 枕套的绸缎可能是穿越了丝绸之路, 从中国运抵法国的。光滑的绸缎让普鲁斯特产生了清新和娇嫩的感受, 然后唤醒了他对自己童年脸庞的记忆。他说他睡在枕头上时, 仿佛是睡在自己童年的脸庞上。这样的记忆就是古希腊人所说的"和谐", 当普鲁斯特的呼吸因为肺病困扰变得断断续续时, 对过去生活的记忆成为了维持他体内生机的气质, 让他的生活在叙述里变得流畅和奇妙无比。(ibid.)

Marcel Proust, dans son œuvre, qui est aussi longue que la vie, *A la recherche du temps perdu*, nous offre une belle description. Très tard, lorsqu'il s'allongeait au lit, il appuyait ses joues contre l'oreiller. *La taie d'oreiller en soie aurait dû traverser la Route de la Soie et être transportée de la Chine en France.* La soie luisante donnait à Proust un sentiment frais et tendre, et suscitait en lui *le souvenir des joues de son enfance*. Il raconte que lorsqu'il mettait sa tête sur l'oreiller, c'était comme s'il dormait *contre les joues de son enfance*. Une telle mémoire est bien 'harmonia' d'après les anciens Grecs. Au moment où la respiration de Proust était rendue intermittente à cause de son asthme, le souvenir de sa vie passée est devenu la substance qui maintiendrait son dynamisme intérieur, et a rendu fluide et merveilleuse sa vie dans le récit.

Proust, in his book *À la recherche du temps perdu*, which is as long as life itself, gives us an exquisite description. Late at night, as he was lying in bed, he rested his cheeks against the pillow. *The pillowcase made of silk might have passed along the Silk Road and been carried from China to France.* The smooth and glimmering silk gave Proust a fresh and tender feeling, and resuscitated *the memory of his childhood cheeks*. He says that when he rested his head on the pillow, it was as though he were *sleeping against the cheeks of his childhood*. Such a memory is what the ancient Greeks call '*harmonia*'. As Proust's breathing was made intermittent by his asthma, the memory of his past life became the substance that would maintain his inner dynamism, and made his life fluid and marvellous in the narrative.[15]

Yu is evidently referring to the second paragraph of *La Recherche* (and onwards):

J'appuyais tendrement mes joues contre les belles joues de l'oreiller qui, pleines et fraîches, sont comme les joues de notre enfance. Je frottais une allumette pour regarder ma montre. Bientôt minuit. C'est l'instant où le malade, qui a été obligé de partir en voyage et a dû coucher dans un hôtel inconnu, réveillé par une crise [...] (*RTP I*, 4, my italics)

I would rest my cheeks tenderly against the lovely cheeks of the pillow, which, full and fresh, are like the cheeks of our childhood. I would strike a match to look at my watch. Nearly midnight. This is the hour when the sick man who has been obliged to go off on a journey and has had to sleep in an unfamiliar hotel, wakened by an attack [...] (*PT I*, 8, my italics)

Yu's passage is a Chinese appropriation of Proust *par excellence*. He overtly implants a new experience into the narrator's childhood memory by evoking a (second) ancient topos, namely the Silk Road, for cultural exchange between China and the West. He further stresses the 'harmonious' aspect of such an operation, as if he were trying to justify his decision to make this rather 'artificial' literary connection between Proust and China.

Proust's voice, or rather Proust's narrator's voice, is displaced and rewritten to suit Yu's purposes, which consequently produces 'a model of the dialogic'.[16] The significance of Yu's fictional implantation is that it recognizes and constructs a frame, a context, a network[17] that allows readers (and indeed the writer too) to imagine themselves and to be imagined, and encourages them to read both Proust's and Yu's works from the perspective of Chinese and world literature right from the start. In this respect, Yu employs the topos of the Silk Road, with his emphasis on communication or communicability ('aurait dû traverser'/'might have passed through'), rather than origin, to symbolize the world of literary relations. Such a cross-cultural intertextual practice—highly common in contemporary Chinese literature—also implicitly expresses the post-Mao cultural complex about Chinese literature's joining of the canon of world literature.

The Greek word 'harmonia' refers to a 'means of joining or fastening', which is immediately relevant to Yu's cross-cultural remark. The Greek concept of harmony is notably associated with Pythagoreanism in origin, as Liba Taub (2003, 18) observes: 'the earliest surviving use of the term to refer to cosmic harmony may be found at the end of Plato's (*c*. 429–347 BCE) dialogue *Timaeus*, where the Pythagorean Timaeus explains that: "the motions which are naturally akin to the divine principle within us are the thoughts and revolutions of the universe"'. More specifically, 'harmonia' refers to 'the cosmic fitting together and to the divine sound of music that can be heard by mortals, allowing them to imitate the cosmic harmony and to be at one with the universe' (ibid.). However, the concept of harmony (*he*, 和) has an ancient root in Daoist and Confucian traditions too. In fact, the earliest Confucian texts also indicate that the meaning of *he* 'mostly has to do with sounds and how sounds interact with one another' (Li 2006, 583). Furthermore, whether it was intended or not, in retrospect Yu's mention of 'harmony' in this new preface written in 2003 could potentially carry a political overtone—it *prefigures* the advent of a new socio-economic vision proposed by HU Jintao, the 'paramount leader' of China between 2002 and 2012, known as the '(Socialist) Harmonious Society' (*hexie shehui*, 和谐社会).[18] Despite Yu's attribution of 'harmony' to the ancient Greeks, most Chinese readers would rather make a connection to the discourse of contemporary Chinese political thought. Such an association indirectly entails another ideological colouring of Proust's work in the Chinese context, from the rise of bourgeois values under the leadership of Deng to the promotion, under Hu, of a 'socialist harmonious society' which aims to retreat from class and class struggle.[19]

The date of this new preface is particularly revealing also in terms of Yu's personal and professional engagement with cross-cultural politics. 2003 was the year in which the French translation of *Cries* was published in France, where it was favourably received. This year also marked the ninetieth anniversary of the first publication of *Du côté de chez Swann*. 2003–2004 was the (*Cross*) *Year of China* in France, as it marked the fortieth anniversary of the establishment of diplomatic relations between France and China, and Yu, along with a few other established Chinese writers, including the Nobel Prize laureate MO Yan, was named a

Chevalier of the Order of Arts and Letters by the French Ministry of Culture. Yu's *Cries* was *the* reason for the honour. In March 2004, *Magazine littéraire* dedicated an entire issue, which also featured Yu, to Chinese and Franco-Chinese literature and philosophy. Back in China, in 2004 and 2005, the publications of two competing new Chinese translations of *Du côté de chez Swann* were ceremoniously launched and attracted considerable media attention. Suddenly, Proust seemed to have become the cultural ambassador of France to China. In this way, the intertextual relation between *Cries* and *La Recherche* evolved from implicit literary allusion to explicit reference to miniature rewriting and finally to the politics of cultural exchange. Could this intercultural literary exchange and mutual recognition be what Yu envisaged as the 'harmonia' of the ancient Greeks?

As has been suggested and will be further demonstrated in an exploration of the prologue of *Cries*, there is a certain personal identification with Proust in Yu's approach which will also be seen in Wei's and Cheng's approaches.[20] However, there is a certain irony in the way they perceive Proust in relation to their own works: on the one hand, they contend that their autobiographical novels are by no means autobiographies; on the other hand, as we have already seen in the passage from Yu, Proust is utterly confounded with his protagonist-narrator, Marcel. There is hence a curious combination between what Roland Barthes (1984, 319) identifies as 'marcellisme', which designates 'cet intérêt très spécial que les lecteurs peuvent porter à la vie de Marcel Proust' ('this very particular interest that readers can take in the life of Marcel Proust'), and 'proustisme', which 'ne serait que le goût d'une œuvre ou d'une manière littéraire' ('would be the appreciation of a work or of a literary style only'). Perhaps it is precisely this irony, generated in the creative reception of Proust, that strengthens Proust's literary posterity not only in the Chinese context but also within world literature. Joseph Brami (2010, 7), in the foreword of *Lecteurs de Proust au XXᵉ siècle et au début du XXIᵉ*, duly observes that the well-established distinctions in Proust Studies between the author and the narrator, between the narrator and the protagonist, 'n'apparai[ssent] pas nécessairement au sein de toutes les lectures des écrivains étudiés' ('do not necessarily emerge in all the readings of the writers studied'). Ultimately, 'chacun d'eux ou presque s'[est] composé des deux ensemble' ('each of them, or almost, was made up of the two together'). Barthes (1984, 319) further clarifies as follows:

La postérité donne de plus en plus raison à Proust: son œuvre n'est plus lue seulement comme un monument de la littérature universelle, mais comme l'expression passionnante d'un sujet absolument personnel qui revient sans cesse à sa propre vie, non comme à un *curriculum vitae*, mais comme à un étoilement de circonstances et de figures. De plus en plus nous nous prenons à aimer non 'Proust' (nom civil d'un auteur fiché dans les Histoires de la littérature), mais 'Marcel', être singulier, à la fois enfant et adulte, *puer senilis*, passionné et sage, proie de manies excentriques et lieu d'une réflexion souveraine sur le monde, l'amour, l'art, le temps, la mort.

More and more, Proust's posterity has proved him right: his work is no longer read only as a monument of universal literature, but as the enthusiastic expression of an absolutely personal subject who ceaselessly returns to his own life—not as in a *curriculum vitae*, but as to a sprinkling of circumstances and figures. Increasingly, we start to love not 'Proust' (the official surname of an author filed in the histories of literature), but 'Marcel', a unique being, a child and adult at the same time, *puer senilis*, passionate and wise, the victim of eccentric and odd habits, and a place of supreme reflection upon the world, love, art, time, and death.

3.3.2 *Prologue to Cries*

Compared to his open acknowledgement of Proust on time and memory in the prefaces, Yu's engagement with *La Recherche* in the prologue is implicit and much more subtle. *Cries* begins:

1965年的时候，一个孩子开始了对黑夜不可名状的恐惧。我回想起了那个细雨飘扬的夜晚，当时我已经睡了，我是那么的小巧，就像玩具似的被放在床上。屋檐滴水所显示的，是寂静的存在，我的逐渐入睡是对雨中水滴的逐渐遗忘. (*Huhan*, 2)

Au cours de l'année 1965, d'indescriptibles terreurs nocturnes s'emparèrent d'un enfant. Le souvenir de cette nuit où flottait la bruine a resurgi dans ma mémoire: je suis couché sur mon lit, posé là comme un jouet, tellement menu et délicat. L'eau dégouttant de l'auvent de la maison révèle l'existence du silence et mon endormissement progressif est un oubli graduel des gouttes de pluie. (*Cris*, 9)

It was in 1965 that nighttime began to stir in me a nameless dread. I am thinking now of that evening when a light rain drifted down. In my bed I

lay, a child so little you could have set me there as easily as a toy. The drip-
ping from the eaves simply called attention to the silence that surrounded
me, and the steady onset of sleep was but gradual forgetting of the rain's
patter. (*Cries*, 3)

Three key elements emerge from these opening lines, which echo the
iconic Chinese title of *La Recherche* (*Pursuing the Memory of Time/Years
as Water/River*): time, memory, and water. From an intercultural perspective, this passage enjoys a *double* cultural referent, especially among
its Chinese readership. First, the association among the three elements
is an 'artistic allusion' according to Annick Bouillaguet's ([1990] 1998,
195) intertextual theory, which is 'beaucoup plus reconnaissable pour le
lecteur' ('a lot more recognizable for the reader') because the material
alluded to 'appartient à un fonds culturel commun' ('belongs to a common cultural heritage'). She continues: 'le lecteur, s'il ne peut identifier
la source, a du moins le sentiment d'être ici en présence d'une légende
que peut-être il connaît, et qui ressortit aux archétypes autour desquels,
selon Jung, se construit l'inconscient collectif' ('if readers are unable to
identify precisely the source, they have at least the feeling of being in the
presence here of a legend they may know of, a legend that belongs to the
archetypes around which, according to Jung, the collective unconscious
is constructed') (ibid., 196). Nevertheless, in previous analyses we have
identified several of the most widely circulated Chinese philosophical and
literary sources for the time/water relation and expression, the existence
of which confirms that 'feeling of a legend' in the Chinese reader's 'collective unconscious'.[21] Then, as Proust's work has become canonized in
China since its integral publication in 1991 (as *Pursuing the Memory of
Time/Years as Water/River* rather than *À la recherche du temps perdu* [*In
Search of Lost Time*]), the prologue of *Cries* has effectively turned from
an 'artistic allusion' to the Chinese cultural heritage, to a 'technical allusion' specifically to Proust, which is then explicitly acknowledged by Yu's
new prefaces. The 'artistic' and 'technical' allusions are mutually complementary rather than exclusive. In Bouillaguet's words, 'la répartition
entre ces deux nouveaux ensembles est peu rigoureuse car ils ne sont
guère étanches' ('the division between the two groups is hardly strict as
they are seldom watertight') (ibid.), and the division is crucially dependent on readers' experience and level of culture ('niveau de culture')
(ibid., 195).

The setting, ambiance, and basic scenario of the prologue of *Cries* closely resemble those of *La Recherche*: a young boy, a wakeful sleeper, is lying in bed alone in the dark, having a series of seemingly illogical flashbacks and manifesting existential anxieties and fears. Yu's depiction of these details even presents several lexical, syntactical, and diegetic parallels to *La Recherche*.

Yu's sentence 'pendant une très longue période, je n'osai m'endormir, couché dans le noir' ('I would lie in the dark for ages, not daring to fall asleep'/'很长一段时间里, 我躺在黑暗的床上不敢入睡') (*Cris*, 11; *Cries*, 4; *Huhan*, 4) is reminiscent of Proust's famous incipit: 'longtemps, je me suis couché de bonne heure. [...] "Je m'endors"' ('For a long time, I went to bed early. [...] "I'm falling asleep"') (*RTP I*, 3; *PT I*, 7). It must be pointed out that the adverbial expression 'pendant une très longue période' in the Chinese original, and its syntactical position, are almost identical to the Chinese translation of Proust's 'longtemps' ('for a long time'/'在很长一段时期里') (*FT I*, 3).[22]

Like Proust's Combray, Yu's book about time and memory begins with a childhood *place*, Nanmen (南门, South Gate). While Proust's narrator recalls 'le bruit de la sonnette du jardin de Combray' ('the sound of the garden bell at Combray') with dizziness ('j'avais le vertige [...] comme si j'avais des lieues de hauteur'/'I felt giddy [...] as if I were miles high') at the very end of *La Recherche* (*RTP I*, 624; *PT VI*, 357), Yu's protagonist physically returns to Nanmen in a 'tangle of voices' ('杂乱的人声'), 'amid clamour and commotion' ('在叫嚷嚷的声音里'), with 'memories from the past' ('残留的记忆') and 'the happy sensation' ('欣喜地感到') (*Cries*, 303; *Huhan*, 276–277). Georges Poulet carried out one of the first book-length studies of the rigorous parallelism that exists in Proust between the dialectic of time and that of space (1982, 88). He notes: 'dès le premier moment—on pourrait presque dire aussi: dès le premier *lieu*—du récit, l'œuvre proustienne s'affirme comme une recherche non seulement du temps, mais de l'espace perdu' ('from the first moment—we could almost also say: from the first *place*—of the narrative, Proust's work establishes itself as a search not only for lost time, but also for lost space') (ibid., 19). Yu's conceptual awareness of place in addition to time, in relation to memory, is evident, and this particular aspect of Yu's Proustian engagement is quite unique among the Chinese and Franco-Chinese authors of our corpus.

The analogy of Proust's narrator to a sick man who feels temporarily relieved at the thought of seeing the first sight of day filtering beneath the door also finds a certain echo in Yu's prologue:

[Proust] C'est l'instant où le malade, [...] réveillé par une crise, se réjouit en apercevant sous la porte une raie de jour. Quel bonheur, c'est déjà le matin! (*RTP I*, 4)

[Proust] This is the hour when the sick man [...] wakened by an attack, is cheered to see a ray of light under the door. How fortunate, it's already morning! (*PT I*, 8)

[Yu] A mon réveil le lendemain à l'aube, je constatais que j'étais encore vivant et comme je regardais le soleil pénétrer par les fentes de la porte, la joie me mettait dans un état d'extrême excitation. (*Cris*, 12)

[Yu] When I woke up the following morning and discovered I was still alive, the sunlight poking through the crack in the door, I was overjoyed to find that I had been spared. (*Cries*, 5)

当我翌日清晨醒来时, 发现自己还活着, 看着阳光从门缝里照射进来, 我的喜悦使我激动无比。(*Huhan*, 4)

Childhood terror haunts the memory of both wakeful sleepers at night:

[Proust] Ou bien en dormant j'avais rejoint sans effort un âge à jamais révolu de ma vie primitive, retrouvé telle de mes terreurs enfantines comme celle que mon grand-oncle me tirât par mes boucles et qu'avait dissipé le jour—date pour moi d'une ère nouvelle—où on les avait coupées. (*RTP I*, 4)

[Proust] Or else while sleeping I had effortlessly returned to a for ever vanished period of my early life, rediscovered one of my childish terrors such as that my great-uncle would pull me by my curls, a terror dispelled on the day—the dawn for me of a new era—when they were cut off. (*PT I*, 8)

[Yu] [...] d'indescriptibles terreurs nocturnes s'emparèrent d'un enfant. [...] [J]'étais gagné par le sommeil, [...] les cris d'une femme, tels des sanglots, me parvinrent du lointain, une voix rauque retentit soudain dans

la nuit jusqu'alors parfaitement silencieuse, faisant trembler ces années
d'enfance dans ma mémoire. (*Cries*, 9)

[Yu] [...] nighttime began to stir in [a child] a nameless dread. [...] I
glided peacefully into slumber, [...]. Then from far away there came the
sound of a woman's anguished wails. When those hoarse cries erupted so
suddenly in the still of the night, the boy [in my memory] then shivered
and quaked.[23] (*Cries*, 3)

[...] 一个孩子开始了对黑夜的不可名状的恐惧。[...] 在我安全而又平静
地进入睡眠时，[...] 一个女人哭泣般的呼喊声从远处传来，嘶哑的声音在
当初寂静无比的黑夜里突然想起，使我此刻回想中的童年的我颤抖不已。
(*Huhan*, 2)

It is through the similar experience of disorientation and confusion
in the darkness, accompanied by a certain detachment of the self, that
we enter both novels. Proust's narrator speaks of a transmigration of
the soul ('métempsychose') and remarks, 'aussitôt je recouvrais la vue
et j'étais bien étonné de trouver autour de moi une obscurité, douce et
reposante pour mes yeux' ('immediately I recovered my sight and I was
amazed to find a darkness around me soft and restful for my eyes') (*RTP
I*, 4; *PT I*, 7). Yu's narrator remarks, 'I can see myself now, a startled
child, eyes wide with fear, the precise outline of my face obscured by the
darkness' ('我看到了自己，一个受惊的孩子睁大恐惧的眼睛，他的脸形在
黑暗里模糊不清') (*Cries*, 3; *Huhan*, 2).

Finally, the structure of both prologues revolves around seemingly
random flashbacks of memory. Uncertainties of time and space permeate
both narrators' accounts:

[Proust] Puis renaissait le souvenir d'une nouvelle attitude [...]. Ces
évocations tournoyantes et confuses ne duraient jamais que quelques
secondes; souvent, ma brève incertitude du lieu où je me trouvais ne dis-
tinguait pas mieux les unes des autres les diverses suppositions dont elle
était faite, que nous n'isolons, en voyant un cheval courir, les positions suc-
cessives que nous montre le kinétoscope. (*RTP I*, 6–7)

[Proust] Then the memory of a new position would be reborn [...]. These
revolving, confused evocations never lasted for more than a few seconds;
often, in my brief uncertainty about where I was, I did not distinguish the
various suppositions of which it was composed, any better than we isolate,

when we see a horse run, the successive positions shown to us by a kineto-scope. (*PT I*, 10–11)

[Yu] Un autre souvenir ne tarde pas à suivre: celui d'agneaux blancs accourant sur l'herbe verte du bord de la rivière. Manifestement, il s'agit d'une impression diurne, d'une caresse après l'inquiétude générée par le souvenir précédent. Mais il m'est difficile de déterminer la place où je me trouvais quand je l'ai éprouvé. (*Cris*, 10)

[Yu] [Another] memory comes hot on the heels of the first: [a few] white lambs trotting across the grass by the riverside, a daytime image, a way of easing the agitation evoked by the previous memory. But I find it hard to decide just where I was when this sight left its mark on me. (*Cries*, 4)

紧随而来的另一个记忆，是几只羊羔从河边青草上走过来。显然这是对白昼的印象，是对前一个记忆造成的不安进行抚摸。只是我难以确定自己获得这个印象时所处的位置。(*Huhan*, 3)

As can be seen, even the exact contents of both narrators' dreamy visions find 'correspondences': Proust's 'running horse' metamorphoses into a few 'trotting lambs'.

As we will see in Part II, Yu's prologue resonates not only with that of *La Recherche*; its key element of an unknown woman's haunting cry is additionally transformed into the mysterious 'voix féminine', a Daoism-inflected feminine voice—hence 'la Voie' (the Way)—in Cheng's prologue, which itself has a distinct Proustian echo, albeit in different ways from Yu's.

3.4   Wei Hui's Short Stories[24]

Wei Hui is a woman writer representative of the literary group gener-ally known in China as 'The New Generation' (sometimes also translated as 'The Late Generation', *wanshengdai*, 晚生代), writers born in the late 1970s and the 1980s, after the economic reform and the opening up of China. Those writers' thematic concerns have come far out of the shadow of the Cultural Revolution and official communist propaganda. Being an ardent Francophile, Wei explicitly cites Proust in her works probably more than any other Chinese writer. Due to her 'decadent'[25] approach to literary representations of sexuality, some of her works are banned in China, which consequently generates media sensationalism once they are translated in the West.[26]

In his seminal study of twentieth-century Chinese literature, Yinde Zhang (2003, 133–156) exhaustively noted Wei's references to Proust in her various short stories, without, however, further commenting on the blatant consumerist ideology that conditions such literary productions, an ideology that was palpably reflected in the new twist of economic reform in the 1990s known as 'marketization' (*shichang hua*, 市场化).[27] My analysis will evaluate the extent to which such an ideological backdrop has given rise to certain aesthetic values in Wei's creative intertextual engagement with Proust. The focus is on the formal and thematic features of those Proustian references in the stories.

The figure of Proust is used primarily for characterization. References to Proust are always concretized in a character's activity of reading *La Recherche*. One of the technical reasons for this intertextual feature is that, in contrast to Wang's and Yu's narratives, which rely heavily on the background material of the Cultural Revolution, all of Wei's stories that contain Proustian echoes are set in cosmopolitan Shanghai in the 1990s, where reading Proust is a realistic activity and even considered chic in some circles of the so-called *dushi chaoren* (都市潮人, urban hipsters).[28] This is consistent with Wei's wide range of references to Western culture in general. Western-style cafés, restaurants, bars, and music venues are among the most popular settings in her stories. The frequency of her citation of a Western writer's work is probably as high as her mentions of Western alcohols (Scotch whisky, Jack Daniels, and popular cocktails) and big fashion and perfume brands (Boss, Louis Vuitton, Chanel, and D&G, to name a few), particularly in the portrayal of her characters, who almost all belong to the same privileged group of urban youths immersing themselves unquestionably in consumer culture. Wei's characters, and to a large extent her writings themselves, manifest a 'carefully cultivated materialism and superficiality in tone, style, and sensibility. The reader feels a palpable flat presentism rather than historical depth' (Lu 2008, 178).

The novella 'Zhi jiezhi' ('纸戒指', 'Paper Rings') begins with the female protagonist's reading of an ostensibly random passage from *La Recherche*:

冬季的壁炉整夜燃着熊熊的火, 木柴毕毕剥剥地响着, 才灭又旺......随手翻开一页, 见到M·普鲁斯特在漫无尽头的追忆中这样的描写。(*WH*, 55)

The winter fireplace was burning all night, the flaming brands kept crackling, gradually going out and soon blazing up again... I thumbed through one page, and found such a description in M. Proust's long and endless *Pursuing Memory* [the usual Chinese abbreviation for *La Recherche*].

As Zhang (2003, 142–143) accurately identifies, this description of a 'winter bedroom'—recurrent in the novella—is a reference to Proust's passage on the narrator's revolving and confused evocations in his 'chambre d'hiver' in *Du côté de chez Swann*: '[...] le feu étant entretenu toute la nuit dans la cheminée, on dort dans un grand manteau d'air chaud et fumeux, traversé des lueurs des tisons qui se rallument [...]' ('[...] the fire is kept burning all night in the fireplace, you sleep in a great cloak of warm, smoky air, pierced by the glimmers from the logs breaking into flame again') (*RTP I*, 7; *PT I*, 11).

This initial context in which the protagonist reads *La Recherche* is significant as it immediately announces her sensual love affair with a married man called Wei (唯, the same pronunciation as 'Wei' but different from the author's surname, which is written卫), which is to be disentangled as the story goes on: 'Wei snored lightly and regularly next to me, but I couldn't sleep at all. While I leafed through this heavy book which has a "soft and gentle" [*yinrou*] style, all sorts of worries came to mind' ('身边的唯发出轻匀的鼾声，我却睡意全无。翻弄着手中这本沉甸甸而格调阴柔的书，心事浩渺') (*WH*, 55). Interestingly enough, it seems that the reason that Wei (the author) considers Proust's work to be particularly relevant to the short story is that *La Recherche* is essentially a 'feminine' book. Indeed, the word *yinrou* is sometimes explicitly translated as 'feminine' or even 'effeminate', derived from the feminine or soft principle of *yin* in ancient Chinese philosophy.[29]

At the end of the Sect. 3.1, the protagonist returns to her reading of Proust in the same bedroom late at night as she is feeling 'lonely' and 'cold':

这一夜，我又捧起了那本漫无尽头的追忆。恍惚中，我的意识随波逐流于时间之河。那个法国人回忆幼时母亲如果没在睡前给他一个吻，他所产生的种种不安、悲伤和孤独。这些纤细而丰盈的感觉栩栩如生地在我眼前突现，我触手可及。

我明白，那正是我自己的灵魂，在寂寞的城市冬夜的写照。(*WH*, 61)

That night, once again, I held in my hands that long and endless *Pursuing Memory*. As if in a trance, my consciousness flew in the river of time. That Frenchman recalled his childhood, when his mum hadn't given him a kiss before sleep, he'd have felt various anxieties, sadness, and loneliness. These delicate and plentiful feelings vividly appeared in front of my eyes all of a sudden, almost tangible.[30]

I understand, that was precisely the portrayal of my own soul in the lonely winter evening of the city.

Evidently this passage refers to the famous episode of the 'bedtime drama' in *Du côté de chez Swann*. Imagery that reflects the impact of *La Recherche*'s water—or river-bound Chinese title is noticeable. The imagery of water is further elaborated at the end of Sect. 3.2, where the protagonist compares herself to 'an anonymous fish' ('一条不知名的鱼') that 'swims from one city to another, floating on the surface, then discovering deep waters everywhere' ('从一个城市游到另一个城市。浮出浮华的水面, 却发现到处是深邃的水'), and suddenly decides to 'pursue the memory of lost love and life' ('陡然追忆远去的爱情和生命') (*WH*, 68).

There are considerable *parodical* values in Wei's insertion of Proust's 'bedtime drama'.[31] The childhood setting of a maternal kiss is transposed into the highly eroticized context of an extra-marital affair. In turn, by comparing her anxiety, sadness, and loneliness—as a result of the temporary unavailability of her lover, whether on the phone or in person—to those of Proust's child protagonist, Wei effectively *infantilizes* the kind of 'unbridled' female sexuality that she deliberately flaunts throughout her writings. This is subsequently confirmed by her male lover's remark: 'very tenderly, he kissed my dishevelled hair and said you're really a child' ('他温柔无比地吻我的散发, 说你真是个孩子') (*WH*, 74).

Literary vocation is a central theme in many of Wei's stories, which signals a very different thematic engagement with Proust from that of Wang and Yu. In Wei, reading Proust is often accompanied by a series of struggles with getting a first book or composition published. Towards the end of Sect. 3.3, the protagonist again mentions Proust and his work:

我把M·普鲁斯特的追忆暂搁一边, 这三本优柔细腻的书总在折磨我脆弱的神经, 令我长久地失眠, 在童年、流水、音乐等富有透明质感的回忆中深深沉溺.[32]

I temporarily put aside M. Proust's *Pursuing Memory*, the three leisurely [*yourou*] and refined volumes were constantly putting a strain on my fragile nerves, making me insomniac for a long time, making me indulge excessively in the memories of childhood, flowing water, music, and so on, which displayed a transparent quality.

The word *yourou* can also be understood to mean 'weak in character' and hence unable to make important decisions (as in the extended collocation, *yourou guaduan*, 优柔寡断). This latter meaning quite suitably conveys the protagonist's irresolution about her love affair at this stage. Incidentally, the mention of 'three' instead of 'seven' volumes also reveals a much later edition of the Chinese integral translation of *La Recherche*,[33] which indicates Wei's slightly belated discovery of Proust compared to Wang and Yu.

It is at this point that the protagonist decides to write a novel:

我也回忆与唯曾有的爱情。[...]   流行歌曲的词作者说为欲望去猎求艳遇为生命去等候爱情, 可欲望和生命难舍难分, 扑朔迷离, 具有哲学的晦涩意味。我再一次想到写作。(ibid.)

I still thought back to the love we had had between us, We and me. [...] The pop song lyricist [Wei] said: 'hunt for affairs out of desire and wait for love for life.' But desire and life are inseparable, complicated, and confusing, with obscure philosophical meanings. Once again, I thought of writing.

Nevertheless, the writer's engagement with a literary vocation remains very shallow and lacks sincerity. The figure of the writer has undergone fundamental changes in Wei's hands, becoming, in Lu's (2008, 178) sharp words, 'a capitalist consumer, a drug addict, a promiscuous lover'. Lu continues: 'the writer has been transformed from an intellectual, the conscience of society, the architect of the soul, to a celebrity in a consumer economy at best, a self-styled outsider at worst'.

Rather like Wang's use of reference to 'time'/'years'—Proust's 'longtemps' and 'les années'/'dans le Temps'—at the beginning and the end of the novella, Wei returns to Proust's prologue at the end of the short story, and her emphasis is now on the passing of time and the advent of another winter:

斗转星移, 时光飞逝。又一个冬季来临的时候, 木柴在M·普鲁斯特的火炉里永远不灭地燃烧着。烟雾中, 爱人的面容依稀如影, 画面至此逐渐淡出。

我知道你这会儿已觉察出故事其实是个平淡老套的故事。(*WH*, 79)

Stars changing their positions constantly, time flying by quickly, as another winter was approaching, the brands kept burning forever in M. Proust's fireplace. The lover's complexion was turning into a shadow in the smoke, and this image was gradually fading away.

I know that you've now realized that the story is just a banal and clichéd story.

Thus, in Zhang's (2003, 138) words, the narrative can be seen as being structured around 'les événements déployés entre deux hivers ressuscitant des souvenirs ravivés par le feu proustien' ('the events spread between two winters bringing back memories revived by Proustian fire'). But on the issue of literary vocation, the reference to Proust in this context is rather ambiguous. For one thing, Proust inspires the protagonist to write. For another, the Proustian conception of art which reveals the essence of life—'la vraie vie'—has completely evaded Wei. In the end, the finitude of the protagonist's literary pursuit appears to resemble the ultimately short-lived love affair. It seems that the power of literary creation to redeem life and to preserve the essence of life has vanished into thin air like the lover's fading image in the smoke; such a conception of writing is no longer desirable, or indeed possible, in the generation and the social milieu that Wei describes and represents. As Zhang (ibid., 148) conclusively comments:

L'art comme essence de la vie l'incite à opposer un refus net à la fois à l'amateurisme et au métier, et à hisser la littérature sur un piédestal sacré, qui implique talent, sacrifice et travail. En dépit de cette prise de conscience, l'heure ne semble pas encore à la révélation. En s'attachant au plaisir, à la mode et à l'argent, la narratrice reste lucide sur la fragilité de son choix littéraire, et ce, jusqu'à la fin lorsqu'elle affirme n'avoir écrit 'qu'une histoire banale'.

Art as the essence of life prompts her to refuse absolutely both amateurism and profession, and to hoist literature on a sacred pedestal, which implies talent, sacrifice, and work. Despite this awareness, this is not yet a moment of epiphany. In attaching herself to pleasure, fashion, and money, the narrator remains quite clear about the fragility of her choice of literature, and does so right to the end, where she claims to have written 'only a banal story'.

The theme of literary vocation is further explored in Wei's novella 'Yuwang shouqiang' ('欲望手枪', 'The Pistol of Desire'), where it is announced right from the incipit: 'even before Mini had wanted to become a writer, she was already enthusiastically working out a list of titles as well as about thirty interesting pen names in her Chinese class' ('在米妮还没有想到要当个作家的时候，她已经在语文课上兴致勃勃地为自己罗列一连串作品的名称，以及近三十个有趣的笔名') (*WH*, 315). The author places an explicit emphasis on the role of memory in novel writing: 'in the period leading to the writing of this novella, Mini felt she was living in a restless state of remembrance. [...] She searched in her memory for the shadows of her ambitious adolescence, including that list of work titles' ('在写这个小说前的一段时间里，米妮觉得自己正处于一个无休止的会议状态。[...] 她在记忆中搜索从前青春年少野心勃勃时的影子') (ibid.). Some of her metaphors of memory are once again reminiscent of the Chinese title of *La Recherche*: 'as she was looking at it [the dark river], some past things came to mind, as if they had emerged from that dark river and were gradually floating towards her' ('她看着看着，就想起了一些往事，仿佛往事徐徐地，从那条肮脏的黑河中，漂浮而来') (ibid., 326). The protagonist did not grow up in a happy family. Her parents were divorced when she was small. Thereafter, her mother moved to a different city, leaving Mini alone to face her alcoholic father and elder brother and witness their abuse of other women. *La Recherche* is the book that the female protagonist was reading while sitting next to her dying father in hospital. Terrified by the dead silence, she seems to read Proust for spiritual consolation: 'she sat in the ward, with a certain *Pursuing the Memory of Time/Years as Water/River* on her knees, feeling that silence which was sharper than a needle' ('她坐在病房里，膝盖上摊着一本《追忆似水年华》，感受着比一枚针见还要尖锐的寂静') (ibid., 386). It is worth reminding ourselves of the obituary connotation of the expression 'to pursue memory' in *La Recherche*'s Chinese title, as this could explain why Wei would consider it to be a poignant reference in this context. Unlike in 'Zhi jiezhi', *La Recherche*'s title is cited in full, but Proust's name is not mentioned. The Chinese title clearly has a semantic function here.

In 'Yinghan bu tiaowu' ('硬汉不跳舞', 'Tough Guy Don't Dance'),[34] reading Proust is an activity intriguingly attributed to a character called EP, who is the lead guitarist of a rock band. EP is frequently characterized as 'the boy who loved M. Proust's *Pursuing the Memory of Time as Water*' (*WH*, 644). Reading Proust makes him feel fulfilled, brings out his poetic sensibility, and eventually inspires him to become a writer—interestingly—of essays rather than novels:

EP已利用休息间隙开始写作, 写的不是小说, (小说在当今已沦落至自慰或
卖俏的手段), EP埋头写的是一篇关于希腊艺术起源或印度宗教探微的
论文, 那些论文可能永远不会发表, 可EP不在乎, 他只听从内心召唤, 按最
朴素的意愿行事。(ibid., 665)

EP already made use of his breaks and started writing. What he wrote was
not a novel (these days, novels have been degraded to an instrument for
self-consolation or coquetry). EP buried himself in the writing of a series
of essays on the origin of Greek art or the discovery of Indian religions.
Those essays would probably never be published, but EP didn't mind, he
listened to his inner calling only, acting according to his most basic will.

Unlike the previous female protagonist readers' attribution of stereotypically 'feminine' qualities to Proust (sensuality, emotions, and irra-
tionality), the male reader in this novella demonstrates a certain and
no less stereotypical 'masculine' take on Proust: uncompromisingness,
self-determination, and solitary existence. This latter view reminds us,
however faintly, of the precarious circumstances under which Proust continued to compose the last few volumes despite his terminal illness. Luo's
Chinese preface certainly emphasizes (and perhaps overstates) Proust's
self-imprisonment and voluntary hermitism in order to write.[35] The lack
of concern over publication also gently reminds us, not without a sense
of irony, of Proust's desperate attempt to find a publisher for *Du côté
de chez Swann* after successive rejections and devastating reports from
Fasquelle, the *Nouvelle Revue Française,* and Ollendorff.[36]

As a woman writer of fiction, Wei in this passage seems to have
taken on board some of the criticisms of her works (i.e. that novels in
her hands 'have been degraded to an instrument for self-consolation
or coquetry'). The word 'self-consolation' (*ziwei,* 自慰) is more commonly understood as meaning 'onanistic activity', especially for women.
This view of novel writing as an intimate self-expression and self-indul-
gence is reiterated elsewhere in her works. For example, in 'Zhi jiezhi'
the protagonist thus speculates: '[I could] try novel writing, perhaps
[one could] thus retreat into one's personal secret language, touching
on something intrinsic while immersed in a certain self-fulfilling enthusiasm' ('尝试写小说这种叙述方式, 也许可以遁入个人的隐秘语词, 在某
种自足的激情中触及实质') (*WH,* 75). Wei clearly thinks that there is a
gender divide in the choice of literary genre. She self-consciously makes
a distinction between the kind of blatantly consumer-oriented 'erotic

chick lit' writers, largely represented by herself, and the more traditional writer-intellectual model that embodies 'the conscience of society' and 'the architect of the soul', mostly written by men. At any rate, the fact that various perceptions of Proust's work can be appropriated to enhance Wei's gender-specific characterizations indirectly reflects the 'androgynous qualities' of Proust's writing.[37]

The rock music scene, in Wei's fictional representation, undoubtedly embodies social and cultural rebellions consisting of drug addicts and libertines. Rock music is the signature passion for real 'cool guys'. However, the lead guitarist, EP, is differently characterized, and reading Proust is certainly one of his most noticeable traits. After the disappearance of the lead singer and songwriter protagonist, a heroin addict, the group is disbanded and EP turns to writing. It seems that Proust is somehow responsible for EP's 'conversion' from the cult of urban rebellious noise to the quiet literary quest for an inner calling. Finally, the rather unusual association between Proust and the lead guitarist of a rock band could perhaps be understood in the context of postmodern consumer culture. The rock music scene was very new to the Chinese public in the 1990s. One characteristic that is shared by both rock music and Proust is their newness and relative marginality in the 'depoliticized culture of urban consumption that has arisen in China in the wake of 1989' (Field and Gronewegen 2008, 24),[38] not so different in essence from other commercial brands and products which feature so prominently in Wei's tales.

Clearly, there is a tendency to 'consume' or 'kitschify' Proust in such intertextual practices, whereby Proust's canonical work is reduced to an almost empty signifier, disconnected from its original signified (Gray 1992, 166). Kitschification is a well-established, paradoxical postmodern phenomenon in the West (Compagnon 1990, 171). Its manifestation in the context of contemporary Chinese literature indicates, albeit rather negatively, China's growing economic and cultural integration into the global system since its reform and opening up. As Lu (2008, 178) sharply observes, the works of what he calls 'beauty writers' like Wei 'signal a shift from the paradigm of national literature to the necessity of globalization. Historical depth is absent, and only a glistening surface remains'. In many ways, this paradigm shift has been well reflected in our study of the three writers of successive generations in post-Mao China. While Wang's and Yu's intertextual engagements with Proust are still thematically grounded in the 'national trauma' of China's recent history, the kind of urban literature represented by Wei can be said to 'partake of a transnational network of postmodern consumer culture', in which 'Chinese history matters less' and 'what matters is the instantaneous surface feeling of a street wanderer, shopper, consumer, and lover in a metropolis' (ibid., 178). In stark contrast to Wei is the Franco-Chinese author François Cheng, whose novel *Le Dit de Tianyi* is to be extensively examined in Part II. Equally written in the late 1990s, Cheng's works also answer the 'necessity of globalization', but with a fundamental intention to put divergent cultural traditions into constructive dialogue.

3.5   Conclusion

As explained in the first section of Chap. 2, Proust was translated in China largely against the backdrop of an emerging Chinese Modernism or 'residual modernism', channelled primarily through translation, as the general intellectual energy of the 1980s wrestled to achieve the 'right' balance between Western cultural influence and Chinese cultural heritage. Proust's *La Recherche* was translated and received as a high Modernist work in China in the 1980s and 1990s, a period in which Chinese society developed exponentially from modernity to postmodernity. The intensity of this socio-economic development was unparalleled in the West. Our intertextual examples are in many ways expressions of the societal and ideological contradictions that mark Chinese postmodernity.

Overall, the mainland Chinese creative reception of Proust seems to offer limited understandings of Proust's work per se. Proust appears almost exclusively in the novellas—rather than long novels—of writers who were still experimenting with Modernist styles and techniques, in a society which was evolving at great speed into postmodernity. None of the works discussed can be said to be the most representative of each author's ultimate literary vision, and the popularity of these texts, with the possible exception of Yu's *Cries*, is relatively small compared to that of some of their later works. None of them demonstrates any particular effort to engage conceptually with or challenge the length and thematic scope of *La Recherche*, something which is also said to be conditioned by the reality of contemporary mainland Chinese literary production—another key difference from Cheng's approach to Proust.[39] In her journalistic article 'Keys to China' (2012) the historian Julia Lovell provocatively concludes:

China today is not the kind of place that encourages the professional dedication to literary craft essential to successful long fiction. Writers rarely revise; editors barely edit; they are too busy blogging, filmmaking, or chasing after the next big literary trend. The short story is the ideal literary form for a country suffering so acutely from attention deficit disorder: long enough to capture a meaningful fragment of this confounding country; (usually) brief enough to prevent authors reaching for melodramatic plot hinges or slack description.

However, making references to Western canonical works such as *La Recherche* is certainly a way to increase the cultural prestige of these mainland Chinese writers' own works, creating a horizon of expectation and a favourable climate of reception. The practice does help promote scholarly as well as creative interest in Proust in China and abroad to some extent. The cross-cultural referencing, which is very common in contemporary Chinese literature, implicitly expresses China's impatient cultural ambition for contemporary Chinese literature to be integrated into the world literature network.

As always, ambiguities permeate such global cultural integration. For many contemporary Chinese writers to be integrated—even just superficially or purely out of commercial interests—is to be successful. As Lovell remarks: 'the possession of an "international" (in reality, a Western or Anglophone) profile through translation was essential to making a literary reputation in China' ('Finding a Place' 2012).[40] Citing and invoking the world and especially the Western canon are the basic strategies that many mainland Chinese writers adopt in order for their writings to be potentially accepted and assimilated in the West, and if they are successful in this, their literary fame back in China is guaranteed.[41] Despite their distinctive aesthetic, as well as marketing concerns, this is equally true for the group of first-generation Franco-Chinese migrant authors, such as the French academician François Cheng, the French Prix Femina winner Dai Sijie, and the Prix Goncourt des Lycéens winner SHAN Sa. Their reputation back in China was boosted dramatically after prestigious Western institutions officially recognized their artistic and intellectual merits.[42]

This integration is of mutual interest. From France's perspective, recognizing and promoting artists and writers from the world's emerging economic powers such as China, India, and Brazil was an important component of French cultural diplomacy in the twentieth century and even more so in the twenty-first century (Lane 2013, 54–55). French cultural authorities are very much conscious of the cosmopolitan vocation of French literature in the national and international literary scenes, especially when faced with the massive and pervading influence of the Anglophone world (Chirila 2012, 68). One of the major scholarly events in 2013 in Paris to commemorate the centenary of the first publication of Proust's *Du côté de chez Swann*, co-organized by the Collège de France and the École normale supérieure, entitled '"Du côté de chez Swann", ou le cosmopolitisme d'un roman français', prominently featured themes such as Orientalism and transnational aesthetics. Western scholars palpably express a desire to expand the field of Proust Studies by reaching beyond their Western context.

Building on our previous observations in Chap. 2, this chapter will end with a few theoretical observations on the *effects* produced by the Chinese linguistic translation and, to some extent, 'cultural translation'—or as some would rather say 'distortions' or 'misappropriations'—of *La Recherche*. As has been mentioned already, Proust was translated in a social and intellectual environment marked by a dynamic tension between an opening up to the West and a rediscovery of Chinese cultural heritage. This tension is well reflected in and supported by an influential Chinese school of literary translation theory which sees translation as fundamentally a 'competition' between two languages and cultures (Xu 2003, 107). The emphasis is on the harmonious 'communicability' between cultures through languages. It is the translator's task and responsibility to strive for such 'harmony',[43] especially when the forward-looking initiative from cultural 'competition' could potentially be brought into a cultural 'conflict' that hinders cross-cultural dialogues. Such a theory does not insist on an 'authentic' understanding of an absolute Other and it in many ways still reflects the 'naturalization' tendency in the Chinese tradition of literary translation since the end of the nineteenth century, which attaches less importance to the notion of 'faithfulness' and imbues the translated text with a higher degree of 'originality'. As André Lefevere (Bassnett and Lefevere 1998, 14) astutely remarks:

> Cultures that are relatively homogenous [such as classical Greece and Chinese] tend to see their own way of doing things as 'naturally', the only way, which just as naturally becomes the 'best' way when confronted with other ways. When such cultures themselves take over elements from

outside, they will, once again, naturalise them without too many qualms and too many restrictions. When Chinese translates texts produced by Others outside its boundaries, it translates these texts in order to replace them, pure and simple. The translations take the place of the originals.

The notion of 'competition' with Western languages and cultures, to adapt Ting Guo's (2016, 48) observation of Pan Guangdan's translation of Havelock Ellis, also 'provoke[s] target readers' cultural memory through retracing and rereading "mirror texts" in the target culture and intervene[s]' in the knowledge of the Other. Such provocation and intervention constitute 'a crucial component in supporting and developing traditional Chinese scholarship'. It is worth pointing out that the scholar XU Yuanchong, who most notably advances this 'competition' theory of translation, was himself involved in the *First Translation* and co-translated *Le Côté de Guermantes* (*The Guermantes Way*). In fact, Xu has authored a Chinese-English bilingual memoir (1996) with the same title as that of *La Recherche* in Chinese (although the English version is titled *Vanished Spring*). According to our earlier observations in Chap. 2, Zhou's new translation would seem closer to this theory in its approach than H. Xu's, and has proved to be more popular with established writers such as Chen Cun and WANG Anyi.[44] Judging by their respective creative engagements with Proust, this particular view of translation would appeal to the three writers of the present corpus too. Wang, Yu, and Wei recycle in various ways some of the Proustian clichés in order to make them appear in the new lights of classical Chinese thought (Wang), contemporary cross-cultural politics (Yu), and the modern Chinese urban landscape (Wei). While the water/river image of time in relation to Proust has started to become a cliché in the reception of *La Recherche* in China, such an aesthetic conception could potentially inspire Western Proust scholars in return, especially when they re-examine passages like the river landscape of the Vivonne, where the narrator associates the river source with aristocratic family ancestries 'venus peut-être il y a bien des siècles d'Asie mais apatriés pour toujours [...] gardant encore [...] un poétique éclat d'orient' ('[who came] from Asia many centuries ago [...] but still retaining [...] a poetic lustre of the Orient') (*RTP I*, 165–166; *PT I*, 168–169).

The three mainland Chinese writers' intertextual practices legitimately constitute and consolidate Proust's literary posterity in China. But it is a retrospective relationship in which the father resembles more and more his son(s) rather than vice versa, as Harold Bloom (1973) observes. Just as Madame de Sévigné is Proust's creation, Proust, too, can be described as these Chinese writers' creation(s), especially for their Chinese readership. Intertextuality can thus be read *backwards* and the posterior texts reveal an additional meaning to the one that preceded them (Bouillaguet [1990] 1998, 255). This is exactly what happened to the Chinese translation and reception of *La Recherche*. Translators of *La Recherche* first (mis)led Chinese writers to create a Proust who could 'speak to' Chinese aesthetic and philosophical traditions. Readers of popular Chinese writers would thus anticipate a 'sinicized' version of Proust before they approached Proust's actual work. As we will see in Part II, on the Franco-Chinese author Cheng, Proust's sinicized posterity will continue to voyage across the waters from China back to France.

NOTES

1. The expression 'kitschification of Proust' is from Margaret Gray. She further explains: 'yet a more anxious energy may be at work here than kitschification suggests, and notions of the part-object or fetish help investigate the unease behind these various reductions of Proust, as in the tendency to conceive the madeleine scene synecdochically for all the *Recherche*. The anxious cultural ambivalence through which we now read Proust cannot but inform and reshape his text' (1992, 12).
2. Most of these works have not been translated into English or French. Unless otherwise stated, all translations are mine. Yu Hua's *Zai xiyu zhong huhan*, which has been translated into both English and French (as *Cries in the Drizzle/Cris dans la bruine*), among many other languages, is an important exception. As we will see, as a result of the translations, this novella, for which he received French institutional recognition, will mark out Yu's international achievement.
3. As clarified in the last chapter, there were earlier studies on this topic in Hong Kong and in the West. See Sect. 2.9.
4. The translators decided to adopt the film title *East Palace, West Palace* as the English title for Wang's novella 'Tender Feelings Like Water' (Zhang and Sommer 2007, viii).
5. Roux-Kieken goes on to explore the various similarities between 'deuil' and 'écriture ('mourning' and 'writing'), such as their dependence on reminiscence, their retrospective proceedings, and their processes of recreating reality (2005, 156–177).
6. In a letter to his young noble friend Georges de Lauris, Proust explicitly states that he does not 'considérer la mort comme une négation'

('consider death to be negative'); death in his work, in fact, 'se manifeste d'une façon terriblement positive' ('manifests itself in an extremely positive way') (Proust 1983, 337–338, my translation).

7. For a discussion of the problems of talking about 'time' in ancient Chinese thought, see Allan (1997, 11–12).

8. In fact, 'most of Wang Xiaobo's protagonists bear the same name, Wang Er' (Zhang and Sommer 2007, iv–x).

9. Unlike the other two writers' works examined in this chapter, Yu's novella has been translated into English (as 'Cries in the Drizzle' [2007]) and French (as 'Cris dans la bruine' [2003]). Where necessary, both translations will be cited for stylistic comparisons. The Chinese original will be abbreviated as *Huhan*, the English version as *Cries*, and the French as *Cris* in the in-text citations.

10. WU Liang, 'Re-membering the Cultural Revolution', in *Chinese Literature in the Second Half of a Modern Century: A Critical Survey*, ed. by Pang-Yuan Chi, David Der-wei Wang (Indiana: Indiana University Press, 2000), pp. 124–136 (pp. 124–125).

11. The Chinese translation of *Du côté de chez Swann* came out in 1989.

12. This is Cheng's rephrasing of a Proustian idea. See Part II, 1.3.

13. The term 'double internal focalization' was popularized in particular by Brian Rogers in Proust Studies, but the idea was based on Gérard Genette's narratological theory. See Rogers (2004, 121).

14. Yu, 'Italian Translation', p. 5.

15. I have chosen to translate Yu's passage into both French and English in order to demonstrate a closer lexical similarity to Proust's original. The italics are mine.

16. I borrow the phrase from Margaret Gray, who herself appropriates this notion from Michel Serres. Gray is more concerned with 'the dialogue as exclusion rather than exchange' in the case of Proust's own practice of 'pastiching' Flaubert's critical language. My focus here, however, is on the dialogic exchange and inclusion through the Chinese writers' creative imagination and fictional reconfiguration. See Gray (1992, 9).

17. I am indebted to Plottel's formulation of intertextuality; see Plottel (1978, xiv).

18. The 'Harmonious Society' was officially propagated from 2005 onwards.

19. See Chap. 2, Sect. 2.1 For a further clarification of Hu's 'Harmonious Society', see Xing (2009).

20. See the summary of Cheng's interview in Part II, 1.3.

21. These cultural sources will be explored further in Part II on Cheng.

22. As can be seen, this Proustian echo is made much less distinct in the English version, hence my insistence on the French version to illustrate the syntactical and lexical similarity.

23. I have slightly modified the English translation to make it appear lexically closer to the Chinese original.
24. The following short stories are cited from *The Complete Works of Wei Hui* (Wei 2000), which will be abbreviated as *WH* in in-text citations. Unless stated otherwise, all the English translations are my own.
25. See Note 4 of Chap. 2 for a qualification of the term. Interestingly, according to H. Wang's doctoral thesis (2012), both Wang and Yu can also be considered as 'decadentist' writers in the Chinese context.
26. A good example would be her novel *Shanghai Baby* (1999), translated into both English (2001a) and French (2001b). The fact that the book was censored in China is used for its Western publicity. This phenomenon may be best captured in Sheldon Lu's words: 'predictably, being "banned in China!" enhanced domestic curiosity about and international marketability of the authors and novels. There was even more reason for people outside "Red China" to pry into texts that "a totalitarian regime" forbade its citizens to read' (2008, 168).
27. See Sect. 2.1 for a brief account of the impact of the 'marketization' on the Chinese translations of Proust. Zhang's section also includes many other Chinese writers' sweeping comments on and references to Proust.
28. Or, given Wei's open Francophilia, she is probably acquainted with the French notion of 'bobo' (for 'bourgeois bohémien'). A strict application of the term to China would be, of course, anachronistic. But this social phenomenon and its basic implications are similar in both Europe and China.
29. See Chap. 2,Sect.2.9.3 for a discussion of the use of *yin-yang* discourse in the Chinese translation of Proust's sexual vocabulary.
30. 'Feelings appearing in front of one's eyes' sounds very awkward in the Chinese original too.
31. This observation is inspired by Bouillaguet's (1996, 86–88) discussion of Proust's parodies.
32. Ibid., p. 75.
33. As mentioned both in the Introduction and Chap. 2, the *First Translation* was published in full in 1991 in seven volumes. Wei's reference is to the three-volume edition published by the same publisher, Yilin, later in 1994. Subsequently there have been several new editions following the same three-volume format. The edition used in this book was published in 2008.
34. The title's English form is explicitly mentioned in the novella. It is supposed to be 'the best song that Miqi [the male protagonist] had written' (*WH*, 646). It is unclear whether it bears any substantial relation to Norman Mailer's novel and film of the same name.

35. Luo (*FT I*, 22) describes Proust as 'someone who willingly buries himself alive in the grave [...], emotionally noting down memories of all sorts of experiences and feelings he lived through in his previous life' ('一个自愿活埋在坟墓中的人 [...] 回想生前种种经历与感受的抒情记录').

36. Bernard Grasset finally agreed to publish Proust's manuscript at the author's own expense. For a summary of the publication trajectory of *Du côté de chez Swann*, see Schmid (2006, 65–66).

37. Section 2.9 of Chap. 2 specifically engages with Proust's discourses on gender and sexuality.

38. For a detailed account of the marginality of Chinese rock music, compared to the hegemonic *tongsu* music (officially approved popular music), in the early 1990s, see Jones (1992, 91–114).

39. Cheng openly speaks of a *démarche proustienne* (Proustian approach). See Part II.

40. Julia Lovell, 'Finding a Place: Mainland Chinese Fiction in the 2000's', *The Journal of Asian Studies* 71 (2012), 7–32 (p. 15).

41. This impression has, however, started to change, most notably with the awarding of the Nobel Prize for Literature in 2012 to Mo Yan, who was already a very well-established writer in China before this weighty Western honour. Like Yu, Mo was also a core member of the Chinese avant-garde literature movement in the 1980s.

42. The Nobel Prize laureate Gao Xingjian is an exception in this regard, as the author's thematic engagement with the events of Tiananmen Square, as well as his comments on the Communist regime, have led to the banning of his works in mainland China.

43. As discussed in relation to Yu's preface, the idea of 'harmony' has a long historical trajectory in Chinese thought, especially in Daoism and Confucianism, and carries strong political overtones in contemporary China. However, it is far beyond the scope of this study to investigate its possible influence on this particular Chinese school of translation theory.

44. For K. Zhou's conversation with Chen Cun, see K. Zhou (2012, 203–222). Wang Anyi openly recommends Chinese readers choose Zhou's translation. Her recommendation is printed on the cover of a different edition of Zhou's translation of *À l'ombre des jeunes filles en fleurs*, published by People's Literature Publishing House.

REFERENCES

Allan, Sarah. 1997. *The Way of Water and Sprouts of Virtue*. New York: State University of New York Press.

Barthes, Roland. 1984. *Le Bruissement de la langue*. Paris: Seuil.

Bassnett, Susan, and André Lefevere. 1998. *Constructing Cultures: Essays on Literary Translation*. Clevedon: Multilingual Matters Ltd.

Bloom, Harold. 1973. *The Anxiety of Influence: A Theory of Poetry*. New York: Oxford University Press.

Bouillaguet, Annick. 1996. *L'Écriture imitative: Pastiche, Parodie, Collage*. Paris: Nathan.

Bouillaguet, Annick. 1990 [1998]. *Marcel Proust: Le Jeu intertextuel*. Paris: Édition du Titre.

Brami, Joseph. 2010. *Lecteurs de Proust au XXe siècle et au début du XXIe siècle*, vol. I. Caen: Lettres modernes Minard.

Cheng, François. 2003 [2009]. *Tianyi yan* 天一言 (Tianyi's Saying), trans. Lianxi Yang. Beijing: People's Literature Publishing House.

Chirila, Illeana Daniela. 2012. La Littérature transculturelle franco-chinoise ou comment réinventer la République des Lettres. In *Traits chinois/lignes francophones*, ed. Rosalind Silvester and Guillaume Touroude, 67–83. Montréal: Presses de l'Université de Montréal.

Colonna, Vincent. 1989. L'autofiction, essai sur la fictionalisation de soi en littérature. *École des Hautes Études en Sciences Sociales (EHESS)*. https://tel.archives-ouvertes.fr/tel-00006609. Accessed 7 Nov 2014.

Compagnon, Antoine. 1990. *Les Cinq paradoxes de la modernité*. Paris: Seuil.

Field, Andrew, and Jeroen Gronewegen. 2008. Explosive Acts: Beijing's Punk Rock Scene in the Postmodern World of 2007. In *Postmodern China*, ed. Jens Damm and Andreas Steen, 8–26. Berlin: Lit Verlag.

Fravalo-Tane, Pascale. 2008. *À la recherche du temps perdu en France et en Allemagne (1913–1958): 'Dans une sorte de langue étrangère...'*. Paris: Champion.

Gray, Margaret. 1992. *Postmodern Proust*. Philadelphia: University of Pennsylvania Press.

Guo, Ting. 2016. Translating Homosexuality Into Chinese: A Case Study of Pan Guangdan's Translation of Havelock Ellis' Psychology of Sex: A Manual for Students (1933). *Asia Pacific Translation and Intercultural Studies* 3 (1): 47–61.

Huang, Hong. 2013. Proust retrouvé. In *D'après Proust*, ed. Philippe Forest and Stéphane Audeguy, 294–304. Paris: Nouvelle Revue Française.

Jones, Andrew F. 1992. *Like a Knife: Ideology and Genre in Contemporary Chinese Popular Music*. Ithaca, NY: Cornell University Press.

Lane, Philippe. 2013. *French Scientific and Cultural Diplomacy*. Liverpool: Liverpool University Press.

Lau, D. C., trans. 1979. *The Analects*. London: Penguin.

Li, Chenyang. 2006. The Confucian Ideal of Harmony. *Philosophy East and West* 56 (4): 583–603.

Lin, Zhou. 1998. *Shengming de baidu* 生命的摆渡 (The Ferry of Life). Shenzhen: Haitian chubanshe.

Lovell, Julia. 2012. Finding a Place: Mainland Chinese Fiction in the 2000's. *The Journal of Asian Studies* 71 (1): 7–32.

Lovell, Julia. 2012. The Key to China. *Prospect*, February. http://www.prospect-magazine.co.uk/magazine/the-key-to-china-literary-magazines-new-chinese-fiction-pathlight-chutzpah. Accessed 7 Nov 2016.

Lu, Sheldon H. 2008. Popular Culture and Body Politics: Beauty Writers in Contemporary China. *Mondern Language Quarterly* 69 (1): 167–185.

Lu, Sheldon H. 2001. *Transnational Visuality, Global Postmodernity*. Stanford: Stanford University Press.

Moretti, Franco. 1983. *Signs Taken for Wonders: Essays in the Sociology of Literary Forms*. London: Verso Editions.

Plottel, J.P. 1978. Introduction. In *Intertextuality: New Perspectives in Criticism*, ed. Jeanne Pariser Plottel and Hanna Kurz Charney, vol. xiv. New York: New York Library Forum.

Poulet, Georges. 1982. *L'Espace proustien*. Paris: Gallimard.

Proust, Marcel. 1983. Lettre à Georges de Lauris [Fin août 1911]. In *La Correspondance de Marcel Proust X*, ed. Philip Kolb, 337–340. Paris: Plon.

Rabut, Isabelle. 2004. Yu Hua. *Magazine Littéraire*, March: 60.

Rogers, Brian G. 2004. *The Narrative Techniques of 'À la recherche du temps perdu'*. Paris: Champion.

Roux-Kieken, Aude le. 2005. *Imaginaire et écriture de la mort dans l'oeuvre de Marcel Proust*. Paris: Champion.

Schmid, Marion. 2006. The Birth and Development of A la recherche du temps perdu. In *The Cambridge Companion to Proust*, ed. Richard Bales, 58–73. Cambridge: Cambridge University Press.

Taub, Liba. 2003. *Ancient Meteorology*. London: Routledge.

Wang, Hongjian. 2012. *Performing Perversion: Decadence in Twentieth-Century Chinese Literature*. PhD dissertation, University of Chicago, ProQuest LLC.

Wang, Shicheng. 2005. *Xiangsi ersheng: Yu Hua* 向死而生: 余华 (Life Through Death: Yu Hua). Shanghai: Shanghai renmin chubanshe.

Wang, Xiaobo. 2011 [1992]. Si shui liu nian 似水流年 (Fleeting Years As Water). In *Huangjin shidai* 黄金时代 (The Golden Age), ed. Xiaobo Wang, 129–198. Beijing: Beijing shiyue wenyi chubanshe.

Wang, Xiaobo. 2011 [1993]. Youguan tongxinglian de lunli wenti 有关同性恋的伦理问题 (About the Ethical Issue of Homosexuality). In *Wo de jingshen jiayuan* 我的精神家园 (My Spiritual Home), ed. Xiaobo Wang, 229–235. Beijing: Beijing shiyue wenyi chubanshe.

Wang, Xiaobo. 2011 [1994]. Guanyu tongxinglian de wenti 关于同性恋的问题 (About the Issue of Homosexuality). In *Wo de jingshen jiayuan* 我的精神家园 (My Spiritual Home), ed. Xiaobo Wang, 224–228. Beijing: Beijing shiyue wenyi chubanshe.

Wang, Xiaobo. 2011. Si shui rou qing 似水柔情 (Tender Feelings Like Water). In *Baiyin shidai* 白银时代 (The Silver Age), ed. Xiaobo Wang, 274–316. Beijing: Beijing shiyue wenyi chubanshe.

Wei, Hui. 2000. *Wei Hui zuopin quanji* 卫慧作品全集 (The Complete Works of Wei Hui). Guilin: Lijiang chubanshe.

Wei, Hui. 2001a. *Shanghai Baby*, trans. Cora Whist. Paris: Philippe Picquier.

Wei, Hui. 2001b. *Shanghai Baby*, trans. Bruce Humes. London: Robinson.

Wu, Liang. 2000. Re-membering the Cultural Revolution. In *Chinese Literature in the Second Half of a Modern Century: A Critical Survey*, ed. Pang-Yuan Chi and Der-wei Wang, 124–136. Bloomington: Indiana University Press.

Xing, Guoxin. 2009. Hu Jintao's Political Thinking and Legitimacy Building: A Post-Marxist Perspective. *Asian Affairs: An American Review* 34 (4): 213–226.

Xu, Yuanchong. 2003. *Wenxue yu fanyi* 文学与翻译 (Literature and Translation). Beijing: Peking University Press.

Yu, Hua. 2002. *Shuohua* 说话 (Talks). Shenyang: Chunfeng wenyi chubanshe.

Yu, Hua. 2003. *Cris dans la bruine*, trans. Jacqueline Guyvallet. Paris: Actes Sud.

Yu, Hua. 2007. *Cries in the Drizzle*, trans. Allan Hepburn Barr. New York: Anchor Books.

Yu, Hua. 2011 [1991]. *Zai xiyu zhong huhan* 在细雨中呼喊 (Cries in the Drizzle). Beijing: Zuojia chubanshe.

Zhang, Hongling, and Jason Sommer. 2007. Introduction. In *Wang in Love and Bondage: Three Novellas by Wang Xiaobo*, ed. Xiaobo Wang, vii–xiv. Beijing: State University of New York Press.

Zhang, Yinde. 2003. *Le Monde romanesque chinois au XXe siècle. Modernité et identité*. Paris: Champion.

Zhang, Yuan. 1996. *East Palace, West Palace*. Directed by Yuan Zhang. Fortissimo Films.

Zhou, Kexi. 2012. *Yi Bian Cao* 译边草. Shanghai: East China Normal University Press.

PART II

Proust in the Chinese Diaspora: François Cheng's *Le Dit de Tianyi*

CHAPTER 4

Intertextual and Paratextual Relations Between *La Recherche* and *Le Dit*

4.1 INTRODUCTION

For mainland Chinese writers, citing Proust enhances the cultural prestige of their own works in China; for Franco-Chinese writers, it signals an imperative assimilation of their 'sinity' into the French culture.
Among this latter group of writers (including Gao Xingjian and Dai
Sijie), François Cheng's engagement with Proust stands out as the most
thorough.[1] The importance of Proust's work as an intellectual and artistic model for Cheng, especially in relation to his novel *Le Dit de Tianyi*
(1998),[2] is crystalized in the author's own words: 'ma démarche, sans
prétention de ma part, est très proche de celle de Proust: avec cette
langue, j'ai pu repenser ma vie, et repenser ma pensée, autrement que
si j'étais resté en Chine' ('my approach, with no pretension on my part,
is very close to that of Proust: with this language, I was able to rethink
my life, rethink my thought, differently from if had stayed in China')
(Cheng 2005, 370–371, my translation). 'This language', of course,
refers to the French language. This 'rethought life' is what Cheng frequently refers to elsewhere as 'une nouvelle vie' ('a new life') (Cheng
2002, 2003). As we will see, the idea of a new language creating a
new life is crucial to our understanding of Cheng's translingual literary
aesthetics.

Cheng's intellectual development mirrors that of Tianyi in *Le Dit*:
predominantly Daoist in his way of thinking (which, in the Chinese context, is never entirely separable from Buddhist and Confucian thought);

© The Author(s) 2017
S. Li, *Proust, China and Intertextual Engagement*,
DOI 10.1007/978-981-10-4454-0_4

very well acquainted with both Eastern and Western literary and artistic traditions; and aspiring to engage equally with the two worlds in order to create something harmonious, which Cheng describes as a ceaseless process of 'transcendance'.[3]

If mainland Chinese writers' encounters with Proust's work appear to be brief, incidental, and, in many ways, 'historical',[4] Cheng's engagement with Proust's work, as well as Proust criticism, can be described as long and inevitable. Proust is arguably one of the most common subjects among members of Cheng's intellectual circle. His master's dissertation (1963–1968) on Chinese poetry made an impact on his examiner Roland Barthes, as well as on Julia Kristeva and Roman Jakobson. This was a time when literary theory was undergoing drastic change. From the 1970s to the 1980s, Cheng was actively involved in structuralist and poststructuralist debates, engaging in intellectual dialogue with Jacques Lacan, Claude Lévi-Strauss, and Gilles Deleuze. For example, many of Cheng's ideas about the arts, as I will later demonstrate in the next chapter, share strong affinities with Deleuze's formulation of Proust's aesthetic conception in *Proust et les signes* (1976).

On the other hand, many of those structuralist and poststructuralist thinkers are known for their interest in Eastern cultures.[5] Barthes's and Kristeva's works also contribute to a wider French discourse on Eastern cultures shared by other scholars from Asian studies, such as François Jullien and Anne Cheng (François Cheng's daughter). Poststructuralist discourses are particularly noticeable in Cheng's creative writings. These varied intellectual connections will help explain the somewhat 'strange' compatibility between Proust and Chinese thought in Cheng's fiction.

If there is one branch of Western philosophy with which Cheng has to associate himself, it is phenomenology as formulated by the French school represented by Maurice Merleau-Ponty and Henri Maldiney. Cheng sees in phenomenology an appreciable communicability with classical Chinese thought, especially Daoism. He remarks:

Je me présente plutôt comme un phénoménologue un peu naïf qui observe et interroge non seulement les données déjà repérées et cernées par la raison, mais ce qui est recelé et impliqué, ce qui surgit de façon inattendue et inespérée, ce qui se manifeste comme don et promesse. Je n'ignore pas que dans l'ordre de la matière, on peut et on doit établir des théorèmes; je sais en revanche que, dans l'ordre de la vie, il convient d'apprendre à *saisir les phénomènes qui adviennent*, chaque fois singuliers, lorsque ceux-ci se révèlent *être dans le sens de la Voie*, c'est-à-dire d'une marche vers *la vie ouverte*. Outre mes réflexions, le travail que je dois effectuer consiste plutôt à creuser en moi *la capacité à la réceptivité*. Seule une posture d'accueil – être *'le ravin du monde'*, *selon Laozi* –, et non de conquête, nous permettra, j'en suis persuadé, de recueillir, de la vie ouverte, la part du vrai. (Cheng 2008, 19, my italics)

I present myself instead as a slightly naive phenomenologist who is observing and interrogating not only the facts already discovered and defined by reason, but also that which I concealed and implied, which arises in unforeseen, unexpected ways, which emerges as gift and promise. I am aware that, within the material order, one can and must establish theorems. But on the other hand I know that within the order of life, it is good to learn to *seize phenomena as they occur*, each time singular, when they reveal themselves to be *following the Way*, that is to say, moving toward *open life*. Beyond my reflections, the work I must accomplish consists rather of hollowing out in myself *the capacity for receptivity*. Only a posture of welcome—to be *the ravine of the world, according to Lao-tzu*—and not of conquest, will permit us, I am persuaded, to gather from open life a share of truth. (Cheng 2009b, 11–12, my italics)

As Part II gradually unfolds, it will become clear that Cheng's interest in phenomenology and a particular trend of phenomenological approaches in Proust Studies opens yet another theoretical and methodological platform on which Cheng's creative Daoist 'import' joins up with Proust critics such as Jean-Pierre Richard and Nathalie Auber. 'The raven of the world' is a concrete representation of the Way 'dans l'ordre du réel' ('in the order of external reality') in Daoism. It symbolizes the idea of a fundamental, generative emptiness in Daoist belief, as Cheng formulates: '[la vallée] est creuse, et, dirait-on, vide, pourtant elle nourrit et fait pousser les choses; et portant toutes choses en son sein, elle les contient sans jamais se laisser déborder et tarir' ('The valley is hollow, and one might say empty, but it makes things grown and nourishes them. Bearing all things within its bosom, the valley contains them without exceeding its capacities or being worn out') (Cheng 1991, 29; 1994, 46). The affinity between Cheng's acculturation of Daoism and the more recent phenomenological approach to Proustian philosophy will allow us to better express 'Eastern' characteristics (long felt by me and other critics like Barbara Bucknall)—albeit epistemologically uncertain—in Proust's Modernist poetics.[6]

Adopting a similar critical approach to the one employed in Part I Chap. 3, the following analysis will first start from a number of empirical observations on Cheng's relation to Proust. Then, largely following up Cheng's vital clue—his *démarche proustienne* (Proustian approach)—it will establish a representative range of conceptual and thematic parallels between *Le Dit* and *La Recherche*, exploring how Cheng's translingual literary aesthetics is effectuated in his creative take on the Western canon in juxtaposition with the Chinese canon. The final section will put Cheng's *démarche proustienne* in relation to his broader intellectual enterprise, which aims at cultural transcendence, and reflect upon a few key critical issues underlying cultural translation and transcultural writing.

4.2   CHENG'S 'À LA RECHERCHE DU TEMPS À VENIR'

Despite the common enthusiasm for Proust in Cheng's intellectual circle, up until the time he started writing *Le Dit* in the late 1980s, Cheng had rarely mentioned Proust in his work. This intellectual silence about Proust could partly be explained by the fact that Cheng was until then mainly preoccupied with poetry rather than prose, as he was translating Baudelaire, Mallarmé, and Verlaine into Chinese, and classical Chinese poetry into French. The publication of *Le Dit* seems to have brought about a drastic change: from then on, references to Proust have proliferated in Cheng's writings. As we have seen in the previous section, it is clearly Cheng's intention to encourage his readers to bear Proust in mind whilst they are reading the novel. *Le Dit*, Cheng's first novel, is often said to have decidedly marked his transition from sinologist to novelist, from his scholarly profession to an artistic vocation. In this light, the impact of Proust on Cheng and his novel can be seen as only more profound. Indeed, this is not the first time in the course of the present study that Proust or the reading of Proust's work has significantly contributed to a writer's intellectual and artistic transition. In Sect. 3.3.1 of Part I, I suggested how the Chinese writer Yu Hua's encounter with Proust's work inspired his thematic and narrative experiments with fictional writings, which decisively led to his generic advancement from short stories to novels.

Le Dit in the French original (1998) consists of a preface ('avant-propos') and three parts—a structure which, as we shall see, is different from the book's Chinese translation (2003). The French preface is attributed to a different narrator, one of Tianyi's former fellow international students in France, who claims to have translated and reconstructed the narrative in French based on the piles of writings given by Tianyi, which would have risked being destroyed had they stayed in China. The apparent inconsistencies and lacunae within these writings are resolved and complemented by Tianyi's verbal recount, which was noted down by the narrator with the help of a basic cassette recorder. This narrator can be seen as the first incarnation of Cheng himself in the novel, especially because of the corresponding details between the narrator's life trajectory and Cheng's biography, such as the decision to settle permanently in France, and a major surgery that both Cheng and the narrator underwent in the early 1990s.

While there is no evidence to suggest that this narrative device is directly influenced by Proust, it is nevertheless worth pointing out its commonality with Proust's earlier unfinished work, *Jean Santeuil*, in the preface of which the narrator claims to have transposed the manuscript of the writer C., with whom the narrator and his friend communicated on a regular basis while staying at a health resort. Just like Proust's narrator, who decided to publish the drafts of a novel they found in the place of the writer C. after the announcement of his death (Proust 1952, 57), Cheng's narrator, after Tianyi's death, 'entrepri[t] alors la rude tâche de reconstituer le récit dont [il avait] la charge [...] Avant que tout ne soit perdu' ('took on the arduous task of putting together the story entrusted to [him] [...] Before all is lost') (*DT,* 11; *RB,* xii).

The three parts of the novel include: 'Épopée du départ' ('Epic of Departure'), which is set in China, spanning the period from 1925 to 1945; 'Récit d'un détour' ('A Turn in the Road'), set in Europe, especially France, between 1948 and 1957; and finally 'Mythe du retour' ('Myth of Return'), leading up to the end of the 1970s. The first two parts are extensively biographical, made up of Cheng's own life experience in China and Europe, whereas the 'myth of return' is based on the author's imaginative reconstruction of catastrophic historical events such as the Great Leap Forward (1958–1961), the Three Years of Natural Disasters (1959–1961), and the Cultural Revolution (1966–1976). Part Three concerns Tianyi's fear that his writings might be destroyed in China, where Tianyi denounces many of the severe mismanagements of the Chinese Communist Party and its leader. Although 'Tianyi's writings'—Cheng's novel—have 'survived', been 'translated' back into Chinese, and even attained considerable fame in the sinophone world, the publication has not circumvented censorship in mainland China.[7]

Cheng explicitly foregrounds his intertextual dialogue with Proust in, quite literally, a pivotal passage connecting the first two parts of the novel. The protagonist Tianyi listens to the 'renowned specialist in Chinese thought', Professor F.—another incarnation of Cheng?—explicate the Daoist conceptions of time, the Void, and the Exchange on the Yangtze River, just before leaving China for France. Tianyi retrospectively makes the following remark:

> Je m'inclinai avec gratitude devant son explication [Prof. F. on different kinds of philosophical 'return'] en bien des points obscurs pour moi. Je retins au moins qu'elle affirmait que rien de la vraie vie ne se perd et que ce qui ne se perd pas débouche sur un futur aussi continu qu'inconnu. Explication dont je me souviendrai lorsque en France il me sera donné de lire *A la recherche du temps perdu*. Contrairement à Proust, j'aurais écrit 'A la recherche du temps à venir'. La loi du temps, du moins ma loi à moi, à travers ce que je venais de vivre avec l'Amante, n'était pas dans l'accompli, dans l'achevé, mais dans le différé, l'inachevé. Il me fallait passer par le Vide et par le Change. (*DT*, 191)

> I accepted his explanation [Prof. F. on different kinds of philosophical 'return'] gratefully, although many points were not clear to me. I did at least grasp the conclusion that nothing in real life is lost and that what is not leads into a future as continuous as it is unknown. An explanation I would remember in France upon reading *In Search of Lost Time*. Differing with Proust, I might have written: 'In search of time to come.' The law of time, for me at any rate, in keeping with what I had just experienced with the Lover, was not based on the accomplished, the finished, but on the postponed [*différé*], unfinished. I had to pass through the Void and the Exchange. (*RB*, 131)

This highly condensed passage self-referentially announces the novel we are reading as Tianyi's 'livre à venir' ('book-to-come'). Cheng evidently attempts to re-examine Proust's sense of time from a Daoist point of view, creatively introducing a critical as well as geographical reorientation of Proust's text. This critical relation, especially in the form of 'commentary', between Cheng's and Proust's texts is what Genette conceives of as *metatextuality*, in addition to their obvious intertextual nature.[8]

The setting of this scene itself is an allusion to a recurrent motif in the founding classical texts of Daoism and Confucianism. Water/river, which share the same character in classical Chinese, 水, as Professor F.

explains, is the 'symbole du temps' ('symbol of time') (*DT,* 190; *RB,* 129) and is essentially cyclical. In classical Chinese thought, the perception of the water/river movement sometimes *is* the definition of 'time' (which is of course different from our modern understanding of it).[9] *The Analects,* again, describes Confucius standing *by* the river—rather than *on* the river—saying, 'what passes away is, perhaps, like this. Day and night it never lets up' (Lau 1979, 98). Let us remind ourselves of the iconic Chinese translation of the title of *La Recherche* as *Pursuing the Memory of Time/Years as Water/River.* Against this backdrop, Cheng's inter-and metatextual introduction of Proust in the above-cited passage appears to be particularly valid in the Chinese context and provokes an intriguing compatibility between classical Chinese thought and Proustian philosophy. Even the alternative, more literal but less well-known rendition of the title by Zhou Kexi as 追寻逝去的时光 (*In Search of Lost Time*) does not escape the water/river reference in the Chinese context. Sarah Allan (1997, 36–37) astutely points out that the verb *shi* (逝, passing away)—which Zhou employs to translate 'perdu' ('lost')—is etymologically linked to the flowing and passing by of water, as is still seen in the expression *shishui* (逝水, passing away of water).

It is worth pointing out that Cheng had actually first intended to employ 'là-bas le fleuve' ('there the river') as the title of his novel. Such a title was rejected by Cheng's editor due to its dearth of literary resonance for French readers. In comparison, the title for the English translation, *The River Below,* makes a conscious effort to return to Cheng's initial intention and further highlights the importance of the passage in question, although 'the river below' is not exactly the same as 'by the river'. Whereas the English translator J. Smith's titular proposal seems to be based on the above-cited pivotal passage alone, Cheng, apart from the Confucian allusion, probably has Tianyi's various experiences with other rivers in the novel in mind, where the subject's position is not always *on* the river.

In our discussion of the intertextual relation between Wang Xiaobo's novella 'Sishui liunian' ('似水流年', 'Fleeting Years as Water') and Proust's work in Part I Chap. 3, we already noted that Wang describes the experience of time as 'a possessed person lying on the riverbed'— rather than *on* the river, like Professor F.'s and Tianyi's position, or like Confucius's *by* the river—'observing dead leaves, driftwood, and empty bottles, flowing by and being carried away by running water'.[10] I suggested that Wang's nuanced version of the time-as-water/river allusion accommodates well Proust's formulation of an existential condition as 'dans le Temps' ('in Time'), the ending phrase of *La Recherche*. In comparison, Cheng's Daoist positioning of time, which, in fact, often hints at a kind of *extra-temporality*—on or above the river—curiously merges with Proust's metaphysical pursuit of truth 'en dehors du temps' ('outside time') (*RTP IV*, 510; *PT VI*, 240) which is, in Deleuze's (2008 [2000], 30) words, 'situated in a primordial complication, veritable eternity, an absolute original time' and is found in art.

Cheng's conception of 'temps à venir' ('time to come') is critically informed by his reading of the *Book of Changes* (*Yijing*, 易经), also known as *I Ching* and *Le Livre des Mutations* in French, a fundamental classical text which significantly predates and exerts huge influence on both Daoist and Confucian scriptures. In *Vide et plein* (1991) (*Empty and Full* [1994]), Cheng explains that whereas 'le Vide originel' ('original emptiness' or 'the Void') corresponds to the 'mutation non changeante' ('non-changing change') (in other words to the primordial and original ontological state of all things to which we constantly return, therefore echoing Deleuze's Proustian time in art), 'le Change' ('the Exchange') refers to both the regular movement of the Cosmos, the 'mutation simple' ('simple change'), and the evolution of particular existents, the 'mutation changeante' ('changing change'). Furthermore, 'in the existence of a particular being, time follows a double movement: linear (in the sense of the changing change) and circular (toward the nonchanging change)' (Cheng 1991, 68; 1994, 58–59). Thus 'on the historical level', time 'unfolds from cycle to cycle' following 'a spiral movement' with 'emptiness' between each cycle (ibid.). As Professor F. teaches Tianyi on the boat, 'le temps procéderait donc par cercles concentriques, ou par cercles tournant en spirale si vous voulez' ('time proceeds in concentric circles, or if you prefer, in spiraling circles') (*DT*, 191; *RB*, 130). The threefold movement of 'time' finds its perfect expression in the water/river metaphor: ongoing, discontinuous, unknowable, and cyclical. The professor further clarifies:

> [...] ce cercle n'est pas la roue qui tourne sur elle-même, sur les choses du même ordre selon la pensée indienne, ni ce qu'on appelle l'éternel retour. Le nuage condensé en pluie n'est plus l'eau du fleuve, et la pluie ne retombe pas sur la même eau. Car le cercle ne se fait qu'en passant par le Vide et par le Change. Oui, l'idée de la mutation et de la transformation est essentielle dans la pensée chinoise. Elle est la loi même de la Voie. Le retour dont parle Laozi [...]. (ibid.)

[...] this circle is not the wheel of Indian thought, spinning endlessly around the same things, nor is it what is known as the eternal return. The cloud condensed into rain is no longer river water, and the rain does not fall back into the same water. The circle is completed only by passage through the Void and the Exchange. Yes, the idea of mutation and transformation is essential to Chinese thought, and is the very law of the Way. Laozi's 'return', [...]. (ibid.)

'La Voie' is the most commonly accepted French translation of the Chinese word *Dao* (道, the Way). But *Dao* also means 'dire' or 'to say', which immediately echoes the title of the novel. Hence 'le dit de Tianyi' should also be understood as 'le Dao de Tianyi'. 'Le dit' in French in this particular substantive form refers to a kind of literary narrative that can be dated back to the Middle Ages.[11]

Although Tianyi ostensibly endeavours to achieve something in opposition to Proust's project ('contrairement à Proust'), most Proust scholars would agree that Proust's 'temps perdu' is never literally 'lost' in the past, and the Proustian sense of time, just like the book the protagonist begins to write at the end of *La Recherche*, revolves around the idea of coming—Cheng's 'le temps à venir'. Deleuze, for example, repeatedly stresses that 'Proust's work is not oriented to the past and the discoveries of memory, but to the future and the progress of an apprenticeship' (2008 [2000], 18).[12] Both the Daoist and the Proustian conceptions of 'time' emphasize the interaction among the unknowable continuity and return of time (and space), as it says in the cited passage: 'rien de la vraie vie ne se perd et que ce qui ne se perd pas débouche sur un futur aussi continu qu'inconnu' ('nothing in real life is lost and that what is not leads into a future as continuous as it is unknown') (ibid., 192; ibid., 131). These ideas are reflected in the basic tripartite design of *La Recherche* as the 'lost', 'sought', and 'regained' time. The novel ends with 'dans le Temps' ('in Time') and begins with 'longtemps' ('for a long time'), with its first volume ending also with a temporal reference, 'comme les années' ('as the years'), which demonstrates a strong sense of continuity and cyclical return. Yet, the 'intermittent'[13] structure of the novel, revolving around spontaneous resurrection of memory, implies a constant disruption of our sense of time as a linear experience.

'Le différé', which Smith translates as 'postponed' rather than 'deferred', is in fact recognizably Derridean, and even Cheng's nuanced formulation of 'un futur aussi continu qu'inconnu' ('a future as continuous as it is unknown') as the 'temps à venir' ('time to come') is strongly reminiscent of Derrida's distinction between 'futur' and 'avenir':

In general, I try to distinguish between what one calls the future and
'l'avenir'. The future is that which—tomorrow, later, next century—will
be. There's a future which is predictable, programmed, scheduled, foresee-
able. But there is a future, l'avenir (to come) which refers to someone who
comes whose arrival is totally unexpected. For me, that is the real future.
That which is totally unpredictable. The Other who comes without my
being able to anticipate their arrival. So if there is a real future beyond this
other known future, it's *l'avenir* in that it's the coming of the Other when
I am completely unable to foresee their arrival. (Derrida 2002)

The exploration of 'the Other' will indeed be Tianyi's primary intellectual preoccupation once he has arrived in Europe in 'Récit d'un détour'
('A Turn in the Road').

In effect, far from contradicting Proust, Cheng's commentary on
Proust, despite his Daoist point of departure, resonates with critical
discourses in Proust Studies. Nathalie Aubert in *Proust: La Traduction
du sensible*, for instance, also concludes that Proust's *La Recherche*
'agite chaque figure du passé par une mise au présent, à la fois mise en
présence et travail constant de l'attente, de l'œuvre qui reste toujours
à venir' ('raises every character of the past to the present, actualizing
both the presence and the constant labour of expectations, of the work
that remains always *to come*') (2002, 134, italics in the original, my
translation).

Thus Cheng provocatively juxtaposes the Daoist vocabulary (and
context) with notable poststructuralist and poststructuralism-inflected
Proustian discourses, which makes the connection between Daoism and
Proust appear all the more compelling in the above-cited passage. As a
result, both French readers and Chinese readers (of *Le Dit* in translation) are pushed to reflect on how those culturally specific and divergent
ideas might converge, despite a sea of epistemic uncertainties—simply
because we do not have enough strong evidence to pin down, especially in the scholarly fashion, the direct empirical influences between
Daoism/Confucianism and the work of Western thinkers like Derrida
and Deleuze. While French readers tend to be intrigued by Cheng's
novel Eastern take on the rather familiar subject of Proust, and aspire to
culturally accommodate such an approach, which is perhaps superficially
reflected in the institutional recognitions of Cheng's work in France
from the Prix Femina to the Académie française, Chinese readers also
benefit from Cheng's creative appropriation of a rather unfamiliar and

abstract foreign subject to Chinese thought. This bilateral process results in an initiation of an intercultural dialogue, in which readers from both cultures are compelled to participate, activating the knowledge of their own cultures while learning about the other. I will return to this intention and the effect of initiating cross-cultural dialogues through the juxtaposition of traditions in later sections of the chapter.

4.3   Proust in Paratexts

In the French edition of *Le Dit*, our cited passage offers Cheng's only explicit reference to Proust. It is the paratexts featuring in the Chinese translation that unequivocally reveal Cheng's ambition to approximate Proust, and there are good reasons for this.

Although Cheng did not translate *Le Dit* into Chinese himself, he did write an additional preface in 2000 for the benefit of his Chinese readership. This new preface no longer has a fictional narrator and the author has signed his name right below the title 'Chinese Preface'. He begins the preface with a succinct discussion of the relationship between fiction and autobiography, and the question of life-writing, which are of course major concerns in Proust Studies. Immediately, in the second paragraph, Cheng reveals that the kind of novel he is about to present is similar to the one that was conceived by Proust (*TY*, 2).[14] Interestingly, what follows then are *Proustian*—rather than Proust's actual—words in quotation marks, as if they were directly taken from *La Recherche*, whereas in reality they are merely a condensed appropriation, at its best, of a Proustian idea by Cheng. This 'quotation' attributed to Proust can be translated into English as follows: 'real life is a relived life, and that relived life is obtained through recreation by memory and language' ('真正的生命是再活过的生命。而那再活过的生命是由记忆语言之再创造而获得的') (ibid.). In fact, Cheng's rendering of Proust's remark has become one of the most celebrated 'Proust quotations' in China, widely circulated among Chinese internet bloggers, and has effectively contributed to a popular Chinese discourse *on* Proust, which is not strictly verifiable *in* Proust. In this 'quotation', Cheng seems to be reading his own linguistic conviction into Proust's philosophy of life, a reading that strongly echoes the idea of a new language creating a new life, which is reiterated, for example, in his inaugural address at the Académie française:

[...] ce qui m'advient [...] signifiera le début d'*une nouvelle vie* [...] surtout à partir de ce moment où j'ai résolument basculé dans la langue française, la faisant l'arme, ou l'âme, de ma création. Cette langue [...] m'a
procuré cette distanciation par rapport à ma culture d'origine et à *mes
expériences vécues* et, dans le même temps, elle m'a conféré cette aptitude à
repenser le tout, à transmuer ce tout en un lucide acte de re-création. (Cheng
2003, my italics)

[...] what has happened to me [...] will signal the beginning of a new life
[...] especially from the moment I resolutely plunged into the French language, making it the weapon, or indeed the soul, of my creation. This language [...] allowed me to distance myself from my culture of origin and
from my real-life experiences, and at the same time, it imparted this aptitude to me for rethinking everything, transmuting everything in a perceptive act of recreation. (My translation and italics)

This Chinese preface adds a new layer of paratextuality to the French
original by formally announcing the author's intention to displace Proust
into the Chinese context, and makes his work's connection with Proust
intelligible to Chinese readers right from the outset.

Once again, this is not the first time in the course of the present
study that we observe the practice of adding an author's preface to the
translated edition(s) of the work, which prominently features a discussion of Proust. In Part I, we already examined Yu Hua's paraphrasing
and appropriation of the prologue of *La Recherche* in the prefaces that he
subsequently wrote for the translations and new editions of his novel.[15]

Besides the new preface, the Chinese translation of *Le Dit* also
includes an interview with Cheng at the back of the book, in which
Cheng further explains his personal relation to the French language
and Proust. Cheng links his necessity of writing novels in French to his
understanding of the 'Proustian state', a reiteration of his 'Proustian
quotation' discussed earlier (i.e. the idea that the real life must be sought
in language and re-experienced so that the mystery and 'fun' of life may
be revealed and clarified). Cheng needs French, a new language for him,
to re-experience the past in a new way, from a new angle, with a new
spirit.[16] For Cheng, the linguistic choice also determines, in this case, the
genre of his work: had it been written in Chinese, *Le Dit* would have
been at best a 'memoir',[17] a book about the past we have lost. However,
Cheng is self-consciously conceiving a book *à venir*, a 'recreation that

transcends time' ('超越年华的再创造') (ibid.) and, as will be explored later, cultural differences.

In fact, in almost every one of his interviews published in Chinese, Cheng comments on Proust at some point. For example, he observes that the philosophical profundity in Proust's work is precisely what traditional Chinese novels lack, except for *Dream of the Red Chamber* (Qian 1999, 7); he relates the Proustian enquiry into mortality, artistic creation and origin—which, for Cheng, is metaphysical in nature—to certain tendencies in Daoist and Confucian philosophies (Zhang 2003); and on a personal level, he thinks that he shares Proust's sensitivity, sense of (self-) alienation, and critique of the superficiality of society life (Zhou 2012, 185). These are just a few of the Proust references which have been singled out from Cheng's Chinese interviews in different contexts and which do not form a coherent argument about Cheng's approximation of Proust. This varied list of comments attempts to convey the idea that the ways in which Cheng engages with Proust are multifarious, without necessarily looking to prove his commitment to Proust, as one would have expected from a Proust scholar. It shows how resourcefully inspirational and intellectually stimulating the figure and the work of Proust are for Cheng to realize his own literary ambition from the most personal to the most abstract levels.

Cheng's intertextual 'play' with Proust's *La Recherche* in the Chinese context does not stop with *Le Dit*. It is worth mentioning that 此情可待, the Chinese title of Cheng's second novel *L'Éternité n'est pas de trop* (literally meaning 'this love that keeps waiting', and which is translated into English as *Green Mountain, White Cloud*), was essentially inspired by the same verse which inspired the iconic 'poetic' translation of 'à la recherche du temp perdu' as 追忆似水年华 ('pursuing the memory of time/years as water/river'). The penultimate line of the classical poem 锦瑟, 'The Beautifully Decorated *Se*',[18] by the well-known poet LI Shangyin (李商隐) (AD 812–858), reads: '此情可待成追忆' ('this love that keeps waiting has become the pursuit of memory'), and it echoes the second line, '一玄一柱思华年' ('every plucking of every string makes one ponder upon the passing years/time'). Therefore, the two elements— 'the pursuit of memory' and 'the passing years/time'—which constitute the main part of the Chinese title for *La Recherche* are found at both ends of 'this love that keeps waiting'. Via the same source of poetic reference, the Chinese title of Cheng's second novel seems to symbiotically join up two canonical texts originating in two very different and often contrastive literary and cultural traditions, especially to the Chinese mind.[19] The importance of Li's poem as a point of reference will be further highlighted when we examine Cheng's 'reorientation' of Proust's aesthetics towards the idea of 'transformation' in classical Chinese thought, as Cheng alludes to the Daoist parable 'the butterfly dream', which is explicitly referenced in Li's poem.[20]

One of the literary sources which supplements the element of 'water/river' in the Chinese title of *La Recherche* is the great classical play *Mudan ting* (牡丹亭, *The Peony Pavilion*), a (mainly) romantic tale by TANG Xianzu (汤显祖) (1550–1616). The line reads: '如花美眷,似水流年' ('beautiful companion like the flower, fleeting years as water').[21] Cheng's *L'Éternité*, frequently advertised as 'a Chinese Tristan and Isolde', is a classical Chinese romantic tale which takes place in the Ming dynasty (1368–1644). The story is presented as the narrator's imaginative reconstruction after his discovery of an old book thanks to a French sinologist of the twentieth century. Cheng may well have taken recourse to available literary models from the late sixteenth and early seventeenth centuries, such as *The Peony Pavilion*, for this *translingual* rewriting of a Chinese literary tradition. The theme of the descent to the underworld that prominently features in *The Peony Pavilion* would have been of great interest to Cheng, as he repeatedly elaborates on this theme—albeit citing different sources—in *Le Dit*.[22] Although exploring Cheng's contrasting novelistic conceptions between *Le Dit* and *L'Éternité* is outside the scope of the present study, it is nevertheless helpful to bear in mind Cheng's alternative mode of cross-cultural rewriting—i.e. the act of writing a classical Chinese romance in French (not without considerable diegetic reconfigurations)—when we, towards the end of this chapter, try to draw a conclusion about Cheng's overall ambition to achieve 'cultural transcendence' through cross-cultural dialogues, which can be initiated by different forms of translating cultures.

At any rate, 'The Beautifully Decorated *Se*' and *The Peony Pavilion* are the two most canonical sources that constitute a key literary expression to culturally displace Proust and accommodate his work in China. The element of 'water/river' as well as the 'pursuit of memory' in the Chinese title of *La Recherche* can be best understood as a Derridean *supplement*—an '*exterior* addition'—as different from the *complement* (Derrida 1976, 145). Just like the title of Derrida's chapter '"…That Dangerous Supplement…"' in *Of Grammatology*, which is taken from

Rousseau's *Confessions*, the Chinese translation of *La Recherche* supplies itself with other texts. Derrida formulates the 'cohabitation' of the two 'strange' yet 'necessary' significations of the supplement as follows:

> The supplement adds itself, it is a surplus, a plenitude enriching another plenitude, the *fullest measure* of presence. It cumulates and accumulates presence. [...] It adds only to replace. It intervenes or insinuates itself *in-the-place-of*; if it fills, it is as if one fills a void. If it represents and makes an image, it is by the anterior default of a presence. [...] it is not simply added to the positivity of a presence, it produces no relief, its place is assigned in the structure by the mark of an emptiness. Somewhere, something can be filled up *of itself*, can accomplish itself, only by allowing itself to be filled through sign and proxy. (ibid., 144–145, italics in the original)

Chinese thought and aesthetic traditions are precisely the 'mark of an emptiness' and the 'anterior default of a presence' in Proust's work, which the Chinese title symbolically fills up.

As mentioned in the Introduction and demonstrated in Part I Chap. 3, this particular supplement of 'water/river' is crucial to our understanding of the critical as well as creative receptions of Proust among Chinese writers and intellectuals. The iconic Chinese title for *La Recherche* provokes an entirely different range of literary and, more generally, cultural associations. Given the extreme complexity and difficulty of Proust's language and the—to some—impossible length of his book, overflowing with unfamiliar cultural references, these Chinese cultural associations paratextually indicate to Chinese readers the kinds of texts they could relate it to, and leave them to pick up the pieces that their own cultural repertoire allows them to understand. Proust's 'water/river' becomes 'virtuous' when related to Daoist teaching (Guo 2011). Proustian laws of transformation and Proustian concepts of time and space resonate with teachings of the *Book of Changes*, as we have seen in Cheng.[23] Proust's unconventional writing style, philosophical enquiry into the novelistic genre, and critique of human vanity are to be understood through *Dream of the Red Chamber*.[24] By contrast, the encyclopaedic cultural references, from the Bible and Greek mythology to philosophers (Schelling, Schopenhauer, Nietzsche, Bergson), artists (Beethoven, Wagner, Vermeer, Giotto), and innumerable other European writers, are, in large part, neglected by a readership with an utterly different cultural upbringing and formation. I have outlined the various strategies adopted by different Chinese translators to tackle the problem of 'cultural negligence' on the readers' part in Chap. 2 of Part I. Perhaps such a phenomenon is best described—not without a sense of irony—in Proust's own words:

> Ce serait même inexact que de dire en pensant à ceux qui le [the narrator's book-to-come] liraient, à mes lecteurs. Car ils ne seraient pas, selon moi, mes lecteurs, mais les propres lecteurs d'eux-mêmes, mon livre n'étant qu'une sorte de ces verres grossissants comme ceux que tendait à un acheteur l'opticien de Combray; mon livre grâce auquel je leur fournirais le moyen de lire en eux-mêmes. (*RTP IV*, 610)

> It would even be a mistake to say that I was thinking of those who would read it [the narrator's book-to-come] as my readers. For they were not, as I saw it, my readers, so much as readers of their own selves, my book being merely one of those magnifying glasses of the sort the optician at Combray used to offer his customers; my book, but a books [*sic.*] thanks to which I would be providing them with the means of reading within themselves. (*PT VI*, 342–343)

Startling though it might sound, this phenomenon of appropriating Proust to Chinese culture is far from unique. In fact, literary theorists have long been aware of such a role of the reader in the production of meaning at stake. Terry Eagleton (1983, 79) makes a strikingly similar remark to the above-cited passage when he explains 'reception theory' and 'the Constance school of reception aesthetics' (including Wolfgang Iser and Hans R. Jauss): 'it is as though what we have been "reading," in working our way through a book, is ourselves'. *La Recherche*, as essentially a *foreign* sign of 'the Other', is therefore read as 'an allegory of internal otherness',[25] an otherness brought out by the temporal distance in the Chinese reader's relation to the Chinese cultural heritage and by the socio-political ideological evolution discussed in the Introduction.

However, Cheng's situation is different. Permanently residing in France, his critically creative take on Proust in *Le Dit* is firmly grounded in his forty-year scholarly learning of Western art and philosophy, but *always* in dialogue with the culture of his origin.[26] Rather like the Derridean supplement, Cheng's ultimate interest in Proust lies precisely in the 'void' of relation of Proust's work with China. *La Recherche* may have achieved its canonical status in the West more than half a century ago. In the Chinese context, Proust could be said to have truly secured his position as an integral part of the Western canon only in the past decade. When Cheng started to draft his first novel in the late 1980s, Proust's *La Recherche* was not yet available in Chinese.[27] It is no coincidence that Cheng wrote a special preface in 2000 for the Chinese translation of *Le Dit* and began it by discussing fiction and autobiography as forms of life-writing, particularly in relation to Proust. On the one hand, Cheng clearly wishes this Western canonical work, which was previously practically unknown to Chinese readers (much like Cheng's own reputation in China until he received the Prix Femina in France and was elected to the Académie française), to attract more attention. On the other hand, the Chinese preface and the interview paratextually supplement the French original, further insisting on a dynamic cross-cultural communication about the differences and common ground between two literary traditions. If the explicit reference to Proust in *Le Dit* (cited earlier) only makes a case for intertextuality, the author's opening indicative remark in the Chinese preface is enough to make *Le Dit* a *hypertext* of *La Recherche*.[28] In other words, Cheng's *Le Dit* spurs on French readers to assimilate a Chinese culture that is *indeterminably* channeled through a French canonical text. At the same time, the novel in translation instructs Chinese readers in the appreciation of the same foreign canonical text, which, for reasons outlined in the Introduction, did not receive its merited national recognition. Such an indeterminable yet hardly ignorable relationship between *Le Dit* and *La Recherche* is what Genette (1997, 397) characterizes as the fundamental ambiguity of hypertextuality, as he explains: 'in every hypertext there is an *ambiguity* [...] That ambiguity is precisely caused by the fact that a hypertext can be read both for itself and in its relation to its hypotext.'

The 'parallel' that Cheng intentionally sets up between *La Recherche* and *Le Dit* is only one of the more developed examples derived from his broader enterprise of 'cultural transcendence'. Subsequent to the paragraph on Proust in the Chinese preface, Cheng evokes the idea of a 'spiritual journey' (*xinlu licheng*, 心路历程) that is shared by all great literary works. He first juxtaposes a few Chinese canonical texts—*Songs of Chu* (*Chu Ci*, 楚辞) and *Dream of the Red Chamber*—with *The Divine Comedy, Paradise Lost*, and *Ulysses*, and rhetorically questions if a similar 'spiritual journey' could still take place on 'this land of hardship cracked open by turmoil' ('这片动荡而裂开的难土') (*TY*, 2). Cheng's 'land of hardship' 'generally refers to the common earth that we all rely on for existence' ('广义是指我们这个共同赖以生存的大地'), but in the context of his book it refers to 'that self-claimed "Middle" Kingdom' ('自名为 "中"的国度') (*TY*, 3). Cheng subtly puns on the historical name of China to suggest a time-space where spiritual journeys could take place, in response to his own question.[29] 'Middle' Kingdom here does not imply, as it used to, China as the centre of the world, but the very opposite of that—the metaphysical and essential 'void' territory or platform in which cultural transcendence takes place through dialogue. Cheng evidently tries to engage Chinese readers in a cultural China *decentred* in the literature of the world, which breaks or indeed transcends the dualist perception of national *versus* foreign literatures. As I shall demonstrate towards the end, this idea goes hand in hand with Cheng's conception of 'le vide médian' ('the median emptiness').

For this reason, despite Cheng's extensive knowledge of European culture, he still chooses to creatively embrace rather than dismiss the various epistemic dangers posed in the Chinese 'self-reading' reception of Proust summarized earlier. Nonetheless, it would seem necessary to make an essential distinction between the cross-cultural imaginings of Proust that are mostly limited to the Chinese traditions in the context of mainland China, and those that set out to connect the Chinese traditions with Proust, to dislocate them only to bring *each other* closer. In *Le Dit*, whilst consciously engaging with a wide range of Proustian themes—time, space, the universal laws of transformation, love and friendship, the role of art—Cheng constantly adjusts his angles to and repositions aspects of Proust's work by simultaneously evoking and analyzing a range of Eastern philosophical and literary texts, including those already mentioned. The specific points of comparison from philosophy to art and to religion are, as will be explored, thought-provoking.

Western scholars working on non-Western thought—arguably since E. Said's *Orientalism*—are haunted by the horror of *inauthenticity*, which often deflates their arguments and other scholarly efforts suspected of exoticism, and the same holds true for Chinese scholars working on Western thought. Inauthenticity further hints at distortion and loss in cultural transfer. But for Cheng, inauthenticity that results from cultural miscommunication is still positively corrigible, through continuous dialogue, for authenticity to come. However, inauthenticity that comes out of the *horror* of communication is self-defeating and fatal.

More importantly, cultural authenticity is not locked in any single monolithic cultural history and tradition, to which only the culture in question should own the key. In fact, cultural authenticity is sought through deliberately crossing, challenging, and rethinking cultural boundaries by both Tianyi and Cheng, as Cheng's new life is a 'rethought life' that is *different* from if he had stayed in China (Cheng 2005, 371). In *Le Dit,* Cheng precisely seizes the opportunity to explore and *rework creatively* elements in both Proust's work and Chinese philosophical and aesthetic traditions, and make them 'speak to' each other. In short, Tianyi's imagined 'A la recherche du temps à venir' is Cheng's determination to search for deep *spiritual*—rather than empirical—correspondences and connections between two very different cultures.

Unlike some of his contemporaries such as Judith Gautier and Pierre Loti, Proust as 'un écrivain tutélaire de l'Occident' ('a tutelary writer of the West') (Fraisse 2010, 633)[30] never claims to have acquired substantial knowledge of the Far East except for the 'japonisme à la mode' in certain Parisian salons. Cheng's critical and creative reorientation of Proust towards the Chinese and Chinese diasporic contexts manifests precisely the powerful fictional reconfigurability and prefigurability of literature.[31] Speaking from the French perspective, Luc Fraisse considers that the discussion provoked by Cheng's explicit fictional approach to Proust:

[...] prendra un tout autre chemin; non celui d'objections ou de reproches, mais celui d'un héritage repensé, celui d'une création décalée par rapport à celle de Proust, revenant sur son œuvre pour extraire de la nouveauté, et aussi pour en rêver la postérité. (2010, 634)

[...] will take an utterly different course, not in the direction of objections or criticisms, but in that of a rethought heritage, in a creative direction brought forward by its relation to Proust's work, a direction that returns to Proust's work in order to extract something new while envisaging a Proustian posterity. (My translation)

Taking the Chinese perspective into account, Cheng's take on Proust could indeed be described as 'deux héritages repensés' ('two heritages rethought through'), which are pushed to converge in Cheng's works, creating novelty and posterity for both cultural traditions.

NOTES

1. Their intertextual references to Proust have been noted by Yinde Zhang (2008, 31–49) (Yinde 2008).
2. The French original of *Le Dit* will be abbreviated as *DT* in in-text citations. The novel's English translation by Julia Shirek Smith, which has a rather different title, *The River Below*, will be abbreviated as *RB*. Where it becomes necessary to compare the Chinese translation, the Chinese translation by Lianxi YANG will be abbreviated as *TY* (for *Tianyi yan*, 天一言).
3. Cheng mentions the idea of transcendence on many occasions. For an example, see Cheng (2008 [2006], 20–21).
4. See Sect. 2.1. of Part I for the translation history of Proust's works in China, which refracts the drastically changing ideological tensions within Chinese society in the twentieth and twenty-first centuries.
5. For example, Barthes's *L'Empire des signes* (1970), *Carnet du voyage en Chine* (posthumously published in 2009), Kristeva's *Des Chinoises* (1973), and many of Lacan's references to Laozi and Chinese symbols.
6. Marguerite Yourceur, for example, describes *La Recherche* as an 'œuvre si bouddhiste, par la constation du passage [du temps], par l'émiettement de toute personnalité extérieure, par la notion du néant et du désir' ('a work so Buddhist, by its observation of the passage of time, by its dissipation of all the external attributes of personality, and by its notion of nothingness and of desire') (cited in Hokenson 2004, 221, my English translation). Similarly, Emmanuel Berl, whose Jewish family is related to Bergson and Proust, calls Proust a 'bouddhiste de l'amour' ('Buddhist of love') (cited in Enthoven 2013, 30).
7. However, the Taiwanese edition of the Chinese translation of *Le Dit* remains uncensored. An example of censored material can be found in Part III Chapter XVI of the novel, where Cheng explicitly comments on the severe mismanagement of the Chinese Communist Party that led to the Three Years of Natural Disaster.
8. Genette (1997, 4) defines *metatextuality* as 'the relationship most often labeled "commentary"' that 'unites a given text to another, of which it speaks without necessarily citing it (without summoning it), in fact sometimes even without naming it. [...] This is the *critical* relationship par excellence.'
9. As cited before in Sect. 3.2 of Part I, a discussion of the problems of talking about 'time' in ancient Chinese thought can be found in Allan (1997, 11–12).
10. See Sect. 3.2 of Part I.
11. *Le Petit Robert* defines 'le dit' as follows: 'au Moyen Âge, Genre littéraire, petite pièce traitant d'un sujet familier ou d'actualité. « *Le dit de*

l'Herberie », *de Rutebeuf'* ('in the Middle Ages, a literary genre, a small piece treating a famliar subject or current affairs. Rutebeuf's *The Tale of the Herb Market'*).

12. Given the close intellectual communication between Cheng and Deleuze, it is perhaps not surprising to notice the affinity between the two writers' readings of Proust. Not only does Cheng's formulation of 'non-changing change' strongly echo Deleuze's classification of Proustian time as 'an absolute, original time, an actual eternity that is affirmed in art' (ibid., 12), Cheng's 'Proustian approach', as will be explored later, also picks up Deleuze's formulation of 'apprenticeship' in *La Recherche*.

13. Proust had first intended to name his novel *Les Intermittences du cœur*.

14. '这里所说的小说, 不是按照通常的理解, 而是如同法国作家普鲁斯特所设想的。' ('The novel in question here is different from our usual understanding of the genre, it is similar to the kind of novel conceived by the French writer Proust.').

15. See Sect. 3.3.1 of Part I.

16. This is a paraphrase of Cheng's following remark: '我写小说时处于普鲁斯特所说的一种状态。他认为真正的生命不止于生命那一瞬间, 当时生活过的要以语言去寻求, 去重新体验。用语言才能给生活以光照和意义, 生活真正的奥秘和趣味才能全面地展示出来。[...] 进行超越年华的再创造, 用新的眼光、从新的角度、以新的精神去看同一个过去' (*TY*, 310).

17. '用中文写反而有点勉强, 最多是一部回忆录' ('If I had written it in Chinese, it would actually have felt a little forced, it would have been a memoir at best') (ibid.).

18. *Se* is an ancient 25-stringed plucked musical instrument, similar to a zither.

19. For the Chinese readership it is essentially a 'game' of literary associations. Given the widespread popularity of the verse, and the line 'this love that keeps waiting has become the pursuit of memory' in particular, as soon as one sees or hears the first part, 'this love that keeps waiting', which is the title of Cheng's novel, one automatically thinks of the second part, 'the pursuit of memory'. One 'pursues the memory' of what? 'Of time as water/river', and one finally thinks of Proust. This chain of association is a most straightforward indicator of the establishment of the canonicity of Proust's work in its Chinese reception. Cheng specifically mentions this literary association in his interview with K. Zhou (2012, 187).

20. It is the third line of the poem: '庄生晓梦迷蝴蝶' ('like the butterfly that obsesses Zhuangzi in his reverie at dawn').

21. As mentioned in Part I Chap. 3, *sishui liunian* (似水流年) is *the* translation advocated by Wang Xiaobo as the Chinese title for *La Recherche*, which he subsequently employs as the title of his own novella.

22. See the section 'Myth of Orpheus'.

23. For an extensive study which uses *The Book of Changes* to engage systematically with the Proustian concept of time, see Bai's (1999) doctoral thesis.
24. For a landmark study comparing *La Recherche* with *Dream of the Red Chamber*, see Tu (2014).
25. This phrase is conveniently borrowed from Christopher Bush (2005, 171), who distinguishes two types of Modernist topoi: those claiming to 'represent the Other' and those citing cultural otherness 'in an allegory of internal otherness'.
26. His entire body of poetic works (in French) engages with the theme of 'dialogue'. He reiterates in all his interviews the necessity of creating and getting involved in East–West cultural dialogues with such essential qualities as equality, tolerance, and openness, and the ultimate goal of achieving cultural harmony, not hegemony, through cultural transcendence. See Niu (2008, 9) and Qian (1999, 13).
27. See the Introduction.
28. Genette's famous example is James Joyce's *Ulysses*, the very title of which propels readers to make all the *indeterminable* connections between his novel based in Dublin and Homer's *Odysseus*.
29. '在这片动荡而裂开的难土上，从此何来空间铺陈心路，何来时间延展历程?' ('In this land of cataclysm, turmoil and hardship, from now on, where do we find the time and space for our spiritual journeys?').
30. Fraisse, *Petite Musique*, p. 633.
31. I echo Spivak's observation of Comparative Literature as a discipline that attempts to 'harness the power of fiction as it approaches Area Studies and the social science disciplines'. She thus continues: 'literature cannot predict, but it may prefigure' (2003, 49). Cheng's writing (which is to be explored in greater detail) not only 'prefigures' a new type of transcultural literary aesthetics, it also 'reconfigures' the intercultural dynamics between France and China at large through, as I hope to have demonstrated by the end of Part II, the process of cultural convergence to cultural transcendence.

REFERENCES

Allan, Sarah. 1997. *The Way of Water and Sprouts of Virtue*. New York: State University of New York Press.

Bai, Gang. 1999. Le langage figuratif du temps dans À la recherche du temps perdu de Marcel Proust: une étude épistémocritique et interculturelle. Doctoral thesis, Montréal: Université de Montréal.

Bush, Christopher. 2005. The Other of the Other? Cultural Studies, Theory, and the Location of the Modernist Signifier. *Comparative Literature Studies* 42 (2): 162–180.

Cheng, François. 1991. *Vide et plein: le langage pictural chinois*. Paris: Seuil.

Cheng, François. 1994. *Empty and Full: The Language of Chinese Painting*, trans. Michael H. Kohn. Boston: Shambhala.

Cheng, François. 2002. *Le Dialogue: Une passion pour la langue française*. Paris: Desclée de Brouwer.

Cheng, François. 2003. Discours de réception de François Cheng. *Académie française*. 19 June. http://www.academie-francaise.fr/discours-de-reception-de-francois-cheng. Accessed 8 Dec 2014.

Cheng, François. 2005. La Double Culture d'un Académicien. In *Débats francophones. Recueil des conférences et actes 2000–2005*, ed. Lise et Paul Sabourin, 357–373. Bruxelles: Bruylant.

Cheng, François. 2008 [2006]. *Cinq méditations sur la beauté*. Paris: Albin Michel.

Cheng, François. 2009a. *Tianyi yan* 天一言. Beijing: People's Literature Publishing House.

Cheng, François. 2009b. *Way of Beauty: Five Meditations for Spiritual Transformation*, trans. Jody Gladding. Rochester: Inner Traditions.

Deleuze, Gilles. 1964. *Proust et les signes*. Paris: Presses Universitaires de France.

Deleuze, Gilles. 2008 [2000]. *Proust and Signs*, trans. Richard Howard. New York: Continuum.

Derrida. 2002. Directed by Kirby Dick and Amy Ziering Kofman. Produced by Zeitgeist Films; Jane Does Films. Performed by Derrida.

Derrida, Jacques. 1976. *Of Grammatology*. Corrected Edition, trans. Gayatri Chakravorty Spivak. Baltimore: Johns Hopkins University Press.

Eagleton, Terry. 1983. *Literary Theory: An Introduction*. Minneapolis: University of Minnesota Press.

Enthoven, Jean-Paul, and Raphaël Enthoven. 2013. *Dictionnaire amoureux de Marcel Proust*. Paris: Plon/Grasset.

Fraisse, Luc. 2010. *La Petite musique du style: Proust et ses sources littéraires*. Paris: Classiques Garnier.

Genette, Gérard. 1997. *Palimpsestes: Literature in the second degree*, trans. Channa Newman and Claude Doubinsky. Lincoln: University of Nebraska Press.

Guo, Guilhua. 2011. Lun Zai Siwan jia nabian zhong de shui yixiang 论《在斯万家那边》中的水意象 [Discussing the Image of Water in Du côté de chez Swann]. *Journal of Xinxiang University (Social Sciences Edition)* 25 (1): 102–104.

Hokenson, Jan Walsh. 2004. *Japan, France, and East-West Aesthetics: French Literature, 1867–2000*. Madison: Fairleigh Dickinson University Press.

Lau, D.C. trans. 1979. *The Analects*. London: Penguin.

Niu, Jingfan. 2008. *Duihua yu ronghe: Cheng Baoyi de chuangzuo shijian yanjiu* 创作与融合:程抱一的创作实践研究 [Dialogue and Fusion: Research on

François Cheng's Creative Practice]. Shanghai: Shanghai Academy of Social Science Press.

Proust, Marcel. 1952. *Jean Santeuil*. Paris: Gallimard.

Qian, Linsen. 1999. Zhongxifang zhexue mingyun de lishi yuhe–Cheng Baoyi: Tianyi yan ji qita 中西方哲学命运的历史遇合-程抱一:《天一言》及其他 (The Historical Encounter of Destiny between Chinese and Western Philosophies–François Cheng: Le Dit de Tianyi and Others). *Kua wenhua duihua* 跨文化对话 (Cross-Cultural Dialogue) 3: 2–14.

Smith, Julia Shirek, trans. 2000. *The River Below by François Cheng*. New York: Welcome Rain.

Spivak, Gayatri Chakravorty. 2003. *Death of a Discipline*. New York: Columbia University Press.

Tu, Weiqun. 2014. *Yanguang de jiaozhi: zai Cao Xueqin yu Masai'er Pulusite zhijian* 眼光的交织: 在曹雪芹与马塞尔·普鲁斯特之间 (Interweaving the Visions: Between Qinxue Cao and Marcel Proust). Nanjing: Yilin.

Yinde, Zhang. 2008. *Littérature comparée et perspectives chinoises*. Paris: L'Harmattan.

Zhang, Ning. 2003. Cheng Baoyi xiansheng yu tade huojiang xiaoshuo Tianyi yan: yu Zhang Ning duihua 程抱一先生和他的获奖小说《天一言》：与张宁对话 [Mr. Cheng Baoyi and His Award-Winning Novel Tianyi yan: Dialogue with Zhang Ning]. *Maya Cafe*. 10 July. http://www.mayacafe.com/forum/topic1sp.php3?tkey=1065524624. Accessed 22 Nov 2016.

Zhou, Kexi. 2012. *Yi Bian Cao* 译边草. Shanghai: East China Normal University Press.

CHAPTER 5

Traits Chinois/Démarche Proustienne

The second half of the title of this chapter ('Proustian approach') is, of course, taken from Cheng's own claim, whereas the first half is inspired by a recent collection of essays, *Traits chinois/Lignes francophones* ('Chinese Traits/Francophone Lines') (Silvester and Thouroude 2012), which promises to be a disciplinary milestone in the ways we conceptualize the generality as well as the particularity of Franco-Chinese literature and art. This present study of the textual relations between Cheng's and Proust's works, which is of a more specialist nature, will hopefully not only reaffirm many of the observations made in *Traits chinois*, but also suggest a few theoretical modifications, as well as new conceptual findings.

Speaking of the first-stage development of Chinese francophony in the 'profoundly conflictual' nineteenth century, Rosalind Silvester and Guillaume Thouroude (ibid., 9, my italics) remark in their Introduction:

> L'arrivée brutale des Occidentaux, dont l'industrie pouvait vaincre l'armée impériale et imposer sa volonté à la Chine, a profondément affecté les Chinois dans leurs croyances, leur confiance, leur système de valeurs. Les Occidentaux, sans coloniser le pays à proprement parler, représentèrent à la fois *le modèle à imiter au niveau de la technique, et l'*autre' auquel s'opposer sur le plan des valeurs.*

> The brutal arrival of Westerners, whose industry was capable of defeating the imperial army and imposing their will on China, profoundly affected the beliefs, the confidence, and the value system of the Chinese. Without colonizing the country strictly speaking, the West represented the *model to*

© The Author(s) 2017
S. Li, *Proust, China and Intertextual Engagement*,
DOI 10.1007/978-981-10-4454-0_5

153

imitate on the level of technology and, at the same time, *the 'other' to oppose in terms of values.* (My translation and italics)

Cheng obviously contributes to the next stage(s) of this development. Throughout the twentieth century, Chinese intellectuals never—perhaps with the significant exception of the later period of Mao's regime—ceased to 'imitate' the West 'on the level of technology'. However, this basic paradigm significantly shifted from 'opposing' to 'joining in with' the values of the Other, in a much larger and increasingly global framework, especially since the 1980s. Indeed, *joining in with the Other from the opposite* captures the central line of enquiry pursued by this very study, from the Chinese translation of Proust to mainland Chinese writers' intertextual engagement with Proust, and finally to a Franco-Chinese writer's transcultural dialogue with Proust. Cheng's *démarche proustienne* does not signify an aesthetic destination, but a critical as well as geographic point of departure, an aesthetic of reorientation and *rapprochement* (the French word for 'bringing closer'). It is also in this sense that one should understand Tianyi's qualification of 'in search of lost time to come' as '*contrary* to Proust' ('contrairement à Proust') (*DT*, 192).

5.1   ARTISTIC INITIATION

Apart from their shared concern over the problematics of life-writing as mentioned in our discussion of Cheng's Chinese preface, one of the other most evident resonances between *Le Dit* and *La Recherche* is the generic conception of their works as both *Bildungsromane* and *Künstlerromane*. Both narratives revolve around the protagonist's individual growth and development through experiences of life. Both protagonists are artists in the making who not only learn to live, but also learn to 'traduire' ('translate')—Proust's own word—the signs of those living experiences. Experience of life then opens the cognitive and affective dimensions of aesthetic experience. Just as 'Marcel becomes a writer' (Genette 1980, 30), Tianyi becomes a painter and calligrapher. It is the creation of artworks that marks out moments of spiritual exaltation for both protagonists, which often provoke ontological discussions in the novels. Cheng in his Chinese preface describes his desire to write his novel as an attempt to search for and create the time and space for a 'spiritual journey', which, in many ways, puts a compelling interpretation on an oft-quoted conclusive remark in the last volume of *La Recherche*: 'la vraie vie, la vie enfin découverte et éclaircie, la seule vie par conséquent réellement vécue, c'est la littérature' ('real life, life finally uncovered and clarified, the only life in consequence lived to the full, is literature') (*RTP IV*, 474; *PT VI*, 204). In fact, according to Maurizio Ascari, literature as fundamentally life-writing marks 'a new stage' of global postmodern and transcultural literature, where 'issues concerning conflict, reconciliation, identity, memory and trauma', as well as 'the relation between the private and the public spheres, imagination and power' (2011, 165), can be fruitfully discussed. The critique states, 'the human is back, right at centre stage' (ibid.).

Largely following the line of exploration of *Le Dit* and *La Recherche* as novels of formation, the following analysis will focus on two key passages of artistic initiation from Proust's and Cheng's respective works, namely the episode of the steeples of Martinville from *La Recherche*, and the mysterious Mount Lu in *Le Dit*. A few key concepts that emerge from this analysis will be more fully developed in our next section, entitled 'Principles of Artistic Creation'. Throughout the two sections, I will demonstrate how the critical language coming from Proust Studies can be interpreted in the light of Daoist ideas through a comparative study of Cheng's work.

Very early in both novels, Proust's protagonist and Cheng's Tianyi share a similar pattern of aesthetic experience: their respective artistic initiation is marked by a shift from the temptation to aesthetically represent an object to the aestheticizing subject's realization of the immanence of the creative activity itself.

Aesthetic experience, as the etymology of the term 'aesthetic' reveals, may be said to start from 'sensory perception'. Common to Proust's protagonist's and Tianyi's perception of mostly ordinary objects and natural phenomena, especially in relation to the general landscape, which respectively inspires the former's first composition and the latter's first drawing, is the subject's experience of *movement*. As Proust's protagonist sits next to the cabman on Dr. Percepied's hackney carriage, which runs at speed 'comme le vent' ('like the wind') (*RTP I*, 177; *PT I*, 180), he observes the rapidly shifting positions of three steeples interacting with the landscape, which provokes in him a 'plaisir spécial qui ne ressemblait à aucun autre' ('special pleasure which was unlike any other'):

[...] les deux clochers de Martinville, sur lesquels donnait le soleil cou-
chant et que le mouvement de notre voiture et les lacets du chemin avaient
l'air de faire changer de place, puis celui de Vieuxvicq qui, séparé d'eux par
une colline et une vallée, et situé sur un plateau plus élevé dans le lointain,
semblait pourtant tout voisin d'eux. (*RTP I*, 177–178)

[...] the two steeples of Martinville, shining in the setting sun and appearing to change position with the motion of our carriage and the windings of
the road, and then the steeple of Vieuxvicq, which, though separated from
them by a hill and a valley and situated on a higher plateau in the distance,
seemed to be right next to them. (*PT I*, 180)

The subject's own physical displacement results in the spatial reconfiguration of the objects in the landscape. Commenting on the same passage,
Sara Danius (2002, 131) considers the high speed at which the protagonist travels to be a key element which 'transforms the surrounding landscape into a phantasmagoria'. While high velocity certainly enhances the
protagonist's sensory experience, or partakes in what Danius formulates
as 'the aesthetics of the windshield', it is fundamentally the movement
of his own body in the landscape which spurs him on to ruminate on
the configurative relation between his being and the world. The expression 'avoir l'air' ('to appear') and the verb 'sembler' ('to seem') (and
later 'paraître'/'to look') are good indicators of the protagonist's suspicion of the phantasmagorical landscape, transformed due to his own
rapid movement. Fascinated though he might be, the subject does not,
however, disintegrate in his own dreamlike vision of the landscape. The
protagonist's implied suspicion enables him to maintain a certain distinction between his being and the world, and consequently this suspicion
leads him to speculate on a quasi-metaphysical relation between the two:

En constatant, en notant la forme de leur flèche, le déplacement de leurs
lignes, l'ensoleillement de leur surface, je sentais que je n'allais pas au bout
de mon impression, que quelque chose était derrière ce mouvement, derrière cette clarté, quelque chose qu'ils semblaient contenir et dérober à la
fois. (*RTP I*, 178)

As I observed, as I noted the shape of their spires, the shifting of their
lines, the sunlight on their surfaces, I felt that I was not reaching the full
depth of my impression, that something was behind that motion, that
brightness, something which they seemed at once to contain and conceal.
(*PT I*, 180)

That 'something', seemingly indeterminable ('at once to contain and conceal'), is characterized by its locus of intermediacy between the protagonist's primary perception of the visible ('shape', 'lines', and 'surfaces') and that which is 'behind' such appearances. That 'something' is not a concrete thing but rather a relation between the phenomena and what may be loosely described as 'noumenal':

> Bientôt leurs lignes et leurs surfaces ensoleillées, comme si elles avaient été une sorte d'écorce se déchirèrent, *un peu de ce qui m'était caché en elles* m'apparut, j'eus une pensée qui n'existait pas pour moi l'instant avant, qui *se formula en mots* dans ma tête, [...]. (ibid., my italics)

> Soon their lines and their sunlit surfaces split apart, as if they were a sort of bark, a little of what was hidden from me inside them appeared to me, I had a thought which had not existed a moment before, which took shape in words in my head, [...]. (ibid., 181, my italics)

The mysterious and frictional ('se déchirèrent'/'split apart') relation between the phenomenal and the noumenal experienced by the subject invokes the necessity for their being realized in words. Proust's simile of the 'bark being torn off' subtly affirms his earlier use of 'derrière' ('behind'), rather than, say, 'au-delà' ('beyond'), to position this 'something', which will later nuance our understanding of the sense of 'being *in* the world'.[1]

In comparison, Tianyi's aesthetic experience of movement is primarily through the subject's inner reflection on, and eventual existential identification with, the clouds. First, Tianyi perceives how the movement of the clouds decidedly affects the human vision of the colours, shapes, and scales of Mount Lu:

> Par leurs mouvements capricieux, imprévisibles, par leurs teintes instables, rose ou pourpre, vert jade ou gris argent, ils transformaient la montagne en magie. Ils évoluaient au milieu des multiples pics et collines du mont Lu, s'attardant dans les vallées, s'élevant vers les hauteurs, maintenant ainsi un constant état de mystère. De temps à autre, subitement ils s'effaçaient, révélant alors au regard des hommes toute la splendeur de la montagne. (*DT*, 20)

> With their capricious, unpredictable movements and their never-fixed hues—pink or purple, jade green or silver gray—they turned the mountain

magical. They developed amid Mount Lu's countless peaks and hills; then, lingering in the valleys or rising toward the heights, they maintained a constant state of mystery. At times they dissipated abruptly, revealing to the human eye the mountain in all its splendor. (*RB*, 6–7)

The movement of the clouds not only constantly changes man's sight of the mountain, but also causes the clouds to change their own ways of existence and, consequently, their different relations to man:

Certains soirs, les brumes denses qui montaient, rencontrant les nuages en mouvement, provoquaient une précipitation et amenaient des ondées, qui déversaient leur eau pure dans les pots et les bocaux déposés par les habitants du village au pied des murs. C'est avec cette eau que ces derniers faisaient le meilleur thé du coin. Une fois averses passées, rapidement, les nuages se déchiraient et, le temps d'une éclaircie, laissaient voir le plus haut mont. (*DT*, 20–21)

Some evenings the heavy mists rose and met up with clouds in motion, producing moisture and bringing showers; the pure water would pour into jars and jugs the villagers set out under their walls. With this water they made the best tea around. Once the downpour had ended, the clouds broke up rapidly, and under clear skies the highest mountain would be briefly visible. (*RB*, 7)

In short, the *manifested* movement of the clouds reveals the 'réalité cachée' ('hidden reality') of the universe: 'il était en perpétuelle transformation. Ce qui était apparemment stable se fondait dans le mouvant; ce qui était apparemment fini se noyait dans l'infini. Point d'état fixe ni définitif' ('it was in perpetual transformation. What was apparently stable melted away into the moving; what was apparently finite sank into the infinite. There was no fixed, final state') (*DT*, 21; *RB*, 7). The movement of the clouds heightens and transforms Tianyi's artistic sensibility—'j'avais l'intuition que le nuage serait mon élément' ('I had an intuition, [...] my element would be the cloud') and 'j'étais nuage' ('I was cloud') (*DT*, 21, 22; *RB*, 7, 8)—producing 'exaltation' ('exaltation') and 'confuse allégresse' ('a confused sort of joy') in Tianyi, which compel him to initiate his own artistic vocation: 'il faut sûrement faire quelque chose de cela' ('one must certainly take advantage of that') (*DT* 22; *RB*, 8). As the condition of vocation converges with the universal principle, the subject is urged to create art to sustain the primordial relation between authentic being and the world. Cheng later reiterates this real-life experience of Mount Lu as a quest for 'la beauté originelle' ('original beauty'), 'un mystère insondable' ('endless beauty'), that 'calls' or summons—the etymology of 'vocation'—him to 'participate in its adventure' (Cheng 2008, 15; 2009, 7).

Proust is certainly not insensitive to the special qualities of the clouds or the mist that draw literary inspiration. In *Contre Sainte-Beuve*, a post-humously published work often read as a statement of his aesthetic principles, Proust characterizes the literary substance of the 'inexprimable' ('inexpressible'), the thing 'qu'on croyait ne pas réussir à faire entrer dans un livre qui y reste' ('one believes one cannot succeed in getting into a book, that remains in it'), 'quelque chose de vague et d'obsédant comme le souvenir' ('something vague and obsessive like the memory'), an 'atmophère' ('atmosphere'), and situates it in the space '*entre* les mots *comme la brume* d'un matin de Chantilly' ('*mixed in between* the words, words, *like the morning mist* in Chantilly') (Proust 1954, 157; 1988, 31–33). Edward Bizub recapitulates Proustian poetics precisely as 'l'esthétique des brumes' ('the aesthetic of the clouds') (1991, 43–66). Exploring the role of Dutch paintings in Proust's works, Nathalie Aubert also affirms that the appreciation of fog and mist was a key feature in the French imagination of Germanic landscape aesthetics even before Proust's time (2011, 135). Citing a range of Chinese expressions— 'nuages et pluies (du Mont Wu)' ('clouds and rain [of Mount Wu]', '巫山云雨'), 'manger brumes et nuages' ('eating mists and clouds', '吞云吐雾'), 'caresser brumes et nuages' ('caressing mists and clouds', '腾云驾雾'), 'dormir parmi brumes et nuages' ('sleeping among mists and clouds', '卧眠云间')[2]—Cheng evidently senses the strong resonance in the Chinese literary and philosophical traditions and explicitly pushes this aesthetic concern of the moving cloud towards an ontological one.

The experience of movement animates and reanimates things. A strong sense of animism[3] manifests itself in both Proust's protagonist's and Tianyi's anagnorisis of the aestheticized objects and the wider landscape. Cheng articulates this idea in terms of Daoist principles: the transformative nature of things essentially revealed by the movement of the cloud points to the primordial ontological state of all beings—the 'souffle vital' ('vital breath') or 'souffle primordial' ('primordial breath') (*yuanqi*, 元气). It is the original source of all beings, as Tianyi rhetorically asks himself: 'n'est-ce pas ce qu'il y a de plus vrai, puisque toutes choses vivantes ne sont que "condensation du souffle"?' ('is that not the real truth, since all living things are but "condensation of the breath"?')

(*DT*, 21; *TY*, 7). In the landscape of Mount Lu, it is 'cette présence éthérée et presque palpable' ('an ethereal and almost palpable presence') of the cloud—'immaterielle et pourtant substantielle' ('immaterial yet substantial') (ibid.; ibid.)—which gives life to the landscape, and this transformed landscape, in turn, reanimates the participating human agent. Cheng (2008, 15–16; 2009, 8) recapitulates this autobiographic experience in *Beauté*:

> [...] à travers le mont Lu, la Nature, de toute sa formidable présence, se manifeste à l'enfant de six ou sept ans que je suis, comme un recel inépuisable, et surtout, comme une passion irrépressible. Elle semble m'appeler à participer à son aventure, et cet appel me bouleverse, me foudroie.

> [...] through Lu Mountain, Nature, in all its formidable presence, revealed itself to the child of six or seven that I was then, as an inexhaustible harbor, and above all, as an irrepressible passion. It seemed to call me to participate in its adventure, and that appeal overwhelmed me, left me thunderstruck.

It should be noted that the cloud and the vital breath are no equivalent, conceptually speaking. The description of the former is only used by Cheng to help assimilate the Daoist concept of the latter. Tianyi, at this stage, is still intuitively observing the natural phenomenon without any proper conceptual understanding: 'dès cette époque, quoique confusément encore, j'avais l'intuition que le nuage serait mon élément' ('dating from then I had an intuition, although still rather vague, that my element would be the cloud') (*DT*, 21; *RB*, 7). He finally learns the idea of the vital breath with references to Daoism, time, water/river, and the cloud from Professor F. at the end of Part I, as the professor expounds:

> Comment concevoir que l'irréversibilité de cet ordre impérieux qu'est le temps puisse être rompue. C'est ici qu'interviennent les Vides médians inhérents à la Voie. Eux-mêmes Souffles, ils impriment à la Voie son rythme, sa respiration et lui permettent surtout d'opérer la mutation des choses et son retour vers l'Origine, source même du Souffle primordial. Pour le fleuve, les Vides médians se présentent sous forme de nuages. (*DT*, 191)

> So what has given us the idea that the irreversibility of time's imperious order can be disrupted? Enter the middle Voids inherent in the Way. Breaths themselves, they impart to the Way its rhythm, its inspiration;

most important, they allow it to effect the mutation of things and to return to the Origin, the very source of the primal Breath. For the river, the middle Voids take the form of clouds. (*RB*, 130)[4]

We notice Cheng's deliberate capitalization of 'Souffles' ('Breaths') here. Tianyi later heuristically applies and refashions these principles to and in his reading of Western art and philosophy. There is a clear sense of linearity in Tianyi's intellectual development throughout the novel from unilateral to lateral thinking.

Proust's protagonist's formulation of animism initially seems less totalizing than Tianyi's intuitive discovery ('toutes choses vivantes ne sont que "condensation du souffle"'/'all living things are but "condensation of the breath"'). It is closely associated with a complex notion of analogy between the external landscape and the calling of the inner self— again the idea of 'vocation'—or what the narrator formulates in retrospect as the 'équivalent profond' ('profound equivalent') (*RTP III*, 877; *PT V*, 347). Firstly, the protagonist tends to grasp this analogy in terms of a representation in words. This hidden something, which he says earlier provokes in him a 'plaisir obscur' ('obscure pleasure'),

[...] devait être *quelque chose d'analogue à une jolie phrase*, puisque c'est sous la forme de mots qui me faisaient plaisir, que cela m'était apparu, demandant un crayon et du papier au docteur, je composai malgré les cahots de la voiture, pour *soulager ma conscience et obéir à mon enthousiasme.* (*RTP III*, 877, my italics)

[...] had to be *something analogous to a pretty sentence*, since it had appeared to me in the form of words that gave me pleasure, I asked the doctor for a pencil and some paper and I composed, despite the jolts of the carriage, and *in order to ease my conscience and yield to my enthusiasm.* (*PT I*, 181, my italics)

What is hidden, mysterious, and inexplicable must be captured in words so that the protagonist can prolong and perpetuate the aesthetic pleasure.

However, this 'pretty sentence' is not yet the '*profound* equivalent', and the actual experience of composition suggests a rather different analogical process:

J'eus fini de l'écrire, je me trouvai si heureux, je sentais qu'elle m'avait si parfaitement débarrassé de ces clochers et de ce qu'ils cachaient derrière

eux, que, comme si j'avais été moi-même une poule et si je venais de pondre un œuf, je me mis à chanter à tue-tête. (*RTP I*, 180)

I had finished writing it, I was so happy, I felt it had so perfectly relieved
me of those steeples and what they had been hiding behind them, that, as
if I myself were a hen and had just laid an egg, I began to sing at the top
of my voice. (*PT I*, 182)

The notion of analogy shifts from 'a pretty sentence'—representational
of that which is hidden behind—to the recognition of a certain thing-
in-itself, present in both the aestheticized object and the aestheticizing
subject. The protagonist realizes that his piece of writing in fact *presents
itself* and has 'perfectly relieved' him of what he has attempted to translate into words. His sense of pleasure does not derive from the *representation* 'in the form of words', which implies a certain intellectualization,
interiorization, or appropriation of the object of aesthetic experience,
but rather as a result of *autopoiesis* after the protagonist's submission
to intuition. The quest for the real 'profound equivalent' is a different
kind of 'translation' from perception to words, as Aubert (2002, 49, my
translation and italics in the original) remarks: 'pour qu'il y ait authen-
tiquement perception, il faut qu'il y ait authentique travail d'écriture. La
perception n'est pas traduite par le moyen de mots et de phrases, mais *se
cherche elle-même dans le langage*' ('in order for there to be an authentic
perception, there has to be an authentic work of writing. Perception is
not translated by means of words or phrases, but it *searches itself in the
language*').

Moreover, by comparing the protagonist's aesthetic pleasure through
creation to that of 'a hen' which 'had just laid an egg' singing at the top
of his voice, Proust twists the usual focus of the hen-and-egg problem,
which in this context would be the question of whether the artist creates the artwork or the artwork makes the artist in the first place, and
effectively locates the aesthetic experience at the level of an inner intuitive *body*. The experience of literary creation, as well as sterility, no different from the biological condition, is *somatic* rather than cerebral. In fact,
prior to this creative experience, the protagonist seems to have believed
in precisely the contrary out of frustration:

Et ces rêves m'avertissaient que, puisque je voulais un jour être un écrivain, il était temps de savoir ce que je comptais écrire. Mais dès que je me

le demandais, tâchant de trouver un sujet où je pusse faire tenir une signification philosophique infinie, *mon esprit s'arrêtait de fonctionner*, [...]
je sentais que *je n'avais pas de génie ou peut-être une maladie cérébrale
l'empêchait de naître*. [...] Ce sentiment intime, immédiat, que *j'avais du
néant de ma pensée*, prévalait contre toutes les paroles flatteuses qu'on pouvait me prodiguer, [...]. (*RTP I*, 170–171, my italics)

And these dreams warned me that since I wanted to be a writer some day,
it was time to find out what I meant to write. But as soon as I asked myself
this, trying to find a subject in which I could anchor some infinite philosophical meaning, *my mind would stop functioning*, [...] I felt that *I had no talent
or perhaps a disease of the brain kept it from being born*. [...] This intimate,
immediate awareness I had of *the worthlessness of my ideas* prevailed against all
the praise that might be heaped on me [...] (*PT I*, 174–175, my italics)

The kind of literary production, like Bergotte's works, which seems to
be 'born' out of a good brain only, is eventually considered to be sterile,
as it does not bring about pleasure. The narrator asserts towards the end
of the novel: 'quant aux "joies de l'intelligence" pouvais-je appeler ainsi
ces froides constatations que mon œil clairvoyant ou mon raisonnement
juste relevaient sans aucun plaisir et qui restaient *infécondes*?' ('as for the
"joys of the intellect", could I use that phrase for these cold observations
which my perceptive eye or my precise reasoning picked out without any
pleasure and which remained *infertile*?') (*RTP IV*, 444; *PT VI*, 174, my
italics). One could indeed argue that it is the intuitive body—'blind',
indeterminable, and unstable in terms of sense-making—that engenders
the enigmas of the external world, which initiates artistic creation in
return for a certain existential certainty. As Merleau-Ponty puts it: '[the
body or the perceiving subject] in the opacity of sensation, reach[es] out
towards things to which [it] has, in advance, no key, and for which [it]
nevertheless carries within [itself] the project, and open[s] [itself] to an
absolute Other which [it] is making ready in the depths of [its] being'
(2002, 380).

From the experience of movement—be it physical displacement or
inner reflection and identification—to animism, what we observe is a
mutually transformative relation between the subject and the thing,
between man and the world. This process, like Cheng's 'perpetual transformation' of water, river, cloud, mist, rain, and the human subject, echoes one of the best-known Daoist parables in *Zhuangzi*, often known as
'the butterfly dream':

Once Zhuangzi dreamt he was a butterfly, a butterfly flitting and fluttering around, happy with himself and doing as he pleased. He didn't know he was Zhuangzi. Suddenly he woke up and there he was, solid and unmistakable Zhuangzi. But he didn't know if he was Zhuangzi who had dreamt he was a butterfly, or a butterfly dreaming he was Zhuangzi. Between Zhuangzi and a butterfly there must be *some* distinction! This is called the Transformation of Things. (Watson, under 'Section Two')[5]

Although Zhuangzi's passage, which in many ways can be considered 'philosophy as fiction',[6] is not directly treating the subject of artistic initiation, it is nonetheless a strikingly similar idea that our analysis of artistic initiation has entailed. As will be examined later, it is precisely the process of artistic creation that fundamentally maintains '*some* distinction' between the artists and the landscapes.

Different from Proust's protagonist's first literary triumph,[7] Tianyi's first drawing is marked as an aesthetic failure—precisely because the latter is far too preoccupied with the representation of the external aesthetic object and landscape, rather than employing his artistic tools such as the Chinese brush and ink to further explore the 'cloudy' intuition *in* him:

Ce jour-là, donc, plongeant mon regard dans le liquide aux reflets sans fond, légèrement irisé, je vis apparaître la vision de la montagne nuageuse que j'avais captée le matin même. Sans tarder, je me mis à dessiner, m'efforçant *d'en restituer aussi bien l'aspect tangible que l'aspect évanescent.* Le résultat, hélas ! *ne correspondit pas, tant s'en faut, à ce que j'escomptais.* (*DT*, 23, my italics)

Thus, the day of my revelation, as I gazed deep into the shimmering, slightly iridescent liquid, the cloud-capped mountain appeared, the very view my eyes had taken in that morning. Without delay I sat down to draw the peak, trying to *reproduce both its tangibility and its evanescence.* The result, alas!, did not *by any means correspond to what I had hoped.* (*RB*, 9, my italics)

As discussed before, representation implies a certain intellectual appropriation, and the quality of representation depends, more often than not, on the question of technique, which is part of the professional formation. For a child of eight or nine such as Tianyi, relatively—though not entirely—innocent of intellectual as well as technical training, it is particularly his own vocational disposition rather than professional formation to which his artistic exploration should be committed.

Indeed, Tianyi's aesthetic failure at this stage is another example of artistic sterility, which demonstrates precisely how the obsession with intellect and technique can counter-productively obfuscate the authentic artistic vision. It is worth reminding ourselves that prior to the episode of the Martinville steeples, Proust's protagonist's unfavourable belief in intellectual quality and abstract truth, too, prohibits his primary sensory impressions from developing into an artistic vision and giving birth to artworks:

> [...] il me parut plus affligeant encore qu'auparavant de n'avoir pas de dispositions pour le lettres, [...] Alors, bien en dehors de toutes ces préoccupations littéraires et ne s'y rattachant en rien, tout d'un coup un toit, un reflet de soleil sur une pierre, l'odeur d'un chemin me faisaient arrêter par un plaisir particulier qu'ils me donnaient [...] Certes ce n'était pas des impressions de ce genre qui pouvaient me rendre l'espérance que j'avais perdue de pouvoir être un jour écrivain et poète, car elles étaient toujours liées à un objet particulier dépourvu de valeur intellectuelle et ne se rapportant à aucune vérité abstraite. (*RTP I*, 176)

> [...] more distressing still [...] did it seem to me than it had seemed before to have no aptitude for literature [...] Then, quite apart from all these literary preoccupations and not connected to them in any way, suddenly a roof, a glimmer of sun on a stone, the smell of the road would stop me because of a particular pleasure they gave me, [...] Of course it was not impressions of this kind that could give me back the hope I had lost, of succeeding in becoming a writer and a poet with no intellectual value and no reference to any abstract truth. (*PT I*, 178–179)

The protagonist does not submit to his intuition, and the kind of aesthetic pleasure that he intuitively senses is left unexplored and too readily sacrificed to the forlorn hope of creating a work of great intellect. The aesthetic pleasure is glossed over as a diversion from boredom and the feeling of powerlessness:

> [...] elles [les impressions] me donnaient un plaisir irraisonné, l'illusion d'une sorte de fécondité et par là me distrayaient de l'ennui, du sentiment de mon impuissance que j'avais éprouvés chaque fois que j'avais cherché un sujet philosophique pour une grande œuvre littéraire. (*RTP I*, 176–177)

> [...] they [the impressions] gave me an unreasoning pleasure, the illusion of a sort of fecundity, and so distracted me from the tedium, from

the sense of my own importance which I had felt each time I looked for a philosophical subject for a great literary work. (*PT I*, 179)

Nevertheless, Tianyi's failed aesthetic experiment serves as an important lesson. Although he does not succeed in producing the artwork he has expected, at the end of the chapter Tianyi becomes acutely aware of the limitless potential of the artistic tools he possesses: 'mais je fus conquis par le pouvoir magique du pinceau et de l'encre. Je pressentis que ce serait une arme pour moi. La seule peut-être que je posséderais pour me protéger de la présence écrasante du Dehors' ('but I was won over by the magical power of brush and ink. I sensed it was to be a weapon for me. Maybe the only one I would have to protect me from the overwhelming presence of the Outside') (*DT*, 23; *RB*, 9). It is no less revealing a remark than Proust's protagonist's realization of the artistic *autopoiesis*. Tianyi is convinced that his brush and ink have the magical power to preserve and enhance his inner sensibility against the pernicious intrusion from the 'Outside', and create artworks that can mark out the 'aesthetic territories' between the inner and the outer—similar to Zhuangzi's 'some distinction'—ultimately establishing a relation between his being and the world.

5.2   Principles of Artistic Creation

The delineation of aesthetic territories is a fundamental paradigm of relation in both Cheng's and Proust's theories of artistic creation. It could be understood as an effective measure against two orientations or movements of aesthetic activity.

First, Cheng's rather violent imagery of a 'weapon' against the 'overwhelming presence of the Outside' is a premonitory reference to the hardship of Tianyi's later life and the human misery during the period of political turmoil in China from the civil war to the establishment of the PRC, leading up to the Cultural Revolution. The external circumstances aggressively intrude into the inner space of artistic sensibility and intuition, leaving little freedom and autonomy for accomplished artistic creation, or even possibility for artistic creation. Tianyi palpably senses the soul-crushing force exerted on the life of his literary companion Haolang: 'dans sa lutte pour la survie, il en était venu à oublier la seule arme qu'il détenait: l'écriture' ('in his struggle for survival, he ended up forgetting the only weapon he possessed: writing') (*DT*, 371;

RB, 258). Equally damaging is the exploitation of inner artistic vocation for external political purposes. Cheng specifically cites Mao's notorious Yan'an Pronouncement in 1942, which autocratically prescribed and imposed the 'correct' conception of art and literature, strictly narrowing down their purpose to the service of the working class and the advancement of socialism (*DT*, 240; *RB*, 166). The kind of aesthetic principle pronounced by Mao turns art into propaganda. Left-leaning writers like Haolang, who are brutally attacked by Mao's pronouncement, nevertheless share similar conceptual limitations of seeing literature 'as a political weapon to be wielded by the individual writer' (Cheek 1997, 10). But Cheng specifically chooses the French word 'arme' ('weapon') to describe literature and art *not* because of their inherently violent nature deployable for political or revolutionary cause, but rather due to the word's near homophonic relation to the word 'âme' ('soul'). The only 'arme'/'âme' possessed by Tianyi and Haolong is their vocation and ability to make art. Cheng explicitly acknowledged such an association of words during his inaugural address at the Académie française, already cited in the last chapter: 'je suis devenu un Français de droit, d'esprit et de cœur, [...] surtout à partir de ce moment où j'ai résolument basculé dans la langue française, la faisant l'arme, ou l'âme, de ma creation' ('I became French, legally, mentally, and emotionally [...] especially from the moment I resolutely plunged into the French language, making it the weapon, or indeed the soul, of my creation') (2003). Interestingly, in doing this, Cheng also gives a French 'spiritual' twist to one of Karl Marx's revolutionary sayings (certainly widely celebrated in China): 'A foreign language is a weapon in the struggle of life' (cited in Lafargue 2002 [1890]).

Conversely, dilettanti in *La Recherche* such as Swann and Charlus, who are seen to instrumentalize and appropriate the external object of aesthetic experience for their own interests, are labelled as 'idolaters of art'. Stéphane Chaudier (2004, 272, my translation) concisely remarks:

L'idolâtre sacrifie son moi profond que l'objet découvre par les résonnances qu'il éveille en lui. Dans une relation féconde à l'objet, c'est à ce dernier que revient l'initiative : c'est lui qui donne 'la joie'. Au lieu de s'attacher au bouleversement que la chose produit en lui, l'idolâtre réalise un projet de maîtrise sur l'objet : la fleur devient sa fleur. L'idolâtre refuse à l'objet son statut de signe.

Idolaters sacrifice their deep selves discovered through the resonances that the object awakens in them. In a fruitful relation to the object, the initiative must return to the object: it is the object that gives 'joy'. Instead of attaching themselves to the disruption that the thing produces in them, idolaters carry through a project of possessing the object: the flower becomes their flower. Idolaters deny the object its status as a sign.

Idolaters of art are essentially self-absorbed and do not recognize the kind of animism in the object which contributes to an authentic aesthetic experience.

When listening to Vinteuil's unfinished work performed by Morel at the Verdurins', the protagonist explicitly names the inner space as 'la patrie intérieure' ('[inner] homeland'), open to artistic *self*-exploration, 'chaque artiste semble ainsi comme le citoyen d'une patrie inconnue, oubliée de lui-même' ('each great artist seems to be the citizen of an unknown homeland which even he has forgotten') (*RTP III*, 761; *PT V*, 236). The artwork, the 'accent unique' ('particular accent') of Vinteuil's work, is 'une preuve de *l'existence irréductiblement individuelle de l'âme*' ('the living proof of the *irreducible individuality of each soul*') (ibid.). The implication of an inner irreducible 'essence' in art[8] is a fruitful way to understand Tianyi's conviction of the magical power of his brush and ink as his only weapon to protect himself against the 'overwhelming presence of the Outside', as the crude communist ideology attempts to crush the sense of individuality and forbid any forms of spirituality other than the communist ideology itself. Just as 'la vision de l'univers' ('the vision of the universe'), 'la patrie intérieure' ('the [inner] homeland'), of Vinteuil's work 'se tradui[t] par une altération générale des sonorités chez le musicien comme de la couleur chez le peintre' ('[is] reflected in a general alteration of sound quality in the musician, as of colour in the painter') (ibid.), so Tianyi's inner space of artistic creation can be 'translated' in a general alteration of Chinese ink in the calligrapher:

Une fois le liquide prêt, je ne me lassais jamais de ce moment où, pour tester son épaisseur, je posais librement le pinceau pleinement imbibé sur le papier fin et translucide, lequel résorbait vite l'encre tout en se laissant 'irriguer' un peu. Puis, durant de longues minutes encore, elle conservait sa fraîcheur lustrée comme pour montrer son contentement de ce que le papier, consentant et réceptif, acceptât de la savourer. Cette magie du papier qui recevait l'encre, les Anciens la comparaient à la peau d'un jeune bambou légèrement poudreuse qui reçoit des gouttes de rosée. (*DT*, 23)

Once the liquid was ready there came the moment of which I never wea-ried, the testing of its flow. With bold strokes I would put my well-soaked brush to thin, translucent paper, which absorbed the black fluid quickly yet allowed it to flood slightly. Then, for several minutes longer the ink retained a fresh glossiness, as if pleased that a receptive and willing paper had consented to savor it. The Ancients compared this magic—paper receiving ink—to the young bamboo's powdery skin receiving drops of morning dew. (*RB*, 9)

Importantly, Tianyi's revelation at the initial stage of his artistic develop-ment emphasizes the artistic medium rather than the *style* of expressing the external world: 'j'eus une soudaine révélation. Tout ce que le monde extérieur provoquait en moi, je pouvais finalement l'exprimer au moyen de quelque chose à ma portée: l'Encre' ('I had a sudden revelation: eve-rything the outside world aroused in me could find expression through an element within my reach. Ink') (*DT*, 23; *RB*, 8–9). While the study of the artistic medium aims at the mastery of technique, the exploration of style reveals an artistic vision, as Proust puts it:

[…] le style pour l'écrivain aussi bien que la couleur pour le peintre est une question non de technique mais de vision. Il est la révélation, qui serait impossible par des moyens directs et conscients, de la différence qualitative qu'il y a dans la façon dont nous apparaît le monde, différence qui, s'il n'y avait pas l'art, resterait le secret éternel de chacun. (*RTP IV*, 474)

[…] style for a writer, like colour for a painter, is a question not of tech-nique but of vision. It is the revelation, which would be impossible by direct or conscious means, of the qualitative difference in the ways we per-ceive the world, a difference which, if there were no art, would remain the eternal secret of each individual. (*PT VI*, 204)

Tianyi's artistic revelations will precisely go from medium to style, from technique to vision.

Common to both Cheng and Proust's aesthetic foundation is the idea that art is not an image *of* the external world; if it is representational at all, its purpose and result are precisely to 'mettre en cause le modèle mimétique' ('call into question the mimetic model') (Aubert 2002, 77, my translation). The maturation of Tianyi's art is marked by his step-by-step development from representational to affective poetics.

Despite its apparent failure, Tianyi's first creative attempt teaches him that a representational approach alone to the relation between the mysterious landscape of Mount Lu and his 'cloudy' intuition is far from sufficient. Tianyi initially receives his technical training of representational visual poetics from his father, who is a schoolmaster and also serves as public scribe in the village, by practicing the art of calligraphy:

A la suite de mon père, j'appris certes à copier les modèles de différents styles laissés par les maîtres anciens mais également à observer les modèles vivants qu'offrait la nature omniprésente : les herbes, les arbres et bientôt les champs de thé en terrasses. (*DT*, 19)

Following my father, I learned not only to copy the various styles from models left by the ancient masters but also to observe the living models afforded by omnipresent nature: the grasses, the trees, and soon the terraced tea fields. (*RB*, 6)

Something special about the art of calligraphy deserves a little clarification. A number of pictograms present in Chinese characters are originally imitative of external objects and natural phenomena. However, throughout history, they have been visually modified, enriched, distorted, formalized, and refashioned according to the evolving human 'visions' such as functionalities, imaginations, conceptions, configurations, and relations of those objects and phenomena. Some of the pictograms are thus further developed into ideograms, or become parts of more complicated characters.[9] That is, the imitation of the external has shifted to the expression of the inner, a fundamental form of *interpretation*, and this shift signals the changing human relation to the external world. The exercise of copying the artwork while observing the living models motivates Tianyi to speculate on the possible relation between man and nature: 'je constatais à quel point ces alignements réguliers et rythmés, apparemment imposés par les hommes, épousaient intimement la forme sans cesse différenciée du terrain, révélant ainsi les "veines du Dragon" qui les structuraient en profondeur' ('I marked how their regular and rhythmic lines, seemingly established by man, followed closely the endlessly varied contours of the terrain, thereby revealing a deeper structure, "the veins of the Dragon"') (*DT*, 19; *RB*, 6).[10] Crucially, very early in Tianyi's artistic training, he heuristically senses that the authentic artistic creation should ultimately create a communal relation between man and nature: 'pénétré de cette vision que nourrissait mon apprentissage de la calligraphie, je commençais à me *sentir en communion charnelle* avec le paysage' ('Thus imbued with a vision nurtured by my apprenticeship in calligraphy, I began to *experience a physical communion* with the landscape') (ibid., my italics). This characterization of man's primordial relation to the world as primarily 'charnelle' ('physical' but more literally 'carnal'), corporeal, or bodily, especially through linguistic as well as aesthetic experience (e.g. the calligraphy), is recurrent in *Le Dit*. For example, in Chapter Eighteen of Part One, Tianyi appreciates that every nook and cranny of Mount Emei and Mount Erlang in Sichuan 'montre, sans retenue, sa *présence charnelle*. Ces vallées profondément creusées, à l'argile tendre et rouge, couleur sang, évoquent, avec leurs sentiers qui se croisent, les entrailles ouvertes *d'un sol originel*' ('bears witness to its *carnality*. Deep valleys, with their delicate bloodred clay and their network of paths, evoke the open entrails of *a primeval soil*') (*DT*, 114; *RB*, 75, my italics).[11]

This vision of the world that sees man's existence as a fundamentally hermeneutic activity is not without resonance in *La Recherche*. Coincidental though it may be, the protagonist does compare his way of knowing the world around him to the deciphering of something similar to a logographic language: 'j'avais suivi dans mon existence une marche inverse de celle des peuples qui ne se servent de l'écriture phonétique qu'après n'avoir considéré les caractères que comme une suite de symboles' ('as I got older, I had developed in the opposite direction from those peoples who adopt a phonetic script only after having used characters as symbols') (*RTP III*, 596; *PT V*, 77). Proust presumably refers to the Western linguistic evolution from the cuneiform and hieroglyphic scripts with prominent logographic elements (such as pictograms and ideograms) to predominantly phonemic scripts (such as the Phoenician), where individual letters do not *mean* much (any more) until they have been grouped together in a deliberate way that delivers a more or less prescribed meaning. The protagonist employs the analogy of phonetic writing to suggest his previous attempt to understand 'la vie et la pensée réelles des gens' ('people's real lives and thoughts') according to what they deliberately express in words, according to existent linguistic conventions—what the protagonist calls 'énoncé direct' ('direct expressions') (ibid.). In other words, the 'suite de symboles' (more literally 'sequence of symbols') determines the meaning of words. But as he grows older, the protagonist realizes that he is actually adopting the reverse approach: every symbol that constitutes a word, and, by extension, a language, is a sign for interpretation, and writing is the *source* of meaning; it creates rather than prescribes meaning. To understand people's 'real lives and thoughts', one simply has to *interpret*. For this reason, Deleuze ([2000] 2008, 59) describes the protagonist as an 'Egyptologist': 'We are not physicists or metaphysicians; we must be Egyptologists. For there are no mechanical laws between things or voluntary communications between minds. Everything is implicated, everything is complicated, everything is sign, meaning, essence.' Just as Proust's protagonist and Tianyi are learning to interpret the symbols and signs in order to create art, 'the Egyptologist', Deleuze adds, 'in all things, is the man who undergoes an initiation—the apprentice' (ibid.).

For Proust, as well as for Cheng, the language—both literal and figurative—that we use to establish and maintain our relation to the world is fundamentally corporeal (or 'carnal', in Cheng's words), as Deleuze points out: 'neither things nor minds exist, there are only bodies: astral bodies, vegetal bodies. The biologists would be right if they knew that bodies in themselves are already a language. The linguists would be right if they knew that language is always the language of bodies' (ibid.). Proust's protagonist remarks himself that 'les paroles elles-mêmes ne me renseignaient qu'à la condition d'être interprétées à la façon d'un afflux de sang à la figure d'une personne qui se trouble, à la façon encore d'un silence subit' ('I relied on words only when I could read them like the rush of blood to the face of a person who is unsettled, or like a sudden silence') (*RTP III*, 596; *PT V*, 77). We have already examined Proust's somatic analogy for literary creation in the previous section: 'comme si j'avais été moi-même une poule et si je venais de pondre un oeuf, je me mis à chanter à tue-tête' ('as if I myself were a hen and had just laid an egg, I began to sing at the top of my voice') (*RTP I*, 180; *PT I*, 182).

The second key moment of Tianyi's artistic formation is found in his fruitful encounter with a hermitic master who admits Tianyi as his disciple. This is when Tianyi receives theoretical guidance on *affective* rather than representational visual poetics. The master first outlines the training route of 'la grande tradition ancienne' ('the great ancient tradition') that Tianyi is already following: 'commencer par la calligraphie, continuer par le dessin qui permet de maîtriser la technique du trait, puis s'attaquer à l'art de l'encre pour aboutir enfin à une composition organique' ('start with calligraphy; go on to drawing, which teaches mastery of line. Then take up working in ink, the end being the creation of an organic composition') (*DT*, 161; *RB*, 108–109). The master's following teaching is evidently informed by Buddhist aesthetic practice:

> [...] avec le regard de l'esprit, ce que les Anciens appelaient le troisième œil ou l'œil de Sapience. Comment posséder cet œil ? Il n'y a pas d'autre voie que celle fixée par les maîtres Chan, c'est-à-dire les quatre étapes du voir: voir; ne plus voir; s'abîmer à l'intérieur du non-voir; re-voir. Eh bien, *lorsqu'on re-voit, on ne voit plus les choses en dehors de soi; elles sont partie intégrante de soi,* en sorte que *le tableau qui résulte de ce re-voir n'est plus que la projection sans faille de cette intériorité fécondée et transfigurée.* Il faut donc atteindre la Vision. *Tu t'accroches encore trop aux choses. Tu te cramponnes à elles.* Or, les choses vivantes ne sont jamais fixes, isolées. Elles sont prises dans l'universelle transformation organique. Le temps de peindre, *elles continuent à vivre, tout comme toi-même tu continues à vivre.* En peignant, entre dans ton temps et entre dans leur temps, *jusqu'à ce que ton temps et leur temps se confondent.* (*DT*, 162, my italics)

> [...] through the eyes of the spirit, what the Ancients called the third eye or the eye of Wisdom. How does one make that eye his own? Only through the way of the Chan masters, namely, the four stages of seeing: seeing; no longer seeing; profound non-seeing; re-seeing. *When we finally re-see, we no longer see objects as outside ourselves. They are now an integral part of ourselves, and the work of art that comes from re-seeing is an exact projection of an enriched and transfigured interiority.* So, it is essential to attain the Vision. *You still hold things too tight. You cling to them.* But living things are never fixed or isolated. They are caught up in the universal organic transformation. In the time it takes to paint them, *they go on living, just as you yourself go on living.* While you are painting, enter into your time and enter into their time, *until your time and their time merge.* (*RB*, 108–109, my italics)

In Buddhism, especially its dominant Chinese school *Chan* (more commonly known in the West as *Zen*, derived from the Japanese pronunciation), the Third Eye is also called the Eye of Wisdom (*huiyan*, 慧眼), in contrast to the Worldly Eye (*fanyan*, 凡眼). Put in a schematic way, the former is a mystical and esoteric concept as it sees the inner spiritual world, whereas the latter sees the external material world. Only a balanced combination of the two eyes allows the artist to achieve the ultimate vision.

The master's teaching sheds light on Tianyi's earlier creative failure. When '[s]'efforçant d[e] restituer aussi bien l'aspect tangible que l'aspect évanescent' ('trying to reproduce both its [Mount Lu's] tangibility and its evanescence') (*DT*, 23; *RB*, 9) in his painting, Tianyi clings too much to the external objects and attempts to fix them in their representation, rejecting their state of life. An authentic work of art should only be 'la projection sans faille de cette intériorité fécondée et transfigurée' ('an exact projection of an enriched and transfigured interiority').

When Tianyi once again endeavours to draw 'la montagne d'en face rayonnant sans fin de verdure' which 'dévoilait, sous mille facettes changeantes, sa figure unique' ('the mountain opposite' which 'shone infinitely green and beneath a thousand changing facets revealed its one face'), he is required by the master to capture 'les poussées internes, les lignes de force qui *animaient* les choses' ('the inner thrusts, the lines of force *moving* things') (*DT*, 163; *RB*, 110, my italics). He again senses the bodily as well as spiritual relation between man and nature that he has felt during his practice of calligraphy: 'à travers ces choses et en correspondance avec elles—les rochers, les arbres, les montagnes, les cours d'eau—les Chinois expriment leurs états intérieurs, leurs *élans charnels aussi bien que leurs aspirations spirituelles*' ('through these things—rocks, trees, mountains, streams—and by affinities with them, the Chinese express their inner states, their carnal urges as well as their spiritual aspirations') (*DT*, 163–164; *RB*, 110, my italics). In order for there to be an authentic artistic creation, there has to be an authentic projection of the inner, a projection that aims at universal harmony:

> En compagnie du maître, j'apprenais donc à observer les choses en leur *devenir*, à sentir, derrière leurs formes solides, l'invisible flux dynamique à l'œuvre. A de rares moments, je ne doutais pas que mes pulsions intimes ne se trouvaient en parfait accord avec les pulsions de l'Univers. (*DT*, 164, my italics)

> In the master's company, I learned to observe the evolution of things [more literally 'the things in their *becoming*'] and to sense behind their solid form the working of an invisible dynamic flow. And at rare moments, I did not doubt that my inner impulses were in perfect harmony with the pulsations of the Universe. (*RB*, 110, my italics)

The universe is in constant transformation. Such a formulation reflects not only Cheng's Daoist belief but also his cross-cultural dialogue with Deleuze. The concept of 'becoming' ('devenir'), together with that of 'difference', is a cornerstone in Deleuzian ontology. As Cliff Stagoll (2010 [2005], 26) concisely explains, 'if the primacy of identity is what defines a world of re-presentation (presenting the same world once again), then becoming (by which Deleuze means "becoming different") defines a world of presentation anew'. If an authentic aesthetic experience changes man's relation to the world, it is because it transforms our sense of being: 'au terme d'un intense travail quotidien, je sentais qu'un nouvel être émergeait, grandissait en moi' ('working so intensely every day, I soon began to feel a new being emerge and grow in me') (ibid.).

Tianyi's remark of 'the working of an invisible dynamic flow' which is 'behind [the] solid form of things' reminds us of Proust's protagonist's observation of that something which is 'behind that motion, that brightness' of the 'shape', 'lines', and 'surface' of the Martinville steeples. Just as the master instructs Tianyi to appreciate the 'life' in things, Proust's protagonist's *analogical* search for the hidden, or what he later reiterates as 'rechercher les causes profondes' ('seeking deep causes') (*RTP IV*, 445; *PT IV*, 175),[12] recognizes what is in the self via the recognition of the hidden behind the steeples of Martinville. The protagonist dismisses neither the material reality of the steeples nor the hidden *thing* behind them that 'corresponds' to what is in him. In other words, the protagonist's affective artistic presentation, rather than representation, does not annihilate—both in the sense of 'reducing to nothing' and 'destroying the soul'—the object of aesthetic experience, which an idolater's practice of appropriation of art does. The relation between what is in him and what is hidden behind the thing constantly undergoes a process of transformation as the protagonist creates his art. Hannah Freed-Thall (2009, 869) has argued that the most striking aesthetic experiences in *La Recherche* involve the most ordinary object which 'defies critical appropriation'.[13] Although the type of aesthetic experience she engages with is predominantly *receptive* and does not seem to include artistic *production*, which is our case here, what her analysis of 'aesthetic disorientation' effectively exposes is that there is clearly an asymmetrical pattern between the perception and the reaction of the aestheticizing subject in those striking experiences. This asymmetry, in the case of artistic production, also characterizes the 'forms' of 'équivalent profond', the relation between the artist's representation and affective presentation, the authentic relation of the individual to the world.

The delineation of aesthetic territories between the inner and the outer is fundamentally *transformative* and there is an asymmetrical correspondence between them. This correspondence is a mode of communication, a communion, bodily and spiritual, perpetuated by the creation of works of art. Our real existence, our fundamental sense of being, is a relation, as Aubert (2002, 81) comments: 'ce que nous appelons la réalité est en fait un certain rapport, notre rapport aux choses, au monde et que c'est ce dernier qu'il faut chercher à éclaircir, et notamment le lien qui unit vérité et images' ('what we call reality is in fact a certain relation, our relation to things, to the world, and it is this relation that we should try to illuminate, especially this connection that unites truth and images').

5.3   PRIMACY OF ART

It is no exaggeration when Richard Bales (2007 [2001], 183) opens his discussion of Proust's relation to art with the following remark: 'few authors foreground the arts quite so comprehensively as Proust; certainly, none made them so central to their own literary production. [...] probably no other work of literature celebrates the arts as totally as his, or is so convincing in his pursuit.' A firm belief in the primacy of the arts in spiritual life, or what both Cheng and Proust should prefer to call 'real life', also represents a central thematic concern in *Le Dit*, although the apparent difference in scale would inevitably make Cheng's efforts seem small when compared to Proust's. Of course, it is far from the purpose of Cheng's 'Proustian approach' to match Proust's *La Recherche* in length. Cheng's approach signals, to borrow Bales's words, 'a keen awareness of the literary possibilities of incorporating the arts in the fabric of [his] own work' (ibid.)—crucially, in the wake of *La Recherche*.

Our previous observations focus on Cheng's critical joining in with Proust's aesthetic theory and his conception of the novel as a *Bildungsroman*. This section will further demonstrate Cheng's artistic ambition to reorient Proust's approach to the arts towards a model of intercultural communication, by developing Cheng's idea of 'cultural translation' as constructions of cultural, and more specifically artistic, 'parallels' or 'equivalents' from both Western and Eastern heritages.

Concerning the engagement with the arts, perhaps the most obvious novelistic parallels between *Le Dit* and *La Recherche* are found in their respective casts of key artist-characters. Just as in Proust, where certain artist-characters stimulate the narrator's discussions of the arts, Cheng's four main characters personify different forms of art. The Table 5.1 summarizes these parallels:

Table 5.1   Corresponding artist-characters in *La Recherche* and *Le Dit*

Art forms	Characters in Le Dit	Corresponding characters in La Recherche
Painting	Tianyi (plus calligraphy)	Elstir
Literature	Haolang	Bergotte and the narrator
Theatre	Yumei	La Berma and Rachel
Music	Véronique	Morel and Vinteuil

The following sections will selectively compare a number of key passages from both novels for each of the four categories.

5.3.1   Painting

Like the protagonist of *La Recherche* and, even more so, like Proust himself, Tianyi makes a number of artistic pilgrimages in Europe. In addition to Paris, he visits Florence and Venice for Italian Renaissance paintings, Amsterdam for Rembrandt, and The Hague for Vermeer. Tianyi's corresponding Proustian character is Elstir in *La Recherche*, whose art most resembles Impressionist aesthetics, which inevitably bear many conceptual differences from ancient Chinese art. Nevertheless, Tianyi's reflections on the similar (re)creative principle of Western paintings to ancient Chinese art resonate with Proust's protagonist's enthusiastic discussions of Elstir's works.

For both Proust's protagonist and Tianyi, artistic creation imitates the creation of the universe. In fact, the former *reconstitutes* the latter—artistic creation is fundamentally a microcosmic *re*creation of the cosmic orders. Proust's protagonist first compares Elstir's studio to

[...] le laboratoire d'une sorte *de nouvelle creation du monde*, où, du *chaos* que sont toutes choses que nous voyons, il avait tiré, en les poignant sur divers rectangles de toile qui étaient posés dans tous les sens, ici une vague de la mer écrasant avec colère sur le sable son écume lilas, là un jeune homme en coutil blanc accoudé sur le pont d'un bateau. Le veston du jeune homme et la vague éclaboussante avaient pris *une dignité nouvelle* du fait qu'ils *continuaient à être*, encore que dépourvus de ce en quoi ils passaient pour consister, la vague ne pouvant plus mouiller, ni le veston habiller personne. (*RTP II*, 190, my italics)

[…] the laboratory out of which would come a kind of *new creation* of the world: from the chaos made of things we see, he had abstracted, by painting them on various rectangles of canvas now standing about on all sides, glimpses of things, like a wave in the sea crashing its angry lilac-shaded foam down on the sand, or a young man in white twill leaning on a ship's rail. The young man's jacket and the splash of the wave had taken on a *new dignity*, in virtue of the fact that they *continued to exist*, though now deprived of what they were believed to consist in, the wave being now unable to wet anyone, and the jacket unable to be worn. (*PT II*, 414, my italics)

The sea, as Jean-Pierre Richard (1976, 128) perspicaciously points out, signifies 'le lieu d'origine' ('the place of origin') in these passages of *Les Jeunes filles en fleurs*. The artistic image of a man at sea symbolically reflects man's primordial relation to the world, which is renewed and perpetuated ('a new dignity, in virtue of the fact that they continued to exist') by Elstir's creation of art. The artist is then directly compared to the divine Creator: 'si Dieu le Père avait créé les choses en les nommant, c'est en leur ôtant leur nom, ou en leur en donnant un autre qu'Elstir les recréait' ('if God the Father had created things by naming them, Elstir recreated them by removing their names, or by giving them another name') (*RTP II*, 191; *PT II*, 415). The protagonist subsequently applies this aesthetic principle to the subjective reading of the changing faces of the young girls he is in love with, 'qui fait penser à cette perpétuelle recréation des éléments primordiaux de la nature qu'on contemple devant la mer' ('reminiscent in its restless contrasts of that perpetual recreation of nature's primordial elements which we witness by the sea') (*RTP II*, 259; *PT II*, 483), which is rephrased again in *Le Temps retrouvé* as 'une création perpétuellement recommencée' ('a creation which is perpetually renewed') (*RTP IV*, 375; *PT VI*, 105). As the narrator's aesthetic reflection matures, he realizes that this perpetual artistic recreation not only sustains one's own authentic relation to the world, but also infinitely opens up other possible worlds: 'grâce à l'art, au lieu de voir un seul monde, le nôtre, nous le voyons se multiplier, et autant qu'il y a d'artistes originaux, autant nous avons de mondes à notre disposition, plus différents les uns des autres que ceux qui roulent dans l'infini' ('Thanks to art, instead of seeing only a single world, our own, we see it multiplied, and have at our disposal as many worlds as there are original artists, all more different one from another than those which revolve in infinity') (*RTP IV*, 474; *PT VI*, 204).

Moreover, Proust repeatedly emphasizes that in order to create authentic art, artists must take refuge in solitude, keeping a distance from society life or even sacrificing friendship, despite people's contempt for them because of that. Elstir 'vivait dans un isolement, avec une sauvagerie que les gens du monde appelaient de la pose et de la mauvaise éducation, les pouvoirs publics un mauvais esprit, ses voisins de la folie, sa famille de l'égoïsme et de l'orgueil' ('lived in a state of isolation and unsociability which fashionable people saw as ill-mannered and affected, the powers-that-be as wrong-headed, his neighbours as mad, and his family as arrogant and inconsiderate') (*RTP II*, 184; *PT II*, 407–408). Elstir 'avait vécu pour lui-même' ('had lived only for himself') (*RTP II*, 185; *PT II*, 408), which Proust later reiterates as 'le devoir' ('the duty') of a real artist: 'or l'amitié est une dispense de ce devoir' ('friendship is a dereliction of that duty') (*RTP II*, 260; *PT II*, 483). In some sense, the artist could be characterized as reclusive and narcissistic: 'la pratique de la solitude lui en avait donné l'amour' ('the practice of solitude had given him a love for it') (*RPT II*, 185; *PT II*, 408).

The corresponding relation between artistic creation and cosmic creation is made crystal clear in Tianyi's following statement: 'les peintres visaient non pas à imiter les infinies variations du monde créé mais à prendre part aux gestes mêmes de la Création' ('the painters aimed not at imitating the infinite variations of the created world, but at participating in the very activity of Creation') (*DT*, 232; *RB*, 160). Initially stimulated by his study of Renaissance paintings, Tianyi's general observation of Western art in some ways proposes a theory that could shed light on Proust's perception of the artist's creative condition of solitude tinged with narcissism:

> Sur fond d'univers objectif, l'homme jouait maintenant le rôle principal. L'univers, tout en participant à l'action de l'homme, était relégué au rôle de décor. [...] je me mettrais dès lors à traquer le long de l'Occident la lignée des peintres qui avaient cherché à restaurer le royaume perdu [...]. Commencement de la grandeur. Commencement de la solitude. Plus tard, je comprendrai pourquoi l'Occident était si hanté par le thème du miroir et de Narcisse. Arraché au monde créé, s'érigeant en sujet unique, l'homme aimait à se mirer. Après tout, c'était désormais sa seule manière de se voir. Se mirant dans le reflet, il captait sa propre image, et surtout l'image de son pouvoir, nourri d'un esprit affranchi. A force de se contempler et de s'exalter, son regard ainsi exercé n'avait de cesse qu'il

ne transformât tout le reste en objet, plus exactement en objet de conquête. Ne reconnaissant plus d'autre sujet autour de lui, il se privait
pour longtemps—volontiers? malgré lui?—d'interlocuteurs ou de pairs.
Pouvait-il réellement échapper à la conscience aiguë de la solitude et de la
mort? (DT, 231–232)

His backdrop the objective universe, man now played the leading role. The
universe, while participating in man's action, had been relegated to the role
of stage set. [...] I would set out to track down the West's long line of painters who sought to restore the lost kingdom [...]. The beginning of greatness.
The beginning of solitude. Later I would understand the West's obsession
with the themes of the mirror and Narcissus. Snatched from the created
world, setting himself up as the only subject, man loved to admire his reflection. After all, from then on it was his own image, with its salient feature the
power fed by a liberated spirit. Steadily contemplating and exalting himself,
he soon acquired a practiced eye that would not stop until it had transformed
all that was not he into object – more precisely into object of conquest. No
longer acknowledging any other subject around him, he long deprived himself – willingly? In spite of himself? – of interlocutors and peers. Could he
really escape a keen awareness of solitude and death? (RB, 159–160)

This is another highly condensed passage which necessarily needs unfold-
ing. First, Cheng evidently traces the development of the Western conceptual and perceptive equation of the artist with the Creator to the
Renaissance theological turn, according to which man—instead of
God—is now the centre of the universe. Cheng implicitly refers to the
birth of the modern human subject ('setting himself up as the only subject') famously announced by Descartes.

Second, 'the lost kingdom' evokes the biblical fall of man, and it is
the artist's task to 'restore' that lost paradise. Although Tianyi does not
generically include Proust in his tracking of the line of Western painters
who endeavour to 'restore the lost kingdom', the idea of retrieving a lost
paradise through art is intrinsic to Proustian aesthetics and spirituality.
Proust's narrator reaffirms at the end of La Recherche:

[Le souvenir] nous fait tout à coup respirer un air nouveau, précisément
parce que c'est un air qu'on a respiré autrefois, cet air plus pur que les
poètes ont vainement essayé de faire régner dans le paradis et qui ne pourrait donner cette sensation profonde de renouvellement que s'il avait été
respiré déjà, car les vrais paradis sont les paradis qu'on a perdus. (RTP IV,
449, my italics)

[The memory] suddenly makes us breathe a new air, new precisely because it is an air we have breathed before, this purer air which the poets *have tried in vain* to make reign *in paradise* and which could not provide this profound feeling of renewal if it had not already been breathed, *for the only true paradise is a paradise that we have lost.* (*PT VI*, 178–179, my italics)[14]

Proust juxtaposes 'les vrais paradis' with 'le paradis'. Incidentally, the latter is capitalized as 'le Paradis' in the Flammarion edition of *La Rercherche*, directed by Milly, which enhances its specifically Christian reference. Proust's nuance is crucial because, ultimately, the real lost par-adise*s* that artists endeavour to restore are not *the* Paradise of the Bible, but *many* paradises—'la création du monde n'a pas eu lieu une fois pour toutes [...] elle a nécessairement lieu tous les jours' ('the creation of the world did not happen once and for all [...] it has to take place, necessar-ily, every day') (*RTP IV*, 375; *PT VI*, 105)—that are essentially recreated *by* and *in* man.

This 'artificial' paradise leads, then, according to Cheng, to man's 'beginning of solitude' and the flourishing of 'the themes of the mirror and Narcissus' in Western art. Although Cheng does not cite any specific artistic examples, critics have long observed this paradigmatic shift to self-reflexivity in Western painting and, by extension, Western thought: from what Foucault characterizes as the 'resembling' representation to the 'pure' representation,[15] and, arguably, from Classical to Baroque and postmodernist aesthetics; from the 'mirror' of the world to that of the self and to the 'mirror of the mirror', or what may be called the met-anarrative structure of knowledge. In this respect, Proust's novel, with its double internal focalization within a first-person narrative, as well as the 'fragment' of 'Un Amour de Swann' seemingly written in the third person, epitomizes the narcissistic game of self-mirroring. To appropri-ate the narrator-protagonist's own words, 'tout tournait autour de moi' ('everything revolved around me') (*RTP I*, 6; *PT I*, 10). In fact, Cheng's work also illustrates such a narrative dynamism—albeit less sophisticated than Proust's—with the multiple reincarnations of the author himself as the narrator (of the preface), the protagonist, Professors C. and F., and Haolang the poet.[16]

But Cheng does not explore Western artistic traditions per se; rather, they signal areas of cross-cultural translation and negotiation. His reflec-tion inspired by Renaissance art is followed by an extensive discussion of Chinese traditional aesthetic theory. He first looks for the Chinese temporal and historic 'equivalent' of the Italian Renaissance because the art 'of his own country', to borrow T.S. Eliot's (2010, 956) formulation, 'has a simultaneous existence and composes a simultaneous order': 'je ne crois pas avoir été autant de connivence avec les peintres chinois des Song et des Yuan que dans les musées de Florence et de Venise' ('I do not think I ever felt as much in harmony with the Chinese painters of the Sung and Yuan Dynasties as I did in the museums of Florence and Venice') (*DT*, 232; *RB*, 160). In doing this, Cheng effectively reorients the preceding European conception of artistic creation towards a Chinese alternative:

> Ne répétait-elle pas à la longueur de siècle, cette cosmologie [...] que la Création provient du Souffle primordial, lequel dérive du Vide originel? Ce Souffle primordial se divisant à son tour en souffles vitaux *yin* et *yang* et en bien d'autres a rendu possible la naissance du Multiple. Ainsi reliés, l'Un et le Multiple sont d'un seul tenant. Tirant conséquence de cette conception, les peintres visaient non pas à imiter les infinies variations du monde créé mais à prendre part aux gestes mêmes de la Création. Ils s'ingéniaient à introduire, entre le *yin* et le *yang*, entre les Cinq Éléments, entre les Dix Mille entités vivantes, le Vide médian, seul garant de la bonne marche des souffles organiques, lesquels deviennent esprit lorsqu'ils atteignent la résonance rythmique. (*DT*, 232)

> Over the centuries this cosmology had reiterated [...] that creation stems from the primal Breath, which derives from the original Void. By splitting into the vital breaths *yin* and *yang* among others, the primal Breath rendered possible the birth of the Multiple. Thus connected, the One and the Multiple are all of a piece. Drawing conclusions from that concept, the painters aimed not at imitating the infinite variations of the created world, but at participating in the very activity of Creation. Between *yin* and *yang*, between the Five Elements, between the Ten Thousand living entities, they strove to insert the middle Void, the sole guarantee of the smooth functioning of the organic breaths, which become spirit upon attaining rhythmic resonance. (*RB*, 160)

Although both European and Chinese traditions share the aesthetic conception of the artist as creator/Creator, the latter significantly differs from the former in its conceptual independence of the human subject. The Chinese conception, to adapt Cheng's (2002) remark on Chinese poetry, 'cherche à laisser parler le paysage et les choses, à laisser transparaître entre les signes un état de communion où l'invisible a sa part' ('tries to let landscape and things speak, to show a state of communion between signs, where the invisible has its part').

Yet the ceaseless and pluralistic recreations of the world through the same primordial principle share a strong affinity with Proust's aesthetic foundation examined earlier. In fact, Cheng's formulation of 'One and Many' ('ainsi reliés, l'Un et le Multiple sont d'un seul tenant'/'thus connected, the One and the Multiple are all of a piece') subtly brings together two epistemologically very different aesthetic and cosmological theories. The notion of 'One and Many' is fundamental in Daoist thought, but Cheng conveniently leaves out the numerical significance of 'Two' and 'Three'[17]—which would have otherwise made this notion specifically Daoist—*in order that* it resonate with certain Western schools of thought, some of which have been extensively employed to study Proustian aesthetics. Deleuze (2008 [2000], 29–30), for instance, notably applies Neoplatonic concepts to the understanding of Proust's idea of 'essence', especially that found in art:

The world enveloped by essence is always a beginning of the World in general, a beginning of the universe, an absolute, radical beginning. [...] Certain Neoplatonists used a profound word to designate the original state that proceeds any development, any 'explication': *complication*, which envelops the many in the One and affirms the unity of the multiple.

More recently, the notion of 'One and Many' in Proust has been most systematically examined by Erika Fülöp in *Proust, the One, and the Many*.[18] She meticulously negotiates these two perspectives in *La Recherche* and formulates them into one coherent structure by engaging with a range of European philosophers from Schelling to Derrida.

Once again, Cheng's aesthetic reflection has shown compelling evidence of both Western (especially French poststructuralist) and Daoist influences. But perhaps more importantly, this 'comparatist' intellectual and artistic energy, channeled through 'cross-fertilization, assimilation, creative adaption, indigenization, translation, and making-new, within and across locally differentiated traditions, through centuries of uneven modernities',[19] has come to define Cheng's literary aesthetic. In this light, Tianyi's Renaissance inspiration is rechanneled literally into a 're-naissance' of art and thought in the present which are preoccupied with a palpable sense of 'to-comeness'. As will be further demonstrated in subsequent analyses, Cheng's 'comparatist' narrative model, which consistently sets up cultural 'parallels' and audaciously constructs 'equivalents' from both Western and Eastern cultural heritages, exemplifies the concept and practice of cultural translation both in form and in content.

5.3.2   Literature

La Recherche provides Cheng with a key formal literary expression of generic hybridity.[20] It is well known that the blurring and blending of literary genres constitutes a vital force behind the evolution of Proust's novelistic conception, from Les Plaisirs et les jours, via Jean Santeuil and Contre Sainte-Beuve, to La Recherche. Proust pushes this generic experiment to such an extreme that he even questions whether he himself is a novelist at all in one of his early notebooks: 'suis-je romancier?' As for Cheng, the titles of each part of the novel—namely 'épopée' ('epic'), 'récit' ('account'), and 'mythe' ('myth')—already demonstrate his conscious engagement with literary genres. Besides the conceptions of the novel as both a Bildungsroman and Künstlerroman like La Recherche,[21] Cheng deliberately challenges the boundaries between biography, autobiography, and fiction, between essay and novel, between history and literature.[22]

Like Bergotte and the protagonist-narrator in La Recherche, Haolang represents the writer and poet in Le Dit. The works by Bergotte, who is often thought to be modeled on Anatole France and Paul Bourget (Hassine 2004), resemble Decadent literature, which has very little stylistic echo in Le Dit. It is Proust's narrator's reflection on the writer's role in relation to national politics, especially in times of war and revolution, that finds its Chinese counterpart in Le Dit.

Haolang is an ardent advocate of politically engaged literature and he becomes a patriotic poet during wartime:

Sur la foi d'une affiche il alla suivre des cours du soir organisés par d'obscurs intellectuels progressistes. C'est là que la guerre, par miracle, est venue le cueillir. Incorporé dans l'un des groupes artistiques 'Résistance aux Japonais et salut de la patrie', il connut la vie itinérante et puis celle du front. Faisant partie des ' petits', mais entouré d'artistes chevronnés, il découvrit la poésie et se découvrit poète. (DT, 78)

Attracted by a posted notice, he enrolled in evening courses organized by some obscure progressive intellectuals. And there, miraculously, the war gathered him up. Enlisting in one of the artists' groups, 'Resistance to the Japanese and Salvation of the Homeland' he experienced the itinerant life, then life at the front. One of the 'youngsters' but surrounded by seasoned artists, he discovered poetry and himself a poet. (*RB*, 49)

He follows in the steps of revolutionary left-wing writers such as LU Xun and HU Feng, and is preoccupied with a new Chinese poetic language, 'pour nous secouer, pour nous arracher à la partie dégénérée pourrie, de nos racines' ('to shake us up, to tear out the degenerate, rotten part of our roots') (*DT*, 97; *RB*, 63). The references to a new language and Lu Xun point to the profound transformation of dominant literary language from classical to modern vernacular Chinese at the beginning of the twentieth century. Lu Xun is a leading figure in this so-called 'Chinese Literary Revolution', which aims to improve and reinvent a modern vernacular written style as the legitimate literary language. Tianyi later witnesses the completion of this transition in Haolang and Yumei's letter: 'début 1950, arriva une lettre de Haolang et de Yumei, assez brève, écrite dans une langue nouvelle' ('In early 1950, a letter from Haolang and Yumei arrived, fairly short, written in a new language') (*DT*, 239; *RB*, 165).[23] At any rate, literary creation is here seen as born out of collective political urgency rather than spiritual concerns, as Haolang decidedly expresses his stance:

> [...] moi, je me range résolument du côté de Lu Xun. L'âme, on l'a ou on ne l'a pas. Si on l'a, on ne l'a perdra pas. Ou alors, c'est au moment où nous nous avisons de la chercher que nous la perdons. Si nous devons renaître, nous renaîtrons. Si nous devons disparaître, acceptons de devenir cendres, d'où naîtra peut-être quelque chose d'autre que nous ignorons. Pour le moment, le salut vient d'ailleurs, de l'étranger. (*DT*, 96)

> I am strongly on the side of Lu Xun. The soul, we have it or we do not have it. If we have it, then we shall not lose it. Or else, it is at the moment we realize we are looking for it that we lose it. If we are to be reborn, we shall be reborn. If we are to disappear, let us accept becoming ashes; perhaps from them something else will be born of which we know nothing now. For the moment, salvation comes from elsewhere, from abroad. (*RB*, 62–63)

Haolang's view of art forms a stark contrast to that of Tianyi, who believes in 'l'aventure de l'âme singulière et à l'errance' ('restlessness of spirit and the peculiar adventure of each soul') (*DT*, 96; *RB*, 62). In a discussion on the 'ideal society', Tianyi reaffirms the different philosophical implications behind their respective artistic activities:

> Instinctivement proche de l'esprit taoïste, j'acceptais plutôt la conception de la création ou de la transformation continue de l'Univers au sein duquel la Terre n'est qu'une halte provisoire. Haolang avançait l'idée que pour le moment il convenait d'aider à détruire l'ordre ancien; une fois le joug levé, on entrerait dans un autre contexte, et on chercherait à s'épanouir autrement. (*DT*, 102)

> Instinctively close to the Taoist spirit, I preferred the concept of the continuous creation or transformation of a Universe where the Earth was only a temporary stopping place. Haolang advanced the idea that for the time being it behooved us to help destroy the old order; once the yoke was lifted, we would be entering a new context, and we could strive to develop our society in a different direction. (*RB*, 67)

It is also the experience of war—in this case, the First World War—that 'allowed Proust to reflect on the connections linking literature, history, and politics' (Hughes 2012, 17).[24] Proust's eventual criticism of patriotic and revolutionary literature and art is well known:

> [...] l'idée d'un art populaire comme d'un art patriotique si même elle n'avait pas été dangereuse, me semblait ridicule. [...] Dès le début de la guerre M. Barrès avait dit que l'artiste (en l'espèce Titien) doit avant tout servir la gloire de sa patrie. Mais il ne peut la servir qu'en étant artiste, [...] N'imitons pas les révolutionnaires qui par 'civisme' méprisaient, s'ils ne les détruisaient pas, les œuvres de Watteau et de La Tour, peintres qui honorent davantage la France que tous ceux de la Révolution. (*RTP IV*, 466–467)

> The idea of a popular art, like that of a patriotic art, seemed to me, if indeed not dangerous, certainly laughable. [...] At the beginning of the war M. Barrès said that the artist (in that instance, Titien) had a duty above all else to serve the glory of his country. But he can serve it only by being an artist [...] Let us not be like the revolutionaries who despised the works of Watteau and de La Tour out of 'good citizenship', painters who do more honour to France than all those of the Revolution. (*PT VI*, 196–197)

The idea of a patriotic art indeed proves to be dangerous and even fatal for Haolang. As the director of the left-wing literary review, Hu Feng is arrested and accused of being anti-revolutionary for having criticized Mao's overpoliticization of art and literature; Haolang, who has contributed to the review, is sent to a 're-education camp'. Later during the Cultural Revolution, he is again absurdly punished by the Red Guards as the 'droitiste le plus ancien et le plus endurci' ('most ancient and the most stubborn rightist') (*DT*, 407; *RB*, 282) for his previous involvement with Hu Feng's left-wing literary review, leading to Haolang's 'death'. Apart from the obvious criticism of the socio-political injustice and absurdity under Mao's regime, Cheng also portrays Haolang as a victim of his own politically engaged poems. For Proust, as well as for Cheng, the only real 'patrie' ('homeland') of an artist is 'la patrie intérieure' ('the [inner] homeland') which proves 'l'existence irréductiblement individuelle de l'âme' ('the living proof of the irreducible individuality of each soul') (*RTP III*, 761; *PT V*, 235).

However, unlike Proust's narrator's total rejection of patriotic literature, towards the end of the novel Tianyi sees a certain complementarity of Haolang's artistic vision to his own. As Haolang works on his 'petite histoire' ('personal history') and Tianyi on his final portrait of Yumei, Tianyi reflects:

> [...] je ressens combien nous sommes différents, combien aussi nous sommes complémentaires. Haolang aura toujours été cet être qui s'arrache de la terre la plus charnelle, qui va droit de l'avant ou qui s'efforce de s'élever vers l'air libre des hauteurs, coûte que coûte, vaille que vaille, fût-ce au prix d'atroces blessures infligées à lui-même et aux autres. Tandis que moi, j'aurai été cet être qui vient d'ailleurs et qui sera perpétuellement choqué par ce qu'offre cette terre. Si en dépit de tout je garde intacte en moi cette capacité d'étonnement et d'émerveillement, c'est que sans cesse je suis porté par les échos d'une très lointaine nostalgie dont j'ignore l'origine. (*DT*, 372)

> I realize how different we are yet how incomplete we are without each other. Haolang is molded of earthly clay and faces life straight on or soars as high as he can, however heavy the cost, however great the wounds he might inflict on himself and others. That is his nature. I on the other hand am from somewhere nebulous and far away, and life in this world never ceases to shock me. Yet at the same time I have an infinite capacity for

astonishment and wonder that wells up from some mysterious inner longing. That is my nature. (*RB*, 258)

If Haolang's poetic ambition entails a rupture with the 'burdensome'
tradition in order to create something radically 'new', Tianyi's artistic vision is marked by the constant return to a quasi-mystic origin. For
Tianyi, 'la vraie vie est un simple retour' ('real life is a simple turning
around') (*DT*, 224; *RB*, 154), and in contrast to Haolang's indifference
to spiritual discourses of art, Tianyi is convinced that 'seule une vision
mythique permettrait aux hommes de prendre en charge ce qu'ils ne par-
viennent pas à dire entièrement. Qui d'entre nous peut prétendre cerner
la vraie vie, savoir jusqu'où elle plonge ses racines et étend ses ramures?'
('Only a mythic vision allows mankind to assume control of what cannot
be fully verbalized. Who among us can claim to take the measure of real
life, to know how deep it sinks its roots, how far it extends its branches?')
(ibid.). If Tianyi's, and by extension Cheng's, literary aesthetic can be
described as 'revolutionary', it is revolutionary in the Proustian sense, as
Antoine Compagnon (1989, 27, my translation) explains:

> [...] en littérature les révolutions ne vont pas toujours vers l'avant, [...] il
> peut y avoir des révolutions en arrière, à rebours pour ainsi dire. Le sens de
> la 'révolution' proustienne aurait été celui-là, le rattachant à la grande tra-
> dition classique, racinienne en particulier, de l'étude des sentiments et des
> passions, par-dessus le roman qui, depuis Flaubert, sacrifiait l'intelligence à
> la sensation.

> [...] in literature, revolutions do not always happen forward, [...] in litera-
> ture there can be backwards revolutions so to speak, and the meaning of
> the one Proust had accomplished lay just there, linking him to the great
> classical tradition, particularly the Racinian tradition of studying passions
> and feelings, going beyond the novel which since Flaubert had been sacri-
> ficing intelligence to sensation.

Indeed, Cheng's 'revolutionary' aesthetic revisits *two* great cultural heritages instead of one, creating something 'new' or, indeed, 'old'.

5.3.3   *Theatre*

Both Proust's and Cheng's engagement with theatre may appear proportionally less significant than with literature and painting. Theatrical art is

nevertheless relevant to both protagonists' own artistic revelations and vocations, and theatrical references permeate both novels. Racine is still one of the most cited writers in *La Recherche*; Yumei or l'Amante, personifying theatrical art, is still the pivotal character of *Le Dit* who inspires Tianyi's final artistic creation.

Tianyi's 'comparatist' observation of theatre in *Le Dit* registers yet another important artistic transition in modern Chinese history owing to Western influence:

> Il s'agissait du 'théâtre parlé', c'est-à-dire à l'occidentale, qui diffère du théâtre ancien en ce que ce dernier comporte outre le dialogue parlé le chant, le mime et l'acrobatie. Dans le théâtre moderne, on ne trouve plus les masques, les accessoires, ni l'ensemble des gestes symboliques qui permettent à l'acteur, sur une scène presque vide, de tirer à lui l'espace et le temps, de se jouer d'eux. Le drame se déroule dans un décor réaliste, sur une durée déterminée. (*DT*, 108)

> Here it was 'spoken theatre', Western style, different from the ancient theatre, which not only has spoken dialogue but also song, pantomime, and acrobatics. Modern theatre does without the masks, the accessories, and the ensemble of symbolic movements through which an actor on an almost empty stage draws space and time to himself and triumphs over them. The modern drama is acted out in a realistic setting, and within strict time limits. (*RB*, 71)

However, instead of elaborating on Western or Western-style theatre, Cheng's discussion almost exclusively focuses on classical Chinese theatre. This aesthetic preference of Cheng's is hardly surprising. Like Haolang's 'revolutionary' poetic language, the 'théâtre parlé', also known in Chinese as *huaju* (spoken drama, 话剧), at the turn of the twentieth century, had its own political agenda:

> La guerre avait fait affluer de toute la Chine un grand nombre d'écrivains, d'artistes et de comédiens vers quelques villes de l'arrière [...] Une majorité d'entre eux, pour ne pas dire la totalité, étaient de gauche ou de tendance 'progressive'; leur propos n'était pas d'amuser. Les uns s'attaquaient directement aux problèmes actuels, d'autres abordaient les grands thèmes, tous étaient conscients de participer à un moment exceptionnel et de préparer la renaissance de la culture chinoise. (*DT*, 108–109)

> The war had driven writers, artists, and actors from all parts of China to a few cities behind the lines [...] The majority were leftists or had

'progressive' tendencies; their purpose was not to entertain. Some attacked contemporary problems directly in their work, others took up the great enduring themes; all were conscious of participating in an unusual moment and of paving the way for the renaissance of Chinese culture. (*RB*, 71)

Both Cheng's and Proust's relative detachment from contemporary politics gives an edge to their appetite for classical theatre. Just as La Berma plays the heroine in Racine's *Phèdre*, Yumei performs the *Legend of the White Snake* (*baishe zhuan*, 白蛇传) in the Sichuan opera. In addition to their shared theatrical genre of tragedy revolving around *l'amour impossible*, there is even a certain 'temporal parallel' between the two pieces. Like Racine's French Classicist recomposition of Euripides's play from Greek antiquity, the earliest written piece of *White Snake* was also published in the seventeenth century, with a long tradition of oral circulation preceding it.[25]

But it would be difficult to talk about *Phèdre/La Recherche* and *White Snake/Le Dit* in interdiegetic terms (as we will do with the myth of Orpheus in a later section). Neither Proust nor Cheng seems to systemically engage with the *plots* of *Phèdre* and *White Snake*. It is the theatricality, the aesthetic performance of the two actresses in particular, that is at the heart of Proust's and Cheng's theatrical observations. In this respect, Cheng's *démarche proustienne* manifests itself in the affinity between Tianyi's admiring description of Yumei's performance and Proust's portrayal of La Berma, especially in the protagonist's second attendance of La Berma's performance of *Phèdre* at the Opéra.[26]

In a strikingly similar fashion, at the appearances of La Berma and Yumei on stage, both protagonists exclaim 'miracle' in relation to their respective mental images:

[Proust's protagonist:] Et alors, *ô miracle*, comme ces leçons que nous nous sommes vainement épuisés à apprendre le soir et que nous *retrouvons en nous*, [...] comme aussi ces visages des morts que les efforts passionnés de notre mémoire poursuivent *sans les retrouver* [...] sont là devant nos yeux. (*RTP II*, 347, my italics)

[Proust's protagonist:] And then *miraculously*, like the lessons which we have vainly spent an exhausting evening trying to learn and which we find we know by heart after a night's sleep, and like the faces of dead friends which the intense efforts of our memory pursue *without success* and appear right there before our eyes. (*PT III*, 45, my italics)[27]

[Tianyi:] *Miracle*, c'est pourtant le seul mot que tout le souffle qui m'animait à cet instant parvint à murmurer. *Miracle*, ma première rencontre avec Yumei dans le jardin au détour d'un sentier. *Miracle, ces retrouvailles.* (*DT*, 138, my italics)

[Tianyi:] And yet *miracle* was the only word that all my inspiration could whisper just then. *Miracle*, my first meeting Yumei at the bend in the garden path. *Miracle*, finding her again. (*RB*, 92, my italics)

From disappointment to revelation, Proust's protagonist learns how to appreciate La Berma's talent in an 'impersonal' way—without any preconceived ideas which would expect, in vain, the performance to answer 'une impression individuelle' ('an individual impression') (*RTP II*, 349; *PT III*, 47). La Berma's acting is marked by a certain transparency, like 'une fenêtre qui donne sur un chef-d'œuvre' ('a window opening on to a masterpiece') (*RTP II*, 347; *PT III*, 46). The spectators are not fascinated by La Berma the person or the technical accomplishment of her acting, but 'une donnée de la vie' ('real life') (*RTP II*, 348; *PT III*, 46), the closeness to real life. The actress's body, voice, attitude, gesture, and veil incarnate (in the etymological sense of 'making flesh') the verses, and her brilliant interpretation makes all the external accessories 'translucides' ('translucent'); instead of 'cacher' ('concealing') the *spirit* of the masterpiece, they make it shine: 'refracter plus richement le rayon central' ('refract more richly the imprisoned, central ray of light') (ibid.).

Impersonality, on the other hand, has always been an important aesthetic in classical Chinese theatre. Brecht, for example, famously explored this aspect of traditional Chinese acting to support his concept of *Verfremdungseffekt*.[28] But Tianyi's aesthetic appreciation of Yumei's theatrical performance is initially caught between an impersonal interpretation of Madame White Snake and his passion for the actress, who is subsequently described as 'une vraie artiste en possession de tous ses moyens, capable d'exprimer tant de passions obscures' ('a true artist in full possession of herself, capable of expressing a myriad of obscure passions'):

Yumei était entièrement maquillée selon les règles du théâtre, portant une coiffe richement ornée. Son visage peint, qui représentait la beauté idéale de la femme chinoise, pour *impersonnel* qu'il fût, comment n'en aurais-je pas reconnue tous les *traits maintes fois imaginés dans mes rêves* durant toutes ces années d'absence: ce parfait ovale, ce nez fin, ces lèvres sensibles et sensuelles, ce regard profond et limpide. [...] une voix plus mûre, un port plus souverain. (*DT*, 139, my italics)

Yumei was heavily made-up in the traditional theatrical manner, and she wore an ornate headdress. The painted face, which represented the Chinese ideal of feminine beauty, could not have been more *impersonal*; yet I did not fail to recognize all the *features of her long-absent face, so often pictured in my dreams*: the perfect oval, the delicate nose, the sensitive and sensual lips, the clear and penetrating gaze. [...] a more mature voice, a more confident bearing. (*RB*, 93, my italics)

Nevertheless, in the end, it is the genius of the theatrical work of art itself that triumphs: Yumei is 'absorbée dans son rôle' ('absorbed in her role'); Tianyi '[se laisse] absorber, [lui] aussi, par l'histoire, dans l'oubli total de soi' ('too [became] absorbed in the story, forgetting [himself] completely'); and Haolang is 'figé par l'émotion, comme hypnotisé' ('transfixed, almost hypnotized') (ibid.).

5.3.4   Music

Both Proust and Cheng place special emphasis on the *affective* aspect of music. Music's apparent lack of external referent and its absolute self-referentiality somewhat paradoxically endow this medium with a tremendous evocative power to express sentiment and desire, to project natural landscapes, and to be easily infused with other artistic media. In Proust's case, the profound influence of Schopenhauer's philosophical aesthetics—according to which music is the most supreme of all the arts—is undeniable (see Leriche 2004; Henri 1981). In Schopenhauer's own words:

Music is as *immediate* an objectification and copy of the whole Will as the world itself is [...] music is by no means like the other arts, namely a copy of the Ideas, but a *copy of the Will itself*, the objectivity of which are the Ideas. For this reason the effect of music is so very much more powerful and penetrating than is that of the other arts, for these others speak only of the shadow, but music of the essence. (1966, 257, italics in the original)

Music, as Ulrich Pothast further explains, 'needs no translation or explanation whatsoever for being "understood" by everybody' (Pothast 2008, 64).

Without explicitly acknowledging Schopenhauer's philosophy any-
where in Cheng's *œuvre*, Tianyi's initial contact with Western music
nonetheless leaves traces of this Schopenhauerian as well as Proustian
characterization of music. Tianyi first remarks that music enjoys a different mode of transmission: 'si la littérature et la peinture nous étaient
plus ou moins accessibles par la traduction et la reproduction, la musique
nous demeurait quasiment inconnue' ('although literature and painting were accessible to us through translations and reproductions, music
remained virtually unknown') (*DT*, 90; *RB*, 58). The foreign Western
music is not 'translated' to be 'understood' by Tianyi and Haolang, it
directly *intrudes* into their inner sense of being: 'ce premier concert de
notre vie fut d'autant plus mémorable qu'il fut marqué par l'intrusion
inopinée—ou miraculeusement opportune—du Dehors' ('This, the first
concert of our lives, was all the more memorable for its being marked by
the unexpected—or miraculously opportune—intrusion of the Outside')
(ibid.).

What follows then is not only a typical Chengian cross-cultural reflection on this medium of art, but, more importantly, the appreciation of
music analogically expressed through man's bodily relation to the natural
landscape:

[...] tant nous étions exaltés. La musique chinoise, retenue et confi-
dentielle, souvent plaintive, ne nous avait guère habitués à ce chant [*La
Symphonie pastorale de* Beethoven] aux accents si souverains, si con-
quérants. Celui-ci n'accompagne pas la nature; il en *déchire la peau, en
transperce la chair pour en devenir la pulsation même.* Ce que cette symphonie évoque, ce sont certes *les champs de blé et les pâturages de la lointaine Europe.* Comme elle était proche cependant du *battement de cœur* de
ces deux marcheurs perdus dans la nuit de Chine! Répondant à nos pas
cadencés, les *rizières en terrasses, inondées de lune, bruyantes de coassements
de grenouilles,* semblaient s'élargir de rond en rond dans un formidable
déploiement rythmique. (*DT*, 91, my italics)

[...] we were too elated. Chinese music, discreet and confidential, often
plaintive, had hardly accustomed us to a song [Beethoven's Pastoral
Symphony] with tones so sovereign, so conquering – one which did not
accompany nature but *tore open its skin, pierced its flesh, to become its very
pulse.* What that symphony evoked of course were the *wheat fields and pas-
tures of far-off Europe.* Yet how akin it was to the measure of our foot-
steps, *the terraced rice fields, bathed in moonlight and noisy with the croaking*

of frogs, seemed to spread out in ever-widening circles with a formidable, rhythmic expansion. (*RB*, 59, my italics)

Moreover, the immediacy of music to the inward human auditory sensation activates cross-cultural imaginings. Music blends freely with other artistic media, without 'translation'. In short, music transcends cultural boundaries:

> Curieusement, cette musique si lointaine, si 'étrangère', me fut d'emblée proche, aussi proche que certains morceaux chinois anciens. Si différence il y avait, c'était sans doute que dans le mouvement lent qui se jouait là, avant chaque retour du motif, il y avait comme un terrible arrachement et du retour fit naître en moi l'image d'un voyageur qui retourne au pays après une long absence, telle qu'elle est maintes fois décrite dans la poésie chinoise. (*DT*, 92)

> Strangely, for me this music from afar, so foreign, was immediately close, as close as some ancient Chinese pieces. If there was indeed a difference, it was probably that in the playing of the slow movement, before each return of the motif there was the sense of a terrible parting, an inconsolable moan. The idea of parting and return gave rise to the image of a traveller returning home after a long absence, such as is so often described in Chinese poetry. (*RB*, 60)

Cheng then goes on to elaborate the topos of *jinxiang qingqie* (近乡情怯)—the complex feelings that come over travellers when they are returning home—many a time articulated in ancient Chinese poetry. As can be seen, what Tianyi's appreciation of music entails is the birth of images and poetry, and more fundamentally, the birth of meaning.

The birth of meaning through music is precisely what marks Proust's devising of 'la petite phrase' ('the little phrase') in *Un Amour de Swann*. This has been most thoroughly explored by Jean-Pierre Richard (1976, 181), as the critic argues:

> Voudra-t-on retrouver, rassemblées en un objet unique, la plupart de ces images de la signification découverte? On songera à la petite phrase de Vinteuil, [...] Voilà bien en effet un objet d'une certaine manière exemplaire puisque [...] il se donne aussi, de par la façon même dont il se manifeste, comme un chiffre, une active figuration de la naissance, et de la naissance du sens.

Will we want to find again most of the images of uncovered meanings which are gathered in a unique object? We think of Vinteuil's little phrase [...] Here is indeed an object of a certain exemplary quality because [...] it also acts, in the very way it expresses itself, like a figure, an active representation of birth, and the birth of meaning. (My translation)

For the purpose of comparison, it would be useful to cite one example (out of many) from *La Recherche* to illustrate Proust's 'landscaped' representation of music, particularly in relation to human desire:

Sous l'agitation des trémolos de violon qui la protégeaient de leur tenue frémissante à deux octaves de là—et *comme dans un pays de montagne, derrière l'immobilité apparente et vertigineuse d'une cascade, on aperçoit, deux cents pieds plus bas, la forme minuscule d'une promeneuse*—la petite phrase venait d'apparaître, lointaine, gracieuse, protégée par le long déferlement du rideau transparent, incessant et sonore. Et Swann, *en son cœur*, s'adressa à elle *comme à une confidente de son amour, comme à une amie d'Odette* [...] (*RTP I*, 260, my italics)

Under the agitation of the violin tremolos protecting it with their quivering extended two octaves above—and *as in a mountainous countryside, behind the apparent and vertiginous immobility of a waterfall one sees, two hundred feet down, the minuscule form of a woman walking*—the little phrase had just appeared, distant, graceful, protected by the long unfurling of its transparent, ceaseless curtain of sound. And Swann, *in his heart, appealed to it as to a confidant of his love, as to a friend of Odette's* [...] (*PT I*, 266–267, my italics)

Similar to Tianyi's poetic imagination inspired by Dvorak's music, the composition of Vinteuil's septet in *La Prisonnière* is described in the language of the visual arts:

[...] c'était le créateur [Vinteuil] qui le conduisait lui-même, puisant dans *les couleurs* qu'il venait de trouver une joie éperdue qui lui donnait la puissance de découvrir, [...] comme au choc d'une étincelle quand le sublime naissait de lui-même [...] tandis qu'il *peignait sa grande fresque musicale*, comme *Michel-Ange attaché à son échelle et lançant, la tête en bas, de tumultueux coups de brosse au plafond de la chapelle Sixtine*. (*RTP III*, 759, my italics)

[...] it was the creator [Vinteuil] who led him on himself, drawing from *the colours* as he found them a wild joy which gave him the power to press on, to discover [...] as if at a spark when sublimity sprang spontaneously [...] *like Michelangelo tied to his ladder and, head down, flinging tumultuous brushstrokes at the ceiling of the Sistine Chapel.* (*PT III*, 233–234, my italics)

Elsewhere Vinteuil's music also constantly evokes Elstir's painting (*RTP III*, 762; *PT V*, 237).

Music's evocative power reaches its apotheosis when it is identified with beloved ones. While Swann 'en son cœur, s'adressa à elle [Vinteuil's little phrase] comme à une confidente de son amour' ('appealed to it [Vinteuil's little phrase] as to a confidant of his love, as to a friend of Odette's') (*RTP I*, 260; *PT I*, 267), Tianyi, listening to Dvorak's music, cannot help but think of the three women in his life: 'l'écoutant, je me laissais porter par la vague d'émotion, celle qui me faisait sentir que d'un instant à l'autre j'allais retrouver les êtres chers qui m'attendaient: ma mère, ma sœur, l'Amante...' ('Listening, I was carried on the music's wave of emotion, which made me feel that at any moment I would be reunited with the loved ones who waited: my mother, my sister, the Lover...') (*DT*, 92; *RB*, 60). Later, in Paris, it is also when listening to Pierre Fournier's interpretation of Dvorak's concerto that Tianyi encounters his 'second love', the clarinettist Véronique. Swann falls in love with 'the little phrase' and then with Odette—only through his subsequent identification of the latter with the former. Likewise, Tianyi's desire for Véronique is first motivated by his enthusiasm for music concerts. Before saying goodbye to Véronique after their first meeting, Véronique hands Tianyi 'un prospectus annonçant un concert de musique de chambre auquel elle participerait' ('an announcement for a chamber music concert in which she was to play'). On the way home, a naissant desire takes place in Tianyi: 'lorsque par hasard je plongeai la main dans ma poche et que je touchai le bout de papier plié, j'éprouvai au bout des doigts une douceur intime, proche du ravissement, un délice si intense qu'il me traversa le cœur comme un jet de feu' ('When I would put my hand in my pocket and touch the folded sheet, through my fingertips I felt a special sweetness, close to rapture, a delight so intense that it went through my heart like a burst of flame') (*DT*, 258; *RB*, 179). But it is not exactly a desire for Véronique, because when Tianyi tries to remember Véronique's face on the same evening, 'le visage recherché devenait flou' ('[the face I sought became] indistinct') (*DT*, 259; *RB*, 179). Reminiscent of Swann's frequent visits to the Verdurins' in order to see Odette, the concert hall becomes *the* meeting point where Tianyi and Véronique find their 'amitié amoureuse', as Tianyi 'pri[t] l'habitude d'assister à tous ses concerts et de la raccompagner' ('would attend all her concerts and escort her home') (*DT*, 260–261; *RB*, 180).

An aesthetic as well as conceptual affinity between Proust and Cheng has become more and more evident: the enchanting, sentimental—and irrational?—quality intrinsic to music seems to be particularly identified with the feminine. Proust thus describes Swann's perception of 'the little phrase':

> Il y a dans le violon [...] des accents qui lui sont si communs avec certaines voix de *contralto*, qu'on a l'illusion qu'une *chanteuse* s'est ajoutée au concert. [...] mais, par moments, on est encore trompé par l'appel décevant de la *sirène*; parfois aussi on croit entendre un génie captif [...] (*RTP I*, 341, my italics)

> There are tones in a violin [...] so similar to those of certain contralto voices that we have the illusion a *[female] singer* has been added to the concert. [...] but at times we are still fooled by the deceptive call of the *siren*; at times too we think we hear a captive genie struggling deep inside [...] (*PT I*, 349, my italics)

The 'feminine mystery' is further enhanced by the mythological reference to the aquatic woman in this passage, which, as Richard (1976, 187) astutely points out, is linked to 'la ligne de plusieurs séries thématiques très actives' ('the line of several very active thematic series') in *La Recherche*:

> Ainsi la série des poissons (poisson-souvenir sous l'herbe de Méséglise), des poissons-femmes (dîneuses de Rivebelle), des poissons offerts par des femmes (la belle pêcheuse de Carqueville); ou la série encore de l'émergence maritime (corps féminin sorti de la vague, tout comme en sortent aussi des phrases mélodiques: ainsi dans le concert sur le quai de Balbec); ou la série du retrait, de l'appel lointain et séducteur (ainsi, et encore, notre petite phrase dans le tableau de Pieter de Hooch). Revoici surgir enfin, lié à la sirène, tout le groupe des êtres incarcérés et des âmes captives.

> In this way, the fish series (fish-memory with the herbs of Méséglise), the series of fish-women (female diners at Rivebelle), and that of women

offering fish (the beautiful fisherwoman of Carqueville); or the series of
the feminine figures emerging at the seashore (feminine body coming out
of the waves, just as melodic phrases come into being: in the concert on
the quay at Balbec, for instance); or the series of retreats, of distant and
seductive calling (our little phrase in Peter de Hooch's painting, for example). Here again is the sudden appearance, linked to the siren, of the entire
group of incarcerated beings and captive souls. (My translation)

Tianyi questionably relates his 'musical' episode with Véronique to the
possibility of a fundamental understanding of a feminine being: 'com-
bien déjà, à la lumière de cet épisode et de l'expérience d'une vie com-
mune, je mesurais la difficulté qu'il y avait à toucher la vraie profondeur
d'un autre, a fortiori un autre féminin' ('But how can I be sure? In the
light of that incident and of our life together, I could already gauge the
difficulty of touching the real depths of another, a fortiori, another who
is woman'). Rather coincidentally, Tianyi's appreciation of Véronique's
music also ends with the aquatic image of an abandoned child listening
to a woman's song by the sea:

L'homme taraudé par le fini, s'échine à rejoindre la femme, envahie par
l'infini, sans jamais y parvenir. Il lui reste à demeurer cet enfant aban-
donné qui pleure au bord de l'océan. L'homme s'apaiserait s'il consentait
à écouter seulement la musique qui résonne là, en lui et hors de lui –
d'écouter humblement la femme devenue un chant trop nostalgique pour
être accessible. (*DT*, 265)

The man—nagged by the finite—struggles to connect with the woman—
assailed by the infinite—without ever succeeding. He remains an abandoned child weeping beside the sea. The man would be soothed were he
willing to listen to the music echoing there, inside and outside him—to listen humbly to the woman become a song too nostalgic to be within reach.
(*RB*, 183)

There is no explicit mythological reference in this passage, but it should
be pointed out that Cheng's association of men with the finite and
women with the infinite is nevertheless informed by the Daoist *yin-yang*
configuration of sexuality. The 'Mysterious Female' or the 'Esoteric
Feminine' is a key theme in Chap. 6 of *Laozi*, and in the *Book of Changes*,
water, one of the Five Elements (*wuxing*, 五行), is classified as *yin* and
feminine *par excellence*.[29]

Despite the Daoist influence on Cheng's vision of the world, Cheng's true religion is art, and this is a vital aspect of Cheng's spiritual connection to Proust. The religion of art in Proust has been most thoroughly explored by Barbara J. Bucknall (1969). My analysis has focused on aspects of Cheng's artistic discourses that 'speak to' Proustian spirituality. Throughout the analysis, we have seen a thought-provoking convergence of cross-cultural ideas of art and literature in Cheng's work. Proust's *La Recherche* is a point of departure from which Cheng constructs his own model of intercultural communication. Perhaps Cheng reorients the artistic aspect of Proustian spirituality further, in the sense that he understands the highest and most sacred achievement of art as creating 'dialogues'—dialogues between cultures, art and nature, the self and others—aiming at 'transcendence' and universal harmony.

Bucknall, in the last three chapters of her book, moves on from the examination of individual artistic media to that of religious language, belief, and structure in Proust. She even extends her discussion of Proust's religion of art to elements of Eastern thought, notably Buddhism, in her final chapter. Our next section follows a similar line of enquiry, exploring Cheng's mythical or mythological engagement with Western traditions epitomized in Proust's work.

5.4   WRITING AND REWRITING THE MYTH

Cheng's intention to devise a mythological structure for *Le Dit* is self-evident. The tripartite narrative—departure, 'detour', and return—is not only reminiscent of such Homeric epics as the *Odyssey*, it is also meant to reflect the *ternary* system fundamental in the Daoist, and to a certain extent, Confucian cosmogonies. Cheng, in the interview appended to the Chinese translation of *Le Dit*, clarifies: 'Chinese thought is ternary, for example, the Confucian tenet of "sky-earth-man", the Taoist "Yin-Yang-Qi"' ('中国思想体系是三元的, 比如儒家的"天地人", 道家的"阴阳充气') (*TY*, 317). He elsewhere cites the Daoist classic text *Laozi* to highlight the significance of the number 'three':

The original Tao gives birth to the one.
The one gives birth to the two.
The two gives birth to the three.
The three produces the ten thousand existents.[30]

Apart from the structure, explicit references to both Chinese and Western myths and folklore permeate *Le Dit*. Cheng is attracted to comparative mythology, especially because the universal and symbolic dimensions of myths, often unbound by time and space, nurture his ambition for cultural transcendence, as Pierre Albouy (1969, 10, my translation, italics in the original) comments: 'les mythes offrent ainsi des images particulièrement riches des *situations* qui se retrouvent dans toute société humaine, ils fournissent encore les images idéales des individus qui affrontent et dénouent ces situations et qui sont les *héros*' ('myths thus offer particularly rich images and *situations* which are found in all human societies, they additionally provide ideal images of individuals, the *heroes*, who confront and resolve those situations').

Proust's passion for myths and mythologies needs no more proof. It is a field of Proust Studies that has been under close scrutiny for many decades and continues to fascinate Proust scholars today.[31] However, perhaps with the exception of *The Arabian Nights*, Proust's mythological references—encyclopaedic though they are—are almost exclusively drawn from the Western heritage (i.e. Greco-Roman, Judeo-Christian, and medieval traditions). This is precisely where Cheng's 'twofold' mythological engagement with Proust comes into full operation, where his literary aesthetic of reorientation and *rapprochement* manifests itself. The following analysis will first focus on Cheng's writing and rewriting of the mythological elements found in the prologue of *La Recherche* and then compare Cheng's and Proust's respective treatments of the theme of Orpheus. Once again, Proust is Cheng's aesthetic departure rather than destination. Cheng does not engage with Proust's individual mythological references per se; rather, they constitute a literary model that reformulates and reincarnates established Western myths, a model which Cheng conveniently adapts to accommodate Chinese myths.

5.4.1   Prologue

It is not the first time in this book that we have studied the attempt to imitate or rewrite (at least elements of) the prologue of *La Recherche*. We have explored in Part I Chap. 3 Yu's stylistic and thematic appropriations of Proust's prologue and discussed how Yu's perception of Proust's work, like Wang's and Wei's, is decidedly influenced by André Maurois's preface, which considers time and memory to be the two central themes of *La Recherche*. In comparison, Cheng's engagement with the prologue demonstrates his additional awareness of the deeper mythological structure that permeates Proust's work.

Le Dit begins with a sentence that carries biblical overtones: 'au commencement il y eut ce cri dans la nuit' ('in the beginning there was the cry in the night') (*DT*, 15; *RB*, 3). Cheng turns the biblical 'void' and 'darkness' on earth into a cry in the night, which takes on other overtones accordingly. As mentioned before, Cheng's special emphasis on a primordial *sound* is connected to his association between *voie* and *voix*, which corresponds to the double signification of the Chinese 'Dao' referring both to 'the way' and 'to say' (and hence 'le *dit* de Tianyi').[32] More subtly, sound declares the existence of the soul. In Cheng's prologue, 'ce cri' ('this cry'), like an incantation, 'une sorte de mélopée à mots répétés' ('a kind of repetitive chant') with 'échos immémoriaux' ('immemorial echoes'), is chanted by the widow to call upon the wandering soul of her husband (ibid.). In fact, the soul exists *as* sound for Cheng, as he writes elsewhere: 'une voix vient nous murmurer à l'oreille que pourtant l'âme pose problème, puisque d'aucuns nient tout simplement son existence! [...] Se faire entendre et résonner, c'est sa manière d'*être*' ('a voice rises to whisper in our ear that the soul poses a problem nevertheless, since there are some who simply deny its existence! [...] To make itself heard, to resonate, is its manner of *being*') (2008, 56; 2009, 48). Significantly, Cheng cites the phrase from Rainer Maria Rilke's *Les Sonnets à Orphée*, 'Chanter, c'est être' ('To sing is to be') (ibid.).[33] Thus, the theme of Orpheus is subtly implied on the first page of the novel. Although Cheng's incipit itself sounds hardly Proustian, Proust does mention the biblical story of Adam and Eve on the first pages of *La Recherche*: 'quelquefois, comme Ève naquit d'une côte d'Adam, une femme naissait pendant mon sommeil d'une fausse position de ma cuisse' ('sometimes, as Eve was born from one of Adam's ribs, a woman was born during my sleep from a cramped position of my thigh') (*RTP I*, 4; *PT I*, 8). Incidentally, this mysterious and ambiguous feminine presence in the prologue is a feature shared by Proust's, Cheng's, and Yu's works.

Cheng's elaboration on the Chinese ritual, namely the reincarnation of the 'âme errante' ('wandering soul') echoes Proust's protagonist's mention of the 'métempsychose' ('metempsychosis') on the first page of *La Recherche*, as well as his imagination of the Celtic belief towards the end of the prologue. Without knowing the ritual taking place next door, Tianyi light-heartedly answers the summoning voice, 'Oui, je viens; oui, je viens' ('Yes, I'm coming, I'm coming'), which angers the adults

of the family, who shout at Tianyi and his sister, 'Tais-toi! Tais-toi! [...]
Couchez-vous maintenant! On vous croyait déjà au lit!' ('Be quiet, child,
be quiet! [...] You two, get to bed now! We thought you were already
asleep!') (*DT*, 16; *RB*, 3). The act of answering that voice results in the
transmigration of souls:

> La bougie une fois éteinte, dans le noir, je ne trouvai pas le sommeil. Je
> réussis à capter quelques paroles échangées entre les grandes personnes, à
> travers lesquelles je finis par saisir à peu près ce qui était en jeu. La femme
> qui criait venait de perdre son mari. Cette nuit, elle appelait l'âme errante
> du mort afin que celle-ci ne s'égarât pas. Selon le rituel, après avoir brûlé
> des papiers-monnaies destinés aux morts, au moment précis de la troisième
> veille, la veuve commence son appel. Si par hasard quelqu'un d'entre les
> vivants répond 'oui' à cet appel, il perd son corps dans lequel s'introduit
> l'âme errante du mort, lequel, du coup, réintègre le monde vivant. Tandis
> que l'âme de celui qui perd ainsi son corps devient errante à son tour. Elle
> erre jusqu'à ce qu'elle trouve un autre corps pour se réincarner. [...] Et
> moi, je me voyais perdant mon corps, déjà mort! (*DT*, 16)

> After the candle had been blown out, I lay awake in the dark. I man-
> aged to catch some of the adults' conversation, and from it I understood
> more or less what was at stake. The woman crying out had just lost her
> husband. That night she called to his wandering soul so it would not go
> astray. According to the ritual, after burning paper money for the dead,
> the widow calls out just as the third watch begins. If by chance someone
> among the living answers her cry with a yes, he loses his body, which is
> quickly entered by the dead man's wandering soul that then returns to the
> world of the living. And the soul of the one thus losing his body becomes
> in turn the wanderer and wanders until finding another body for its rein-
> carnation. Soon I heard the voices of the adults again, reassuring one
> another: 'But an innocent reply does not count!' 'How can they feel reas-
> sured?' I wondered. As for me, I saw myself already dead, losing my body!
> (*RB*, 3–4)

The first sentence of the quoted passage is evocative of Proust's protagonist's situation in the prologue of *La Recherche*: 'à peine ma bou-
gie éteinte [...] la pensée qu'il était temps de chercher le sommeil
m'éveillait' ('my candle scarcely out [...] the thought that it was time to
try to sleep would wake me') (*RTP I*, 3; *PT I*, 7). The protagonist later
ascribes his initial unintelligible experience of metempsychosis to the
Celtic belief as follows:

Je trouve très raisonnable la croyance celtique que les âmes de ceux que nous avons perdus sont captives dans quelque être inférieur, dans une bête, un végétal, une chose inanimée, perdues en effet pour nous jusqu'au jour, qui pour beaucoup ne vient jamais, où nous nous trouvons passer près de l'arbre, entrer en possession de l'objet qui est leur prison. Alors elles tressaillent, nous appellent, et sitôt que nous les avons reconnues, l'enchantement est brisé. Délivrées par nous, elles ont vaincu la mort et reviennent vivre avec nous. (*RTP I*, 43–44)

I find the Celtic belief very reasonable, that the souls of those we have lost are held captive in some inferior creature, in an animal, in a plant, in some inanimate thing, effectively lost to us until today, which for many never comes, when we happen to pass close to the tree, come into possession of the object that is their prison. Then they quiver, they call out to us, and as soon as we have recognized them, the spell is broken. Delivered by us, they have overcome death and they return to live with us. (*PT I*, 47)

The Chinese superstition and the Celtic belief may seem, at first glance, worlds apart. A close examination does however reveal that Cheng's and Proust's accounts share a similar 'pattern' of perception and conception. In both ritualistic accounts, the soul calls upon us and requires an answer or recognition, so that it can return from the world of the dead to that of the living. The two souls—one lost and wandering and the other lost and incarcerated—are examples of transmigration. Just like the infant Tianyi's conviction of his own death, Proust's protagonist later observes in retrospect: 'depuis mon enfance j'étais déjà mort bien des fois' ('since my childhood I had already died a number of times') (*RTP IV*, 615; *PT VI*, 347).

Both protagonists palpably feel and experience the separation between the soul and the body. Tianyi sees himself losing his own body ('Et moi, je me voyais perdant mon corps, déjà mort!'/'As for me, I saw myself already dead, losing my body!') and concludes at the end of the prologue:

Je me sentis tout d'un coup étranger à moi-même: j'avais conscience que mon corps antérieur avait été pris par quelqu'un, et ce corps étendu là, presque inerte, que je pouvais éventuellement tâter de la main, était celui d'un autre, auquel mon âme s'était, coûte que coûte, accrochée. [...] c'était une âme égarée qui logeait comme elle pouvait dans un corps

d'emprunt. Tout chez moi, depuis, sera toujours décalé. Jamais les choses
ne pourront coïncider tout à fait. (*DT*, 17)

But suddenly I felt a stranger to myself. I was aware that my previous body
had been taken by someone; what lay on the bed nearly inert—and could
perhaps be felt with my hand—was another person's body, to which my
soul had attached itself, come what may. [...] [it was] a stray soul dwelling
in any body it could borrow. I was convinced that from then on everything
in me would be perpetually out of joint. Things would never match up
perfectly. (*RB*, 4–5)

The stray or wandering soul adds to our understanding of Cheng's
description of the writing process of *Le Dit* as a 'spiritual journey' in the
Chinese preface.[34]

Similarly, Proust's protagonist also puts special emphasis on the dis-
cordance between his 'esprit'/'pensée' and his body.[35] While his mind in
half-sleep travels 'à toute vitesse dans le temps et dans l'espace' ('at top
speed through time and space') (*RTP I*, 5; *PT I*, 9), his body is confined
to a room and surrounded by furniture:

Mon esprit s'agitant pour chercher, sans y réussir, à savoir où j'étais, tout
tournait autour de moi dans l'obscurité, les choses, les pays, les années.
Mon corps, trop engourdi pour remuer, cherchait, [...] à repérer la position
de ses membres pour en induire la direction du mur, la place des meubles,
pour reconstruire et pour nommer la demeure où *il* se trouvait. (*RTP I*, 6,
my italics)

My mind restlessly attempting, without success, to discover where I was,
everything revolved around me in the darkness, things, countries, years.
My body, too benumbed to move, would try to locate [...] the position of
its limbs in order to deduce from this the direction of the wall, the location
of the furniture, in order to reconstruct and name the dwelling in which it
found itself. (*PT I*, 10, my italics)

The protagonist continues to address his body in third person as though
it were a different entity: '*sa* mémoire, la mémoire de *ses* côtes, de *ses*
genoux, de *ses* épaules, *lui* présentait successivement plusieurs des chambres où *il* avait dormi, tandis qu'autour de *lui* les murs invisibles, [...]
lui, – *mon corps*, – se rappelait pour chacun le genre du lit' ('*its* memory, the memory of *its* ribs, *its* knees, *its* shoulders, offered in succession

several of the rooms where *it* had slept, while around *it* the invisible
walls [...] *it—my body*—would recall the kind of bed in each one') (ibid.,
my italics).

The image of 'childhood terror'—a point we have already treated in
relation to Yu's appropriation of Proust's prologue—is resurrected in
both Proust's and Cheng's accounts. Proust's protagonist remarks:

> J'avais rejoint sans effort un âge à jamais révolu de ma vie primitive,
> retrouvé telle de mes terreurs enfantines comme celle que mon grand-
> oncle me tirât par mes boucles et qu'avait dissipée le jour—date pour moi
> d'une ère nouvelle—où on les avait coupées. (*RTP I*, 4)

> I had effortlessly returned to a for ever vanished period of my early life,
> rediscovered one of my childish terrors such as that my great-uncle would
> pull me by my curls, a terror dispelled on the day—the dawn for me of a
> new era—when they were cut off. (*PT I*, 8)

The terror of being forced to have one's hair pulled is transformed into
that of having one's *head* cut in *Le Dit*, as Tianyi associates his own
'transmigrated' death with his previous experience of witnessing the capi-
tal execution of a 'revolutionary bandit': 'j'apprenais déjà, à ce moment-
là, qu'il ne fallait surtout pas se laisser mordre par la tête fraîchement
coupée. Car celui qui est mordu remplacera le mort; il mourra et le mort
reviendra vivant' ('I had learnt that one must at all costs avoid being bitten by a freshly severed head. For anyone so bitten replaces the deceased
and will die, while the dead man shall rejoin the living') (*DT*, 16–17;
RB, 4).

The significance of Proust's evocation of the Celtic belief in the
prologue is often overlooked, probably because there is only one such
occurrence in the entire novel and therefore a lack of cross references
to suggest Proust's deeper engagement with Celtic myths. However, as
Miguet-Ollagnier (1982, 268) points out, this Celtic reference, despite
its singular occurrence, is consistently present in all versions of the madeleine passage, and the legend is similarly presented in *Contre Sainte-
Beuve* without being specifically qualified as 'Celtic':

> Il y a là [...] un 'fonds invariable' de la pensée proustienne car depuis le
> 8ᵉ cahier, dans toutes les rédactions de l'épisode de la madeleine (d'abord
> pain grillé) nous trouvons mentionnée la croyance en l'âme captive en

un objet matériel. La préface du *Contre Sainte-Beuve* la présente de cette façon sans faire référence à un corpus de croyances celtiques.[36]

There is [...] an 'invariable cultural heritage' in Proust's reflections, as since *Cahier 8*, in all the drafts of the madeleine (initally toast) episode, we find mentioned the belief in a soul being incacerated in a material object being. The preface to *Contre Sainte-Beuve* also introduced this belief in such a way without making any reference to works on Celtic belief. (My translation)

There is more at stake than finding out whether Proust is a great lover of Celtic culture.[37] Firstly, this Celtic myth offers a valuable system of belief, a form of ritual that *complements* Proust's aesthetic foundation (Topping 2007, 118). It elucidates the strong sense of animism in the protagonist's perception of the aestheticized object, which we have explored in earlier sections. The acknowledgement of the soul trapped in the tree echoes the protagonist's later observation of the brightened lines and surfaces of the Martinville steeples: 'comme si elles avaient été *une sorte d'écorce*, se déchirèrent, un peu de ce qui m'était caché en elles m'*apparut*' ('as if they were *a sort of bark*, a little of what was hidden from me inside them *appeared to me*') (*RTP I*, 178; *PT I*, 181, my italics). We can now understand that which is hidden behind the aestheticized object as a soul, and the protagonist's vocation not as God's 'calling' but that of a soul who communicates with his own. Thus, what 'appears' to the writer-to-be protagonist is not just the *appearance* of things but, more importantly, their *apparitions* which, as the myth recounts, after having been recognized by us ('sitôt que nous les avons reconnues'/'as soon as we have recognized them'), come back to life ('reviennent vivre avec nous'/'return to live with us')—as a work of art, 'la vraie vie' ('real life').

Secondly, situated right before an essential passage of *La Recherche*—that of the *Petites Madeleines*—this Celtic myth serves as a mythical analogy to Proust's theory of involuntary memory:

Il en est *ainsi* de notre passé. C'est peine perdue que nous cherchions à l'évoquer, tous les efforts de notre intelligence sont inutiles. Il est caché hors de son domaine et de sa portée, en quelque objet matériel (en la sensation que nous donnerait cet objet matériel), que nous ne soupçonnons pas. Cet objet, il dépend du hasard que nous le rencontrions avant de mourir, ou que nous ne le rencontrions pas. (*RTP I*, 44, my italics)

It is *the same* with our past. It is a waste of effort for us to try to summon it, all the exertions of our intelligence are useless. The past is hidden outside the realm of our intelligence and beyond its reach, in some material object (in the sensation that this material object would give us) which we do not suspect. It depends on the chance whether we encounter this object before we die, or do not encounter it. (*PT I*, 47, my italics)

The 'lost' time and memory may be 'dead', but are they 'mort à jamais' ('dead forever') as the protagonist asks himself? '[C]'était possible. Il y a beaucoup de hasard en tout ceci' ('There is a great deal of chance in all this') (*RTP I*, 43; *PT I*, 46–47). They are like the lost soul; one has to listen to their 'calling' to resurrect them, and such resurrection—in Proust's metaphorical handling of the myth—leads to the creation of artworks—in this instance, the protagonist's book-to-come. However, one may never encounter any lost soul, because 'un second hasard, celui de notre mort, souvent ne nous permet pas d'attendre longtemps les faveurs du premier' ('a second sort of chance, that of our death, often does not let us wait very long for the favours of the first') (ibid.). This is a very important detail, since the protagonist, towards the very end of *La Recherche*, is finally urged to write his book precisely at his realization of everyone's aging in time as well as his own mortality. The protagonist's book-to-come is compared to 'un monument druidique au sommet d'une île' ('a druidic monument on the high point of an island') (*RTP IV*, 618; *PT VI*, 350) on these final pages of the novel, echoing again the Celtic reference at the beginning.

Finally, Proust engages with this particular Celtic myth because of its commonality with other beliefs and rituals that he evokes in *La Recherche*, notably Orphism, featuring also metempsychosis and the transmigration of souls. Indeed, Proust's quasi-architectonic engagement with the myth of Orpheus is so profound that it leads Albouy (1976, 345) to call Proust's protagonist's vocational realization a 'schéma orphique' ('Orphic pattern'), and Aubert (2002, 109) to define Proust as an 'écrivain orphique' ('Orphic writer'). If seeing the inherent structure of *La Recherche*, on both microcosmic and macrocosmic levels, as essentially mythical or Orphic relies on certain scholars' informed hypotheses,[38] Cheng's (2002, my translation) enthusiasm for the myth of Orpheus is self-confessed and it is certainly an important aspect of his 'Proustian approach', as he comments: 'Orphée, le poète à la lyre, ordonne par son incantation le mouvement des rochers, des arbres et des animaux et, par là même, insère le destin de l'homme dans l'ordre de la Création' ('Orpheus, the poet with the lyre, through his incantations ordains the movement of rocks, trees, and animals, whereby he attaches the destiny of man to the order of Creation'). The myth of Orpheus is emblematic of the structures of both *Le Dit* and *La Recherche*.

5.4.2   Myth of Orpheus

Central to the myth of Orpheus is this legendary musician and poet's descent to the underworld to retrieve his wife, Eurydice. The 'schematic' connection between this myth and *La Recherche* is best encapsulated in Pierre Albouy's (1976, 383, my italics) words as follows, where he singles out three key episodes of *La Recherche* that share the same dynamic process of literary creation:

> Marcel, en devenant écrivain, utilise le langage comme moyen d'une création mythique; l'écriture est création mythique. L'épisode des arbres est à mettre aussi en rapport avec celui de la madeleine; alors que l'épisode des clochers insiste sur le rôle de l'écriture dans la transfiguration mythique qui pourvoie les objets d'une essence (qui est leur secret), l'épisode de la madeleine met en lumière l'expérience existentielle qui correspond à cette découverte du secret des choses. Or, si l'on relit les pages fameuses où il est raconté comment la madeleine évoque des profondeurs Combray mort et ramené à la vie, on y découvre, de nouveau, *les images, la thématique, la structure orphiques qui caractérisent la mythologie proustienne: images d'une 'grande profondeur', de 'distances traversées', de la 'nuit' dont on remonte difficilement; bref, on nous suggère une descente aux enfers et la remontée d'Eurydice.* En rapprochant les trois épisodes parents de la madeleine, des clochers de Martinville et des arbres de Balbec, nous sommes amené à conclure que la création littéraire chez Proust—ou, pour mieux dire, l'écriture—constitue une *aventure orphique,* laquelle nous fournit la structure dominante de *la Recherche.*

In becoming a writer, Marcel uses language as a means of mythic creation; writing is creating myths. The episode of the trees is put in relation to that of the madeleine. While the episode of the Martinville steeples insists on the role of writing in the mythical transfiguration that endows objects with an essence (which is their secret), the madeleine episode illuminates the existential experience that corresponds to the discovery of the secret of things. If we just reread the famous pages which describe how the madeleine evokes from depths a dead Combrary brought back to life, we discover there, again, *Orphic images, thematics, and structure which characterize Proustian mythology: images of a 'great depth', of 'distances travelled', of the 'night' from which we try to get away with difficulty; in short, these passages suggest a descent to Hell and the return of Eurydice.* By bringing the three related episodes together (i.e. the madeleine, the Martinville steeples, and the trees of Balbec), we can come to the conclusion that literary creation in Proust—or, put in a better way, writing—constitues *an Orphic adventure* which gives us the dominant structure of *La Recherche*. (My translation)

Out of these three key episodes, we have extensively studied one (the Martinville steeples) and touched upon one other (the Celtic myth leading to the madeleine passage), and our findings are consistent with Albouy's observation.

Largely developing Albouy's strong line of enquiry, Miguet-Ollagnier (1982, 87–88) exhaustively examines the Proustian reincarnations of the myth of Orpheus, especially in her chapter 'Les Mythes de la remontée à la lumière' ('The Myths of Ascent to Light'). She convincingly argues for the identifications of Swann/Orpheus and Odette/Eurydice, lost in a dark and infernal Paris that is sometimes explicitly mistaken for the Tartarus in Book Four of *Georgics*, and how Proust in *Un amour de Swann* effectively transforms Parisian figures into the mythical ones found in Virgil's poem. Similar mythical identifications, between the protagonist and Orpheus on the one hand and Albertine and Eurydice on the other, are also found in *Albertine disparue* (*The Fugitive*) (ibid., 273). Furthermore, Proust accentuates the *sonorous* aspect of the myth, particularly in the episode of the telephone call with the protagonist's grandmother. 'Le téléphone accomplit' ('The telephone performs'), as Albouy (1976, 345) puts it, 'le mystère orphique de l'évocation des absents, des êtres lointains comme le sont les morts' ('the Orphic mystery of calling up the absent ones, the distant beings such as the dead'). Not only does Proust's description of the grandmother's voice imply the ascent from or descent to the underworld ('il m'a semblé que cette voix clamait des profondeurs d'où l'on ne remonte pas'/'I have felt that the voice was crying out to me from depths from which it would never emerge again') (*RTP II*, 432; *PT III*, 130), it culminates in the protagonist's exclamation, 'Grand'mère, grand'mère' ('Grandmother! Grandmother!'), after the sudden disconnection of the phone call, which finds a distinct echo in Virgil's 'Eurydice, Eurydice'. Orpheus

is explicitly referred to, for that matter: 'il me semblait que c'était déjà
une ombre chérie que je venais de laisser se perdre parmi les ombres,
et seul devant l'appareil, je continuais à répéter en vain: "Grand-mère,
grand-mère", comme Orphée resté seul, répète le nom de la morte' ('I
felt as though it was already a beloved ghost that I had just allowed to
disappear into the world of shadows, and standing there alone in front of
the telephone I went on vainly calling: "Grandmother! Grandmother!"
like the abandoned Orpheus repeating the name of his dead wife') (*RTP
II*, 434; *PT III*, 132). As Miguet-Ollagnier (1982, 278, my translation)
further comments: 'la présence de la voix, séparée de l'être physique,
donne au narrateur-Orphée, à la fois la joie de ramener Eurydice et la
frustration déchirante de ne pouvoir pas regarder, toucher, embrasser la
femme aimée' ('the presence of the voice, separated from the physical
being, gives the narrator-Orpheus, at the same time the joy to bring back
Eurydice and the harrowing frustration of not being able to to see, to
touch, and to kiss the beloved woman'). This phrase is reminiscent of
Tianyi's last oral communication with l'Amante: 'Yumei, Yumei, accep-
tons la terrible épreuve de la séparation. Nous nous retrouverons. Nous
nous sommes déjà retrouvés, à jamais retrouvés' ('Yumei, Yumei, let us
accept the terrible ordeal of separation. We shall find each other. We have
already found each other, found each other for all time') (*DT*, 187; *RB*,
127). This connection between *la voix sonore* (the sonorous voice) and *la
voie mythique* (the mythical way) would be of further interest to Cheng.

The 'Orphic pattern' applies to *Le Dit* too. Just as the Orphic myth
can be linked to the Celtic belief in *La Recherche*, Cheng explicitly relates
it to the Buddhist legend of Mulian: 'tout comme lors de la mort de ma
mère, je pense à la légende bouddhique qui relate les séjours de Mulian
en enfer. A cette légende vient d'ailleurs se mêler le mythe d'Orphée
appris en Europe' ('just as when my mother died, I think of the Buddhist
legend of Mulian in hell. Mixed into it now is a European legend, that of
Orpheus') (*DT*, 275; *RB*, 191).[39] Elsewhere in his essays, Cheng (2002,
my translation) compares the *voix/voie* (voice/way) of Orpheus to that
of Chan Buddhism more broadly:

[…] il y a donc deux voix/voies auxquelles je me suis référé, celle du *chan*
et celle d'Orphée. Quelle que puisse être la différence qui les sépare, je
crois déceler un point commun qui les unit: toutes deux impliquent de la
part de celui qui chante qu'il subisse le passage d'une 'néantisation'.

[...] there are therefore two kinds of voice/way (*voix/voie*) that I referred to, the one of Chan and the other of Orphism. Whatever the difference that separates them, I think I see a shared feature that unites them: both of them imply, on the part of the singing teller, that one has to undergo the passage of a certain 'nihilation'.

As far as the macrocosmic structure is concerned, the theme of the descent to and return from the underworld features in each part of the novel. In fact, the preface, written by a different narrator who claims to know Tianyi personally, already paves the way for such a thematic development. The narrator decides to visit Tianyi in a 'special' care home in post-Cultural Revolution China. After returning to France, the narrator himself suffers from grave illness and is at death's door. But awaking from a surgical operation, he is surprised to 'rediscover' himself 'living'. The narrator, as if 'indebted' to Tianyi, undertakes the task of 'restituer' ('putting together') Tianyi's life story and 'le transposer en français' ('[rendering] it into French') (*DT*, 11; *RB*, xii). It seems that the composition of the narrative itself has something to do with the transmigration of Tianyi's soul, as previously discussed in relation to Proust's mention of metempsychosis and the Celtic belief on the first page of *La Recherche*.

Towards the end of Part One, after learning of his mother's death in Tchoungking (described as 'une fournaise infernale'/'a hellish furnace'), Tianyi continues to describe his 'voyage de Lanzhou à Tchoungking dans la chaleur et la poussière' ('journey from Lanzhou to Tchoungking in the heat and the dust') as 'une longue descente aux enfers' ('a long descent into the underworld') (*DT*, 181–182; *RB*, 123). At the beginning of Part Two, perhaps more relevant to Proust's Orphic reference in *Un amour de Swann*, Tianyi recounts his initial experience of Paris as another descent to Hell (until he has encountered 'un visage féminin, [...] être qui sache [lui] sourire'/'a woman's face, [...] someone who could make [him] smile') (*DT*, 256; *RB*, 178):

> Oui, j'apprendrai à aimer cette ville où je vais vivre un certain temps. J'apprendrai à aimer ce pays qui se trouve au cœur de l'Europe occidentale. Ce sera une longue initiation. En attendant, il faut passer—je le pressens, je le sais déjà—par le purgatoire, sinon par l'enfer. (*DT*, 196)

> Yes, I would learn to love this city where I was to live for a time. I would learn to love this country in the heart of Western Europe. But it would be

a long initiation. While waiting—and I felt it, I knew it already—I would
have to pass through purgatory, if not through hell. (*RB*, 135)

Elsewhere in Part Two, Tianyi infrequently evokes 'cet enfer parisien'
('the Parisian hell') (*DT*, 256; *RB*, 178). At the beginning of the final
part, Tianyi remarks: 'retrouver l'Amante! [...] Je sais que retourner en
cette Chine dénaturée que je ne reconnaîtrai plus, ce sera pour moi une
véritable descente aux enfers' ('to rejoin the Lover! [...] I know that
returning to an altered, unrecognizable China will be a veritable descent
into hell') (*DT*, 275; *RB*, 191). Towards the end, after Tianyi eventually
finds his Ami (Friend) (instead of Amante [Lover])—supposedly already
dead—in Northern China, he says, 'j'accompagne littéralement mon ami
dans sa traversée de l'enfer' ('I am accompanying my friend on his journey through hell') (*DT*, 369; *RB*, 256).

On the microcosmic level, too, the Orphic myth is reflected in intra-
diegetical terms. Just as Orpheus travels as an Argonaut ('sailor of
the Argo') in search of the Golden Fleece, with his lyre being his sole
weapon, Tianyi sails to Europe in search of a certain 'spiritual knowledge', relying on his 'weapon': 'le pouvoir magique du pinceau et de
l'encre' ('the magical power of brush and ink') (*DT*, 23; *RB*, 9). The
suggestion of a search for spiritual knowledge in the West strongly
echoes the idiom *xitian qujin* (西天取经, pilgrimage to the West for
Buddhist Sutra), derived from a significant historical event in the early
Tang dynasty, which is now generally used to mean 'learning from the
West'. In ancient China, 'the West' is generally used to refer to today's
India. For centuries, Chinese Buddhist monks made the pilgrimage
along the Silk Road to the 'Western regions' (*xiyu*, 西域) in order to
obtain sacred Buddhist scriptures. The archaeological site, the Dunhuang
Caves, rediscovered in the twentieth century, where Tianyi is sent by his
Chan master to work briefly, was a major stop on the Silk Road. From
around the fifth century, the prosperous city of Dunhuang 'a servi de
lieu d'échanges entre la Chine et l'extérieur, et de halte pour les pèler-
ins bouddhistes' ('began serving as a place of exchange between China
and the outside world as well as a stop for Buddhist pilgrims') (*DT*, 167;
RB, 112). Tianyi's Chan master draws Tianyi's attention to the analogy between China's profoundly consequential encounter with Indian
thought and art centuries before, and that between China and the West
today: 'nos maîtres, du VIIIe au XIe siècle, n'avaient-ils pas justement

intégré l'art indien? [...] C'est là où je veux en venir, car toi, tu ne peux pas éviter d'affronter l'autre. Je sens qu'à l'issue de cette guerre, la rencontre de la Chine et de l'Occident en profondeur est inévitable' ('didn't our masters of the eighth through the eleventh centuries assimilate Indian art? [...] I'm telling you this because you, you will have to face what is different. Once this war is over, I think it inevitable for China and the West to encounter each other on a deeper level') (*DT*, 165; *RB*, 111). Or, elsewhere, Tianyi remarks: 'nous savions qu'au point où était parvenue la culture chinoise, après son long dialogue avec l'Inde et l'Islam, l'Occident était l'interlocuteur plus qu'essentiel, incontournable' ('we knew that, after its long dialogue with India and Islam, Chinese culture had reached a point where the West was an essential voice and could not be ignored') (*DT*, 83; *RB*, 53).[40]

Tianyi returns to China after Yumei's calling ('reviens! [...] Te voilà enfin! Nous voilà enfin!'/'return! [...] Here you are at last! Here we are at last!') (*DT*, 272; *RB*, 188), only to find out, like Orpheus looking back at Eurydice near the threshold of the underworld, that Yumei is lost forever. However, it is Tianyi's male companion, Haolang (Ami/Friend), who miraculously 'returns' from the dead, as Yumei has previously misinformed Tianyi about Haolang's death. Thereafter, Tianyi's 'destin' ('destiny') to 'retrouver l'Amante' ('rejoin the Lover') (*DT*, 275; *RB*, 191) is transferred to that of 'joining' the Friend:

Quelle fatalité! Quelle absurdité! Quelle est cette réalité capable d'engendrer des situations aussi cruelles qu'inattendues? Je suis revenu en Chine à cause de la mort de Haolang et de la survivance de Yumei. Voici Haolang vivant et Yumei morte. [...] Tant que je resterai en vie, en cette vie, je n'aurai qu'un but: le rejoindre. (*DT*, 297)

The absurdity of fate! How can I be in such a cruel, unexpected situation? I came back to China because Haolang was dead and Yumei had survived him. But Haolang lives and Yumei is dead, [...] As long as I am alive in this world I shall have but one goal: to join him. (*RB*, 206)

Resonating with Orpheus's turning of passion to boys after his eventual failure to retrieve Eurydice, there is an intense development of homoeroticism between Tianyi and Haolang: 'si j'aime Yumei, n'est-ce pas une raison de plus d'aimer aussi Haolang?' ('isn't my love for Yumei one more reason to love Haolang?') (*DT*, 340; *RB*, 235).

Haolang is the actual poet, the Orphic bard, of the novel.[41] He is the one to whom Yumei feels more sexually attracted. Yumei's feeling for Tianyi shows a 'sisterly' leaning, as she declares: 'je suis ta soeur, je suis ton amante. [...] Ah! Comme j'ai aimé notre amitié, elle est plus noble que l'amour. N'aurions-nous pas pu demeurer tous les trois dans l'amitié?' ('I am your sister, I am your lover. [...] Ah! How I loved our friendship; it was finer than love. Couldn't the three of us have stayed as we were, friends?') (*DT*, 185; *RB*, 125). There is an undeniable attraction between Tianyi and Haolang right at the beginning of their encounter. Tianyi explicitly compares their 'friendship' with his love for Yumei:

Cette amitié ardemment vécue me fit prendre conscience que la passion de l'amitié, vécue dans des circonstances exceptionnelles, peut être aussi intense que celle de l'amour. Je ne manquai pas de comparer ma rencontre avec Haolang à celle que j'avais eue avec Yumei. Si cette dernière m'avait ému jusqu'à l'extrême racine de mon être, les larmes de nostalgie ou de gratitude qu'elle avait suscitées étaient pareilles à une source jaillie d'une terre native, pleine d'une douceur confiante. A travers le regard de l'Amante, tous les éléments qui composent l'univers se sont révélés sensibles, reliés par une lumière diffuse, mais unique et par là unifiante. La rencontre avec mon ami, en revanche, fut une véritable irruption qui provoquait en moi de violentes secousses, m'entraînant vers l'inconnu, vers de continuels dépassements. L'attirance physique, confusément ressentie, n'était pas dans l'urgence de nos soif et faim l'aimant principal. Ce que l'autre ouvrit devant moi était un univers insoupçonné, insondable, celui de l'esprit. A côté de la nature brute, il y a donc une autre réalité, celle des signes. Les paroles exaltées du jeune poète, ainsi que ses écrits m'ont fait comprendre qu'à l'homme qui pense et crée tout demeure non clos mais infiniment ouvert. En compagnie de l'Ami, mon être littéralement éclaté avançait désormais vers un horizon lui aussi éclaté. (*DT*, 79–80)

The fervor of our friendship made me aware that the passion of friendship can be as intense as that of love when the circumstances are out of the ordinary. I did not fail to compare my encounter with Haolang to my encounter with Yumei. She had moved me to the very roots of my being, but the tears of longing and gratitude aroused were like a sure and gentle spring gushing from one's own earth. Seen through the Lover's eyes, all the elements composing the universe proved tangible, connected by a light that was diffused, but unique and thus unifying. In contrast, the encounter with my friend was a veritable irruption, jolting me fiercely, carrying me toward the unknown, toward continual challenges. Our vaguely felt physical attraction was not the main force that compelled our pressing hunger and thirst. What the other opened up to me was an unsuspected, unfathomable universe, that of the mind. Alongside untouched nature, there was another reality, that of language. The young poet's impassioned words and writings made me realize that, for the man who thinks and creates, all remains not closed but boundless open. In the Friend's company, the self in me that had literally exploded would henceforth march toward a horizon which itself had exploded. (*RB*, 50–51)

Prior to this dense and elegant passage, Tianyi's attention is specifically drawn to Haolang's reading of *Leaves of Grass* by the American poet Walt Whitman: 'je remarquai qu'il s'agissait d'un recueil de poésie portant le titre *Feuilles d'herbes* (de Whitman). Nous avons ri tous deux de bon cœur à cause de la coïncidence entre ce titre et l'endroit où le livre venait d'être ramassé' ('I noticed that it was a collection of poetry entitled *Leaves of Grass*. We both laugh heartily [de bon cœur] at the connection between the title and the spot from which the book had just been retrieved') (*DT*, 79; *RB*, 50). Whitman, like Proust, is known for his homo—or bisexuality, and *Leaves* features extensive discussions of delight in sensual pleasures. It is perhaps no 'coïncidence' that Cheng makes this particular reference, where his two male characters laugh 'de bon cœur' at their first meeting—physical intimacy is where their relationship develops in Part Three of the novel:

A bout de souffle, il titube sur quelques pas, se laisse choir dans les feuilles sèches, bras ouverts, face au ciel. Je le rejoins, me couche à côté de lui, tenant sa main dans la mienne. Je sens sa respiration haletante et la puissante pulsation de ce corps ami, alourdi par plus de dix ans d'épreuves physiques. [...] Haolang m'écoute sans mot dire. Je sens seulement la pression de sa main qui serre maintenant la mienne plus fort, au point de me faire mal, de me broyer les os. Un long moment se passe. [...] Tout, amitié et amour confondus, y est accepté, exalté comme un mystère fatal. (*DT*, 368–367)

Out of breath, he staggers, then collapses into the dry leaves, arms outspread, face to the sky. I join him and lie beside him, taking his hand in mine. I am aware of his panting and of the heart pounding in the familiar body weighed down by ten years and more of physical ordeal. [...] Haolang listens without a word. But I can just feel the pressure of his hand, now so tight that it hurts, crushes my bones. A long moment passes. [...] Friendship and love mingled, in these pages everything is accepted and exalted like a fateful mystery. (*RB*, 255–256)

The setting of this homoerotic scene echoes precisely the imagery of Whitman's 'leaves of grass', although, instead of quoting Whitman's work, Cheng actually inserts his own poem in the above-cited passage (indicated by the first ellipsis).

It should be noted that later in the Orphic myth, after Eurydice's final death, especially in Ovid's version, a strong sense of misogyny prevails, as the protagonist is eventually dismembered by the frustrated female followers of Bacchus, who are enraged by Orpheus's passion for young boys and his indifference to those women's love pursuit. The misogynist element is nowhere to be found in Cheng's Daoist engagement with the myth, which is arguably—at least in part—due to the general affirmation of women's role in Daoism, a philosophy which is 'unworldly and basically matriarchal in orientation' (Gulik 1961, 44). At any rate, as Albouy (1969, 190, my translation) comments on the Orphic myth: 'c'est moins de misogynie qu'il faudrait parler que de la quête de l'androgynie idéale' ('it is less misogyny than the quest for an ideal androgyny that we should be concerned with').[42]

Our ultimate purpose of exploring the Orphic myth is to relate Cheng's mythical engagement back to *La Recherche*. It is therefore worth further developing Cheng's treatment of love, sexuality, and friendship in *Le Dit*. Similar to Proust's fluid conception of love, notably his famous connection between adults' love for partners and children's love for parents (Finch 2007 [2001], 171), Cheng explicitly associates his 'filial piety'—a core tenet in Confucian teaching—with his passion for Yumei. In addition, this adults' love for partners is frequently compared to that between siblings. While listening to Dvorak's music, Tianyi states: 'l'écoutant, je me laissais porter par la vague d'émotion, celle qui me faisait sentir que d'un instant à l'autre j'allais retrouver les êtres chers qui m'attendaient: ma mère, ma sœur, l'Amante...' ('Listening, I was carried on the music's wave of emotion, which made me feel that at any moment I would be reunited with the loved ones who waited: my mother, my sister, the Lover...') (*DT*, 92; *RB*, 60). The protagonist, as he intrepidly returns to an altered, unrecognizable China, explicitly compares his search for the Lover with his previous attempt to reunite with his dying mother: 'en ai-je peur? Pas vraiment. Tout comme lors de la mort de ma mère, je pense à la légende bouddhique qui relate les séjours de Mulian en enfer. A cette légende vient d'ailleurs se mêler le mythe d'Orphée appris en Europe' ('Am I afraid? Not really. Just as when my mother died, I think of the Buddhist legend of Mulian in hell. Mixed into it now is a European legend, that of Orpheus') (*DT*, 275; *RB*, 191). This amalgamation between 'filial piety' and passionate love is crystalized in the intercultural mixing of the two myths. Furthermore, this particular Buddhist legend, with its emphasis on 'filial piety', can already be regarded as a *sinicized*, and more precisely, *Confucianized*, version of the original myth, an exemplar of cultural translation between ancient India and China.[43]

Just like Proust, Cheng explores the 'malleable borders between love and friendship', taking full advantage of the shared etymology of 'aimer', 'amour', 'amitié', 'ami(e)', and 'amant(e)' in the French language, as Alison Finch accurately explains:

> 'aimer' means both 'like' and 'love' and the second meaning of 'ami/e' is 'one who has a sexual relationship with another'. But Proust also constantly stretches the meaning of the word 'amitié' so that it too becomes ambiguous and reinterpretable. ('Amitié' can, rarely, have the same amorous application in French as 'ami', but when it does it is far slyer and more self-consciously euphemistic [...]) (2007 [2001], 180)

Cheng's decision to nickname Yumei 'l'Amante' ('the Lover') and Haolang 'l'Ami' ('the Friend') cannot make this malleable vision of love and friendship more explicit; to recap an already-cited sentence: 'tout, amitié et amour confondus, y est accepté, exalté comme un mystère fatal' ('Friendship and love mingled, in these pages everything is accepted and exalted like a fateful mystery') (*DT*, 368; *RB*, 255–256).

However, it would be slightly misleading to continue to investigate Tianyi's homo- or bisexuality *à la proustienne* (i.e. applying Proust's as well as his contemporaries' sexological theories to the reading of *Le Dit*),[44] for this is precisely where Cheng *reorients* the established Western line of enquiry into sexuality by introducing a Daoist alternative. Yumei/l'Amante and Haolang/l'Ami can be read as allegorical figures of *yin* and *yang*, which are two primordial cosmic forces of *qi*—Cheng's *souffle vital* (vital breath). In the context of sex and sexuality, *yin* is predominant in women and *yang* in men. But as Charlotte Furth (1988, 3) stresses:

> [...] there was nothing fixed and immutable about male and female as aspects of yin and yang. [...] They are interdependent, mutually reinforcing and capable of turning into their opposites. This natural philosophy would seem to lend itself to a broad and tolerant view of variation in sexual behavior and gender roles.

Wah-shan CHOU (2000, 18) further clarifies: 'yin and yang are not ontologically binary, as what they produce are not generic women and men, but persons in specific relations such as mother and father, husband and wife, brother and sister, emperor and favorite'. In other words, *yin* and *yang* are fundamentally relativistic.

Hence, Tianyi is *yang* relative to Yumei, but *yin* relative to Haolang. Tianyi's first description of Yumei particularly emphasizes the *yin* force in her by associating Yumei with the fertile and regenerative spring: 'elle dit sur un ton naturel: "Regarde ces primevères, le printemps est là!" Avec le printemps, elle aussi renaît à la vie' ('[she said] in a natural tone: "Look at the primroses. Spring is here!" With spring, she too was coming back to life') (*DT*, 52; *RB*, 30). After this first encouter, Tianyi 'ressen[t] un tressaillement presque serein, comme si Yumei était attendue et que de toute éternité elle devait venir, un peu à la manière de ces arbres d'hiver qui accueillent, légèrement surpris mais ne doutant nullement de son arrivée, la brise printanière' ('[experienced] a serene sort of shudder, as if Yumei had been expected and as if from time immemorial she had been supposed to come; I was a little like a tree in winter greeting the spring breeze with mild surprise but never doubting that it would arrive') (ibid.). By contrast, Haolang's first appearance in the novel already manifests strong masculine features: 'homme du Nord, il était d'une taille plus haute que la moyenne. De teint légèrement foncé, comme coulé dans du bronze, il en imposait par sa seule présence, sombre et tranquille' ('a man of the North, he was taller than average. His skin was dark, as if he had been cast in bronze. By his mere presence, solemn and quiet, he inspired respect') (*DT*, 78; *RB*, 49–50). More specifically, Haolang is identified with the element of fire, *yang par excellence* (according to the *Book of Changes*): 'l'adolescent de seize ans qu'il était alors avait tout de même assez de lucidité pour savoir que sa vie n'était pas faite de la seule force brute, qu'un feu sans complaisance le brûlait de l'intérieur' ('the then-sixteen-year-old adolescent had sufficient clarity of mind to know that there was more to him than mere brute force, that an uncompromising inner flame consumed him') (ibid.). Because of his outstanding physical force, Haolang, meaning 'l'Homme à l'esprit vaste' ('the man with the wide-ranging mind'), is later nicknamed 'le Loup hurlant' ('the howling wolf') through a word game based on homophones (*DT*, 295; *RB*, 205). By portraying the eroticism between Tianyi, l'Amante, and l'Ami, as well as making connections between 'filial piety' and passionate love, Cheng effectively recasts well-established Proustian thematics (love, friendship, homo- and bisexuality) from the Chinese perspective, offering alternative visions and theories. A Modernist aesthetics in Proust which reflects, in Finch's words, 'a "modern" acceptance of paradoxical or polymorphous sexuality' (2007 [2001], 177), is thus injected with a fresh dose of ancient Daoist and Confucian elements when we read *Le Dit* against *La Recherche* as a kind of 'Chinese shadow'.

Finally, love, friendship, and sexuality are always accompanied by the signs of art. Tianyi's longing to reunite with his mother and later with Yumei is compared to the Buddhist legend of Mulian, which he learns from the wall painting at the archaeological site of Dunhuang; his spiritual and physical intimacy with Haolang leads to his spontaneous chanting of poetry; his love for Yumei is crystalized in his final unfinished fresco of Yumei's portrait; even Tianyi's 'amitié amoureuse' ('relationship as friends and lovers') (*DT*, 261; *RB*, 180) with the slightly secondary character Véronique is preceded by the recital of the violoncellist Pierre Fournier. This is because, to return to Deleuze (2008 [2000], 10), knowing another being is fundamentally deciphering and interpreting the signs it sends out, and 'at the deepest level' the essence of life is 'in the signs of art'.

5.5   Transcendence Through the Void

This investigation of Part II on Cheng and Proust has proceeded from 'empirical' textual findings to conceptual comparisons. The latter exploration is a concerted attempt to 'verify' Cheng's self-proclaimed 'Proustian approach' (*démarche proustienne*), in a manner which is rather similar to scientific speculation that can be confirmed by detailed analysis.[45] But additionally, Cheng's Proustian hypertext also demonstrates a strong sense of alterity, a kind of fundamental intention towards the Other.[46] Further still, Cheng's aesthetic of reorientation and *rapprochement* aims at 'transcendence' and universal harmony, as he asserts: 'la vraie transcendance, paradoxalement, se situe dans l'*entre*, dans ce qui jaillit de plus haut quand a lieu le décisif échange entre les êtres et l'Être' ('true transcendence, paradoxically, is located in the *between*, in that which bursts forth most intensely when decisive exchange between beings and Being takes place') (2008 [2006], 23; 2009, 18). This idea is reiterated elsewhere in Cheng's writing: 'L'*entre* fécond est bien le lieu de l'enjeu de l'être et de son devenir. C'est là que la vraie vie révèle sa capacité à transformer certains hasards en événement-avènement, que l'invisible s'inscrit sur l'écran de l'espace et que l'infini s'engouffre dans la brèche du temps' ('the fruitful *between* is just the crucial place of being and its becoming. It is there that real life reveals its capability to transform certain happenstance into event-advent, that the invisible inscribes itself in the shade of the space, that the infinite steps into the breach of time') (Cheng 2009 [2004], 14, my translation). At the beginning of the section on Cheng's mythical engagement with Proust, I cursorily suggested *ternarism* as the way to understand Cheng's broader literary and cultural enterprise. In Cheng's own words, 'all art is ternary' ('艺术都是三元的') (*TY*, 317). With references to Cézanne and Shitao (a Chinese painter of the seventeenth century), Cheng (2009 [2004], 13, my translation) comments: 'toute oeuvre d'art est justement un Trois qui, drainant la meilleure part du Deux, permet aux deux—l'artist et son sujet—de se transcender' ('all works of art incarnate the idea of a Three, which, bringing in the best part of the Two, allows the two—artists and their works—to transcend each other'). Elsewhere, appropriating an expression from John Keats which involves the image of a 'valley', Cheng further characterizes the empty yet generative space of the Three as 'le royaume de l'intervalle' ('the kingdom in between') and 'la vallée où poussent les âmes' ('the vale of soul-making') (ibid., 16, my translation). Ternarism will now be properly developed to help further conceptualize Cheng's cross-cultural Proustian hypertext.

Cheng's vision of transcendence is grounded in his interpretation of the Daoist notion of *yin-yang*, which is associated with the *vide médian*, which has been variably translated into English as 'the middle Void', 'the median Void', or 'the median emptiness'. The Daoist cosmogony and ontology are founded on the idea of *qi* (or *ch'i*, 气), literally 'breath, air', or 'souffle' in French, 'à la fois matière et esprit' ('both substance and spirit') ([2006] 2008, 74; 2009, 66). The primordial *qi* (or *yuanqi*, 元气) signals the Original Void, a void that aims at plenitude, as it says in *Laozi*: 'la grande plénitude est comme vide; alors elle est intarissable' ('the great fullness is as though empty; thus it is inexhaustible') (cited in Cheng 1991, 29; 1994, 46). According to Cheng, the complex relationship among Dao, *qi*, void, *yin, yang*, and the *vide médian* can be summarized as follows:

> Le Souffle primordial assurant l'unité originelle continue à animer tous les êtres, les reliant en un gigantesque réseau d'entrecroisements et d'engendrement appelé le Tao, la Voie.

Au sein de la Voie, la nature du Souffle et son rythme sont ternaires, en ce sens que le Souffle primordial se divise en trois types de souffles qui agissent concomitamment: le souffle Yin, le souffle Yang et le souffle du Vide médian. Entre le Yang, puissance active, et le Yin, douceur réceptive, le souffle du Vide médian—qui tire son pouvoir du Vide originel—a le don de les entraîner dans l'interaction positive, cela en vue d'une transformation mutuelle, bénéfique pour l'un et pour l'autre. ([2006] 2008, 74–75)

The primordial Breath that ensures the original unity continues to animate all beings, linking them into a gigantic, inter-woven, engendering network called the Tao, the Way.

Within the Way, the nature of the Breath and its rhythm are threefold in the sense that the primordial Breath is divided into three types of Breath that act concomitently: the Yin Breath, the Yang Breath, and the Breath of the Median Void. Between the Yang, the active power, and the Yin, gentle receptivity, the Breath of the Median Void—which draws its power from the original Void— has the gift of pulling them into positive interaction, with a view toward a mutual transformation, as beneficial for one as for the other. (2009, 66)

This transformative process signals a spiritual exaltation and a form of ceaseless transcendence. It may be advisable to stick to Cheng's *vide médian* in its French form throughout the discussion; this is essentially because the *vide médian*, as an individual concept, is very much Cheng's own conceptual development based on the dynamics between *yin* and *yang*. This idea is most noticeably derived from the following already-cited passage in *Laozi*:

Le Tao d'origine engendre l'Un
L'Un engendre le Deux
Le Deux engendre le Trois
Le Trois produit les dix mille êtres
Les dix mille êtres s'adossent aux [*sic.*] Yin
Et embrassent le Yang
L'harmonie naît au souffle du Vide médian. (Cheng 1991, 62)

The original Tao gives birth to the one.
The one gives birth to the two.
The two gives birth to the three.
The three produces the ten thousand existents.
The ten thousand existents carry yin and embrace yang.
Harmony is born with the breath of median emptiness. (Cheng 1994, 49)

This is Cheng's own French translation of Chap. 42 of *Laozi* in verse. Cheng clearly places the *vide médian* as a separate concept alongside *yin-yang*. However, according to the original text, whether the *vide médian* should stand as a 'conceptual equal' to *yin-yang* is rather debatable. To clarify the point, it would be helpful to show the original text in Chinese and compare D.C. Lau's and, more recently, Edmund Ryden's English translations of the same passage:

道生一; 一生二; 二生三; 三生万物. 万物负阴而抱阳, 充气以为和.

The way begets one; one begets two; two begets three; three begets the myriad creatures.
The myriad creatures carry on their backs the *yin* and embrace in their arms the *yang* and are the blending of the generative forces of the two. (Lau 1989 [1963], 63)

The Way generates the Unique;
The Unique generates the Double;
The Double generates the Triplet;
The Triplet generates the myriad things.
The myriad things recline on *yin* and embrace *yang*
While vacuous *qi* holds them in harmony. (Ryden 2008, 89)

As can be seen, the *vide médian* does not ostensibly feature in Lau's translation; it is simply understood as a process instead of a concept. Whereas Cheng explicitly acknowledges *three* types of Breath, Lau sees only 'the generative forces of the *two*'. On the other hand, Ryden's 'vacuous *qi*' corresponds to Cheng's 'primordial Breath' and 'original Void' rather than his *vide médian*, although Cheng does define the *vide médian* in relation to them: 'ce Vide médian, un souffle lui-même, procède du Vide originel dont il tire son pouvoir' ('the Median Void [...] draws its power from the original Void') (Cheng [2006] 2008, 75; 2009, 49).

Cheng's reinterpretation of *yin-yang* and his insistence on the *vide médian* largely foreground his literary aesthetic and artistic vision. While the *yin-yang* dynamics is incorporated into his construction of intercultural dialogues between China and the West, the *vide médian* could be seen to metonymically refer to not only the inherent fictionality of literature as a kind of essential void, but also Cheng's humble role as the creative intermediator, who, like his description of the *vide médian*, 'a le don de les [China-West] entraîner dans l'interaction positive, cela en vue d'une transformation mutuelle, bénéfique pour l'un et pour l'autre' ('has the gift of pulling them into positive interaction, with a view toward a mutual transformation, as beneficial for one as for the other') (ibid.). Like the Daoist priest who spends his life pursuing personal transcendence (*Le Dit*, 28–30),[47] Cheng searches for deep spiritual correspondences between Chinese and Western cultures by envisaging as well as tentatively creating the literature to come, a literature which, as I hope my analysis has shown, enables us to rethink and enrich both cultural traditions.

This 'transcendent' cultural enterprise behind Cheng's engagement with Proust marks a qualitative difference from mainland Chinese writers' intertextual practice. While mainland Chinese writers' references to Proust are examples of cross-cultural intertextuality, the effect of which seems to be limited to the Chinese context, what we see in Cheng is a *transcultural* rewriting which speaks to two cultural traditions and aims to reorient both Western and Chinese literary aesthetics. Of course, one can always read *Le Dit* independently, which is also a key trait of the Genettian hypertext mentioned at the beginning of Part II. But reading *Le Dit* against *La Recherche* certainly enhances the experience of cross-fertilization and empowers us to concretely understand Cheng's literary ambition. The eminent Proust scholar Luc Fraisse entitles his chapter on Cheng and Proust '*Le Dit de Tianyi*, palimpseste de *La Recherche?*' (2010, 633), with a question mark signaling the ambiguity and uncertainty of such a reading, which I hope can now be seen as being no longer necessary. If, etymologically and symbolically, the word 'palimpsest' still only reflects the Greco-Latin, and by extension European, heritage, we could perhaps replace it with a Chinese metaphor, describing *Le Dit* as *La Recherche* in the Chinese shadow.

NOTES

1. Furthermore, this idea of 'something behind the bark' is related to the Celtic belief. See the section of this chapter 'Writing and Rewriting the Myth'.
2. The French translations of these Chinese expressions, which are in inverted commas, are slightly modified by Cheng. The corresponding Chinese expressions cited here are from Yang's translation (*TY*, 6).

3. The idea of animism in Proust's time was developed by Edward Tylor (1871), often regarded as the founder of modern anthropology, in his evolutionary theory of religion. He borrows the term 'animism' from Aristotle to explain the function of religion in primitive societies.

4. There are different English translations for Cheng's concept of the 'vide médian'. Here in the novel, it is translated as 'the middle Voids', whereas in *Empty and Full* (1994) it is translated as 'the median emptiness'.

5. As I mentioned in the last chapter, this Daoist parable explicitly features in Li Shangyin's classic poem—an essential literary source for the Chinese title of *La Recherche* as well as that of Cheng's second novel (Cf. Sect. 4.3 of Part II).

6. This is also the title of Joshua Landy's [2004] illustrious book on Proust. It is a common practice in ancient Chinese philosophy to start with a concrete model, through the process of analogy, to formulate an 'abstract' idea, whereas in the Western tradition we tend to use analogy to *illustrate* or understand an 'abstract' idea.

7. Still, this triumphant piece of 'prose poem' by the protagonist is later met with severe criticism from M. de Norpois, which deeply dampens the protagonist's spirit for his literary vocation: 'atterré par ce que M. de Norpois venait de me dire [...] Je me sentais consterné, réduit; et mon esprit comme un fluide qui n'a de dimensions que celles du vase qu'on lui fournit, de même qu'il s'était dilaté jadis à remplir les capacités immenses du génie, contracté maintenant, tenait tout entier dans la médiocrité étroite où M. de Norpois l'avait soudain enfermé et restreint' ('I was devastated by what M. de Norpois had said [...] I felt deflated and dumbfounded; and just as my mind, like a fluid whose only dimensions are those of the container into which it is poured, had once expanded so as to fill the vast vessel of my genius, so now it shrank and fitted exactly into the exiguous confines of the mediocrity to which M. de Norpois had suddenly consigned it') (*RTP I*, 466; *PT II*, 49).

8. The notion of 'essence' in art in *La Recherche* is most famously elaborated on by Deleuze, who sees it as a Platonic conception of Idea or Form. We will return to Deleuze's reading of the 'Proustian essence' in a later Section.

9. Not all Chinese characters are pictograms and ideograms. There are many more complicated character formations which nevertheless bear certain relations with the basic pictograms and ideograms. Modern linguistics often categorizes the Chinese language as a *logographic* system, in which a *grapheme* is used to represent a word or morpheme. However, the phonetic dimension of many graphemes is often present. In contrast, the Latin alphabet belongs to a phonographic system in which graphemes play a small role. As a result, the *symbolic* values of individual letters are

significantly lowered. For a detailed introduction to the Chinese writing system, see DeFrancis (1984).

10. 'The veins of the Dragon' in classical Chinese characters look like this: 龍脈. Such a calligraphic 'revelation' can be understood in the light of the *fengshui* concept—a philosophical system which aims to harmonize inhabitants, humans and animals alike, with their surrounding environment.

11. This erotically charged and seemingly feminizing depiction of landscape, such as the valley (echoing Laozi's 'ravine of the world'), is in fact part of Cheng's Daoism-inflected fictional discourse. I will later return to the Daoist themes of the 'valley' and the 'esoteric feminine'. For an extensive discussion on the conditioning of the body as we learn to master the art of calligraphy, see Billeter (2010, 111–242).

12. The translation of this phrase is mine. The syntax of Ian Patterson's English rendition does not suit my purpose here.

13. An obvious example, as the title of Freed-Thall's article indicates, is the protagonist's nonsensical interjection 'zut, zut, zut' in front of the pond at Montjouvain.

14. Note that Proust actually uses the plural form 'paradises' in the last sentence, which is not reflected in the Penguin translation.

15. Foucault ([1970] 2002, 19) bases this observation particularly on his analysis of Vélasquez's painting *Las Méninas*. He says, 'up to the end of the sixteenth century, resemblance played a constructive role in the knowledge of Western culture'. Vélasquez's work marks 'the representation as it were, of Classical representation', or what Foucault otherwise formulates as 'representation in its pure form' (ibid., 18).

16. The point about Haolang being an alter ego of Cheng will be properly addressed in Sect. 5.4.2. of this part.

17. In short, it concerns the following passage from Chap. 42 of *Laozi*: 'le Tao d'origine engender l'Un /L'Un engender le Deux /Le Deux engender le Trois /Le Trois produit les dix mille êtres' (The original Tao gives birth to the one /The one gives birth to the two /The two gives birth to the three /The three produces the ten thousand existents'). This French translation is provided by Cheng himself. I will return to this passage in the final section of this chapter.

18. Erika Fülöp, *Proust, the One, and the Many: Identity and Difference in* A la recherche du temps perdu (London: Legenda, 2012).

19. I borrow Christine Froula's (2012, 76) accurate remark on the Western 'modernist' aesthetics of the early twentieth century. Froula thoroughly explores the Chinese art objects ('china') mentioned in *La Recherche*.

20. I am aware that critics such as CHU Xiaoquan (2014, 39) refuse to employ the term 'hybridity' to describe the generic status of *Le Dit*, because such a qualification seems to go against Cheng's

Daoism-informed conception of the artwork as one single entity. However, for me 'hybridity' is not necessarily the opposite of 'the one'. We *can* analyze individual generic elements and explore how their various inner dynamics contribute to an artistic organic whole.

21. See Sect. 5.1. of Part II.

22. I would like to add that Cheng's tripartite novelistic conception is redolent of travel writings. Notions such as 'parting', 'journey', 'arrival', and 'return' are typical of a travelogue. Exploring *Le Dit* in the light of travel writings will require a fundamental change of critical framework established by the present book (which centres around Proust), but it promises to be another fascinating line of enquiry: for example, the translation of cultural forms of expression of the Other into one's own language; the transformation from individual experience into collective reservoirs of knowledge; and the issue of authentication problematized by the tension between the immediate experience and seeing (a narrated 'I') and the discursive mediation that considers the dissemination of knowledge about cultures and societies (a narrating 'I'). For a brilliant account of these features of the travelogue, see Ette (2003, 25–38).

23. For a discussion of this linguistic transformation, see Note 3 of Sect. 3.1. of Part I.

24. In the original passage, Hughes cites Tadié's biography as support. See Tadié (1996, 787, 826).

25. Its earliest printed form is found in a collection of stories entitled 'Stories to Caution the World' (*Jingshi tongyan*, 警世通言) compiled by FENG Menglong (冯梦龙, 1574–1646). Various theatrical adaptations of *White Snake* became popular from the mid-Qing Dynasty (1644–1912) onwards.

26. Proust's protagonist's first disappointing experience with La Berma's performance—due to the discrepancy between La Berma's interpretation of *Phèdre* and the way he imagines those familiar lines to be delivered—is 'unparalleled' in *Le Dit*. Whereas Proust overall tends to highlight Racine's poetic genius and prioritize the 'côté de l'écriture' of theatre, Cheng hardly fleshes out the connection between theatre and literature or painting like Proust. See J. Guérin, 'Théâtre', in *Dictionnaire Marcel Proust*, pp. 997–1000 (p. 999).

27. This English rendition of Proust's expression 'ô miracle' and his use of the word 'retrouver', which strongly echo Cheng's passage, do not quite suit my analytical purpose here.

28. Interestingly, in his essay, Brecht (2008, 181) is actually trying to adapt the actor's *Verfremdungseffekt* in classical Chinese theatre to 'revolutionary' theatre.

29. For an overview of the Five Elements and their corresponding degree of *yin* and *yang*, see Gulik (1961, 40). For a more systematic discussion of 'the feminine' in Cheng's works, see Bertaud (2014, 117–132).

30. This is (the English translation of) Cheng's own translation of Chapter XLII of *Laozi* (Cheng 1994, 49). I will return to this ternary way of thinking as the way to understand Cheng's enterprise of creating dialogues for cultural 'transcendence' in detail in the final section of this chapter.

31. To name but a few book-length studies from the fifties to now: Eliott Coleman's *The Golden Angel, Papers on Proust* (1954), Claude Vallée's *La Féerie de Marcel Proust* (1958), David Mendelson's *Le Verre et les objets de verre dans l'univers imaginaire de Marcel Proust* (1968), Richard Bales's *Proust and the Middle Ages* (1975), Marie Miguet-Ollagnier's *La Mythologie de Marcel Proust* (1982), and more recently, two works by Margaret Topping, *Proust's Gods* (2000) and *Supernatural Proust* (2007).

32. Elaborations on the special immaterial quality of sound are not absent in Daoism, but they have not necessarily been granted a central position in the traditional understandings of Daoism. Major references can be found in *Zhuangzi* (Chap. XIV) and numerous references to music in *Liezi*. *Laozi*, *Zhuangzi*, and *Liezi* are all fundamental Daoist texts.

33. I thank Prof. Joachim Gentz for pointing out that Rilke's original remark in German is 'Gesang ist Dasein', and the choice of the French word 'être' ('being') instead of 'existence'—'dasein' literally means 'being there' in German, usually associated with the idea of being-in-the-world—in the French translation used by Cheng already has an enhanced transcendence-inflected ontological implication, which suits Cheng's elaboration on 'soul' and 'sound' here even better.

34. See Sect. 4.3. of Part II.

35. Although Proust in the following passage does not exactly use the word 'âme' ('soul'), one should note that the protagonist's ideas of soul and metempsychosis are closely associated with 'pensée' ('thought') and 'esprit' ('mind'), as he says on the opening page of the prologue: 'comme après la métempsycose les pensées d'une existence antérieure' ('as after metempsychosis do the thoughts of an earlier existence') (*RTP I*, 3; *PT I*, 7).

36. The critic is recapitulating J.-F. Reille's (1979, 96) observation.

37. The new Pléiade edition of *La Recherche* notes that Proust may have come across this Celtic legend from Michelet's *Histoire de la France* (*RTP I*, 1122). Miguet-Ollagnier (1982, 267) also suggests that there was a resurgence of interest in Celtic myths at the end of the nineteenth and the beginning of the twentieth centuries.

38. Topping, in *Supernatural Proust* (2007, 11), for example, suggests, with reference to Albouy's article, that the mythical or mythological structure or unity should be placed within a much wider framework of 'supernatural' images and references. In her words, 'incongruity, exuberant

abundance and a refusal of closure characterize Proust's handling of these sources as much as do pattern and structure, and all find their place within this singularly intricate work, the novelistic embodiment of the dramatist's maxim: "I am human so nothing human is strange to me'''. My own concern here is not so much whether the myth of Orpheus is *the* central structure of *La Recherche*; rather, my primary focus is Cheng's intercultural engagement with *a* particular myth that features prominently in Proust's novel.

39. This Buddhist legend, in Tianyi's words, 'racontait comment Mulian, l'ardent bouddhiste, était descendu aux enfers pour affronter mille épreuves afin de délivrer l'âme de sa mère défunte' ('told the story of Mulian, the devout Buddhist who had descended to the underworld, facing a thousand trials to free his deceased mother's soul') (*DT*, 182; *RB*, 123–124).

40. Again, the topos of the Silk Road has already been evoked by Yu in his appropriation of Proust's prologue. See the relevant section in Part I Chap. 3.

41. This particular aspect would make the character another alter ego of the author. Cheng is of course the real poet, some of Haolang's poems cited in the novel being adapted from Cheng's actual poems.

42. Albouy, *Mythes*, p. 190.

43. The earliest source of the Buddhist legend 'Mulian en enfer' is indeed, as Cheng describes in *Le Dit*, found in the Dunhuang Caves. It is generally suspected to have a certain Indian origin, but we do not have any concrete evidence except for its diegetic similarity—i.e. the descent to Hell—to the story of Ksitigarbha, one of the four principal bodhisattvas in Mahayana Buddhism. Incidentally, the latter legend is also depicted in the Dunhuang Caves. For an introduction and analysis of the manuscripts found in Dunhuang, where these legends were first recorded in China, see Mair (1989).

44. For a discussion of the influence of the *Zwischenstufen* theory on Proust, see Sect. 2.9.1. of Part I.

45. I borrow this methodological analogy from Orr's reconceptualization of 'influence studies'. See Orr (2003, 85).

46. This remark is particularly informed by Spivak's theory of 'planetarity'. She explains: 'the planet is in the species of alterity, belonging to another system; and yet we inhabit it, on loan. [...] To be human is to be intended toward the other' (2003, 72–73).

47. Transcendence in this case can be narrowly understood as the Daoist's cultivation of detachment and mastery of *yin-yang* forces to reach the status of a saintly immortal, known as *xian* (仙) in Chinese.

REFERENCES

Albouy, Pierre. 1969. *Mythes et mythologie dans la littérature française*. Paris: Armand Colin.

Albouy, Pierre. 1976. *Mythographie*. Paris: Librarie José Corti.

Ascari, Maurizio. 2011. *Literature of the Global Age: A Critical Study of Transcultural Narratives*. Jefferson, CO: McFarland & Company.

Aubert, Nathalie. 2011. La peinture hollandaise de notre mémoire. In *Marcel Proust Aujoud'hui 8: Proust et la Hollande*, ed. Sjef Houppermans, Manet van Monfrans, and Annelies Schulte Nordholt, 131–147. New York: Edition Rodopi.

Aubert, Nathalie. 2002. *Proust: La Traduction du sensible*. Oxford: Legenda.

Bales, Richard. [2001] 2007. Proust and the Fine Arts. In *The Cambridge Companion to Proust*, 183–199. Cambridge: Cambridge University Press.

Bales, Richard. 1975. *Proust and the Middle Ages*. Genève: Droz.

Bertaud, Madeleine. 2014. Le Féminin selon François Cheng. *François Cheng à la croisée de la Chine et de l'Occident. Colloque de Paris-Shanghai*. Bibliothèque nationale de France, ADIREL, Université Fudan, 117–132. Genève: Droz.

Billeter, Jean François. 2010. *Essai sur l'art chinois de l'écriture et ses fondements*. Paris: Editions Allia.

Bizub, Edward. 1991. *La Vénise intérieure*. Neuchâtel: La Baconnière.

Brecht, Bertolt. 2008. Alienation Effect in Chinese Acting (1936). In *Theatre in Theory 1900–2000: An Anthology*, ed. David Krasner, trans. John Willett, 178–184. Oxford: Blackwell.

Bucknall, Barbara J. 1969. *The Religion of Art in Proust*. Urbana: University of Illinois Press.

Chaudier, Stéphane. 2004. *Proust et le langage religieux: la cathédrale profane*. Paris: Champion.

Cheek, Timothy. 1997. *Propaganda and Culture in Mao's China: Deng Tuo and the Intelligentsia*. Oxford: Clarendon Press.

Cheng, François. 1994. *Empty and Full: The Language of Chinese Painting*, trans. Michael H. Kohn. Boston: Shambhala.

Cheng, François. 2002. *Le Dialogue: Une passion pour la langue française*. Kindle Ebook. Paris: Desclée de Brouwer.

Cheng, François. 2008. *Cinq méditations sur la beauté*. Paris: Albin Michel.

Cheng, François. 2009. *Way of Beauty: Five Meditations for Spiritual Transformation by François Cheng*, trans. Jody Gladding. Rochester: Inner Traditions.

CHOU, Wah-shan. 2000. *Tongzhi: Politics of Same-Sex Eroticism in Chinese Societies*. New York: The Haworth Press.

Christine, Froula. 2012. Proust's China. In *Modernism and the Orient*, 74–109. Orleans: University of New Orleans Press.

Chu, Xiaoquan. 2014. Le Langage romanesque de François Cheng dans Le Dit de Tianyi. In *François Cheng à la croisée de la Chine et de l'Occident. Colloque de Paris-Shanghai*. Bibliothèque nationale de France, ADIREL, Université Fudan, 39–48. Genève: Droz.

Coleman, Elliot. 1954. *The Golden Angels: Papers on Proust*. New York: C. Taylor.

Compagnon, Antoine. 1989. *Proust entre deux siècles*. Paris: Seuil.

Danius, Sara. 2002. *The Senses of Modernism: Technology, Perception, and Aesthetics*. Ithaca, NY: Cornell University Press.

DeFrancis, John. 1984. *The Chinese Language: Facts and Fantasy*. Honolulu: University of Hawaii Press.

Deleuze, Gilles. [2000] 2008. *Proust and Signs*, trans. Richard Howard. New York: Continuum.

Eliot, T.S. 2010. Tradition and the Individual Talent. In *Anthology of Theory and Criticism*, ed. The Norton, 955–961. New York: W. W. Norton & Company.

Ette, Ottmar. 2003. *Literature on the Move*, trans. Katharina Vester. Amsterdam: Rodopi.

Finch, Alison. [2001] 2007. Love, Sexuality and Friendship. In *The Cambridge Companion to Proust*, 167–182. Cambridge: Cambridge University Press.

Foucault, Michel. [1970] 2002. *The Order of Things: An Archaeology of the Human Sciences*. London: Routledge.

Fraisse, Luc. 2010. *La Petite musique du style: Proust et ses sources littéraires*. Paris: Classiques Garnier.

Freed-Thall, Hannah. 2009. Zut, Zut, Zut: Aesthethic Disorientation in Proust. *Modern Language Notes* 124 (4): 868–900.

Fülöp, Erika. 2012. *Proust, the One, and the Many*. London: Legenda.

Furth, Charlotte. 1988. Androgynous Males and Deficient Females: Biology and Gender Boundaries in Sixteenth- and Seventeenth-Century China. *Late Imperial China* 9 (2): 1–30.

Genette, Gérard. 1980. *Narrative Discourse: An Essay in Method*, trans. Jane E. Lewin. Ithaca, NY: Cornell University Press.

Gulik, Robert Hans van. 1961. *Sexual Life in Ancient China*. Leiden: Brill.

Hassine, J. 2004. Bergotte. In *Dictionnaire Marcel Proust*, ed. Annick Bouillaguet, 130–132. Paris: Champion.

Henri, Anne. 1981. *Marcel Proust: Théories pour une esthétique*. Paris: Klincksieck.

Hughes, Edward J. 2012. *Proust, Class, and Nation*. Oxford: Oxford University Press.

Lafargue, Paul. [1890] 2002. Reminiscences of Marx. *Lafargue Internet Archive (marxists.org)*, September. https://www.marxists.org/archive/lafargue/1890/xx/marx.htm. Accessed 28 Nov 2016.

Landy, Joshua. 2004. *Philosophy as Fiction: Self, Deception, and Knowledge in Proust*. Oxford, NY: Oxford University Press.

Lau, D.C., trans. [1963] 1989. *Chinese Classics: Tao Te Ching*. Hong Kong: The Chinese University Press.

Leriche, F. 2004. Musique. In *Dictionnaire Marcel Proust*, ed. Annick Bouillaguet and Bryan Rogers, 664–666. Paris: Champion.

Mair, Victor. 1989. *T'ang Transformation Texts*. Cambridge: Cambridge University Press.

Mendelson, David. 1968. *Le verre et les objets de verre dans l'univers imaginaire de Marcel Proust*. Paris: J. Corti.

Merleau-Ponty, Maurice. 2002. *Phenomenology of Perception*, trans. Colin Smith. London, NY: Routledge.

Miguet-Ollagnier, Marie. 1982. *La Mythologie de Marcel Proust*. Paris: Les Belles Lettres.

Orr, Mary. 2003. *Intertextuality: Debates and Contexts*. Cambridge: Polity.

Pothast, Ulrich. 2008. *The Metaphyisical Vision: Arthur Schopenhauer's Philosophy of Art and Life and Samuel Beckett's Own Way to Make Use of It*. New York: Peter Lang.

Proust, Marcel. 1954. *Contre Sainte-Beuve*, ed. Bernard de Fallois. Paris: Gallimard.

Proust, Marcel. 1988. *Against Sainte-Beuve and Other Essays*, trans. John Sturrock. London: Penguin.

Reille, Jean-François. 1979. *Proust: Le Temps du désir*. Paris: Editeurs français réunis.

Richard, Jean-Pierre. 1976. *Proust et le monde sensible*. Paris: Seuil.

Ryden, Edmund, trans. 2008. *Laozi: Daodejing*. Oxford: Oxford University Press.

Schopenhauer, Arthur. 1966. *The World as Will and Representation*, trans. E.F.J. Payne, vol. I. New York: Dover.

Silvester, Rosalind, and Guillaume Thouroude. 2012. *Traits chinois/lignes francophones: écriture, images, cultures*. Montréal: Les Presses de l'Université de Montréal.

Spivak, Gayatri Chakravorty. 2003. *Death of a Discipline*. New York: Columbia University Press.

Stagoll, Cliff. [2005] 2010. Becoming. In *The Deleuze Dictionary*, ed. Adrian Parr, 25–27. Edinburgh: Edinburgh University Press.

Tadié, Jean-Yves. 1996. *Marcel Proust: Biographie*. Paris: Gallimard.

Taylor, Edward. 1871. *Primitive Culture: Researches into the Development of Mythology, Philosophy, Religion, Art, and Custom*, II vols. London: John Murray.

Topping, Margaret. 2000. *Proust's Gods: Christian and Mythological Figures of Speech in the Works of Marcel Proust*. Oxford: Oxford University Press.

Topping, Margaret. 2007. *Supernatural Proust: Myth and metaphor in A la recherche du Temps perdu.* Cardiff: University of Wales Press.

Vallée, Claude. 1958. *La féerie de Marcel Proust.* Paris: Fasquelle.

Watson, Burton, trans. n.d. The Complete Works of Chuang Tzu. *Terebess Asia Online.* http://terebess.hu/english/chuangtzu.html. Accessed 25 Nov 2016.

CONCLUSION

Proust would probably never have envisaged the round trip between France and China enjoyed by his novel, propagating literary 'descendants' that have witnessed and themselves epitomized contemporary Franco-Chinese intellectual and artistic transaction. Echoing a number of classical sources, the iconic Chinese title for *La Recherche*, as has been thoroughly investigated in this book, signifies a long line of Chinese philosophical and literary traditions to a sinophone readership. The choice and composition of this 'traditional' title for a canonical foreign work has symbolically reflected major post-Mao intellectual preoccupations with cultural 'renewal' and 'opening' in and since the 1980s. As expounded at the beginning of my enquiry, the translation and critical reception of Proust's work in China has been shaped by socio-political vicissitudes of modern and contemporary China; equally, they have synecdochically reflected Chinese intellectual and artistic developments before and after the establishment of the PRC in 1949, and subsequently following two successive phases of economic reform in post-Mao China from 1979 until now. Critical preferences for Proustian themes of time and memory in the Chinese reception of *La Recherche* were brought to light by our examination of traditional Chinese literary discourses. Meanwhile, the lexical and discursive shift regarding homosexuality and sadomasochism-manifested in the first and more recent translations of Proust's work was also evidently informed by contemporary sociological works on sexuality in China, many of which were directly influenced by Western sexological

© The Editor(s) (if applicable) and The Author(s) 2017
S. Li, *Proust, China and Intertextual Engagement*,
DOI 10.1007/978-981-10-4454-0

discourses. In this respect, the 'knowledge of the socio-historical context' of Proust's work in translation 'furnishes the starting point for interpretation itself' (Moretti 1983, 8).

If we compare the mainland Chinese creative reception of Proust to the transcultural dialogue with *La Recherche* initiated by the Chinese diaspora in France, their commonalities and qualitative differences quickly emerge. While manifesting a similar ambition for Chinese cultural heritage to 'go global', the two groups' varied approaches to Proust demonstrate contrasting senses of alterity, which carry rather different cross-cultural implications. The three mainland Chinese writers' intertextual engagement with *La Recherche*, which has necessarily been filtered through the Chinese translations, signals, to borrow Christopher Bush's (2005, 171) expression, 'cultural otherness in an allegory of internal otherness'. Proust, as a relatively new, foreign sign of canonical otherness, signifies a difference to them, or indeed, his novel enters into a relation of *différance* with these Chinese writers' works. That is, the sign of Proust, which only represents a 'deferred presence' (Derrida 1982, 9) of Proust's original work, interacts with the Chinese writers' works by entering a 'playing movement' which produces cultural differences as well as the effects of such differences.[1] Such a sign can only be secondary and provisional, as Derrida explains: 'secondary due to an original and lost presence from which the sign thus derives; provisional as concerns this final and missing presence toward which the sign in this sense is a movement of mediation' (ibid., 9). The geographic and cultural topoi[2] in which Proust's text originated seem rather inconsequential to these writers' interpretations; or, in the light of Derridean conception, such a relation of *différance* is 'the non-full, non-simple, structured and differentiating origin of differences', and 'thus, the name "origin" no longer suits it' (ibid., 11). These writers do not attempt to represent a 'truthful' Proust or an 'authentic' West at large. Their personal (re)interpretation, (mis)appropriation, and creative (re)imagination of Proust exemplify their impatient embracing of their newly found intellectual, artistic, and in Wei's case, sexual freedom. Additionally, their responses to Proust mark their self-conscious distancing from the 'Red China' under Mao by engaging—albeit superficially—with the canon of world literature (dominated by the West). Although Wang's and Yu's overall understanding of Proust remains limited, their attempts to re-enact certain Chinese cultural traditions in their creative reading of *La Recherche* are nevertheless noticeable. Their engagements still help to expand the Chinese 'horizon of expectations' over which Proust's work could potentially 'speak to' the Chinese sense of 'time-as-water/river' (in Wang) and connect China and France through the (re)creation of a Silk Road in memory (in Yu). Comparing Wang's and Yu's perceptions of Proust's work with that of Wei, we also notice a 'horizon of change' within the same framework of contemporary China. Wei's receptive appreciation of the literary qualities of *La Recherche* as stereotypically 'masculine', 'feminine', or 'hipstery'— which can then be related to drugs, sex, and the rock music scene in her respective short stories—marks out an 'aesthetic distance' from Wang's and Yu's previous receptions and creates a new horizon of expectations.[3] The readings and understandings of Proust's work reflect the literary and intellectual development of post-Mao China more than that of France and Europe. But these writers' cross-cultural intertextual practice affected by the Chinese translation is unilateral: its effect is for the most part limited to the Chinese context.

In contrast, Cheng has been settled in France since the beginning of Mao's era, and the historical specificities of contemporary China and their associated ideological factors, though crucial to Cheng's diegetic configuration in *Le Dit*, do not seem to manifest themselves in his engagement with Proust. In fact, as noted in Part II, Cheng's reformulation of Proust's novel as 'in search of time to come', with its emphasis on 'le différé' ('the deferred') and 'l'inachevé' ('the unfinished') for 'un futur aussi continu qu'inconnu' ('as continuous as it is unknown') (*Le Dit*, 191; *RB*, 131), strongly indicates the French poststructuralist prism of perception rather than the shifting of ideological tensions in contemporary Chinese society. Moreover, different from mainland Chinese writers, the representation of the Other becomes both a literary aesthetic and a cultural responsibility for Cheng. Indeed, Cheng's double perspective on Franco-Chinese literary and cultural interaction undertakes to represent not just the Other, but also, in some sense, to borrow Bush's expression again, 'the Other of the Other'.[4] The geographic, cultural, and epistemic topoi of both Proust's and Cheng's texts become essential critical ingredients of a transcultural dialogue. Such a dialogue disconcerts not only the historical time, but also the immediate cultural contexts and their associated values which Cheng ultimately aims to transcend.

Cheng's conception of dialogue is redolent of other contemporary thinkers of cosmopolitanism. The philosopher Kwame Anthony Appiah, for example, favours the idea of 'conversation' as the 'primacy of practice' for cross-cultural engagement, especially through literature and art, as he observes:

> [...] conversations across boundaries of identity—whether national, religious, or something else—begin with the sort of imaginative engagement you get when you read a novel or watch a movie or attend to a work of art that speaks from some place other than your own. So I'm using the word 'conversation' not only for literal talk but also as a metaphor for engagement with the experience and the ideas of others. And I stress the role of the imagination here because the encounters, properly conducted, are valuable in themselves. (2006, 85)

Allowing oneself, or daring to imagine and to be imagined is also one of the central tenets of Spivak's reconception of comparative literature (2003, 52; 81; 99). However, Cheng's ambition to 'transcend' cultural differences through a dialogic process may make him seem much more of an 'idealist' when compared to Appiah, as the latter expresses: 'conversation doesn't have to lead to consensus about anything, especially not values; it's enough that it helps people get used to one another' (2006, 85).

Malcolm Bowie, in his seminal work *Proust Among the Stars* (1998), employs the interstellar allegory—informed by Proust's narrator's own observation during a dinner at Rivebelle in *À l'ombre des jeunes filles en fleurs*—to characterize Proust's way of 'linking the multifariousness of human experience with the kaleidoscopic variety of his own writing' (319). The elaborate and polyphonic texture of Proust's prose is seen and read as 'stars' that are 'a pure scattering of luminous points' at one moment, and at the next moment, 'constellations, gigantic intimations of structure' (ibid., 320). Bowie's interstellar allegory is further in harmony with Proust's own *telescopic* (as opposed to *microscopic*) perception of 'truths': 'des choses, très petite, en effet, mais parce qu'elles étaient situées à une grande distance, et qui étaient chacune un monde' ('things which were indeed very small, but only because they were situated a long way away, each of them a world in itself') (*RTP IV*, 618; *PT VI*, 350). Both the astronomical and the modern popular senses of 'star' apply to the way Proust is situated in relation to established contemporary mainland Chinese and Franco-Chinese writers by the present book. Proust's work travels to China through translation and is conditionally received and (re)canonized along with the ideological shift of modern and contemporary Chinese society; and a Chinese creative response in French is simultaneously brought forth and well received back in France via the Chinese diasporic community, initiating a transcultural dialogue characteristic of contemporary migrant literature.

This circular trajectory fruitfully delineates a dynamic model of international canonization which manifests 'a different logic and different values' from national canonization (Thomsen 2008, 3). In the course of the present study, I have demonstrated not only how Proust has come to be canonized in China, but also how mainland Chinese writers have both contributed to, and profited from, Proust's Chinese canonization, largely in the attempt to raise their 'international' profiles in order to strive for their own canonicity at home. Or, in Cheng's case, engaging with the French canon from a migrant and transcultural perspective created new positions in the literary field and proved to be an effective pathway to contemporary French national canon formation.[5] His fame and success within and through the diasporic community in France then led to his Chinese canonization, in which Proust now plays only a small part. Therefore, the geopolitically circular line of enquiry pursued by this book has effectively mapped a *constellation* of works that, to continue in Thomsen's (ibid., 3) words, 'share properties of formal and thematic character, where canonized works can bring attention to less canonized, but affiliated, works, and draw them into the scene of world literature'. In this respect, Bowie's interstellar allegory of Proust's writing has a much extended implication for my comparatist approach in this study. A constellation is

[…] a group of stars visibly related to each other in a particular configuration. In three-dimensional space, most of the stars we see have little relation to one another, but can appear to be grouped on the celestial sphere of the night sky. Humans excel at finding patterns and throughout history have grouped stars that appear close to one another into constellations. (Cited in Thomsen 2008, 139)

A 'constellational' approach to world literature insists then on 'using international canonization as an analytical resource' (ibid.), as has been done in my study of Proust and China. A 'strong' constellation, according to Thomsen, should excel in the following attributes:

First, it is 'realistic', especially in terms of its empirical grounding;

second, it is 'innovative' in its

> [...] capacity for finding similarities in works that are usually not thought of as belonging together, but which will have a greater chance of being connected, because the canonical imperative directs the gaze towards a limited body of works, and because the idea of the constellation is not to find an almost complete coherence among works, but to connect central attributes that can also be said to define the work, in contrast to other, less canonical works from the same authors or the same literatures;

third, it is 'pluralistic' in its

> [...] ability to connect less circulated literature with the most internationally canonized works, and describe how they belong to the same wave in a certain period, and focus on the evolution of literature in time, [...] or how they have been canonized as an expression of a certain interest in the literary community in the longer process of canonization, [...] how the voice of migrant writers display properties that were appealing in the history of twentieth century literature;

and finally, it is 'didactic' in its 'ability to establish a point of view and reduce complexity by the use of international canonization, while at the same time facilitating unlikely meetings of texts across cultures' (ibid., 139–142).

Our paradigm of constellation constructed around Proust and China through translation, intertext, and transcultural dialogue hopes to become an effective model for other specialist and comparatist works to follow. For example, its discursive framework could immediately be adapted to support the study of many of Proust's fellow Modernist writers such as Virginia Woolf and James Joyce. What about the translation and reception of their works in China? Are they more of the same as Proust's? Have their respective thematic foci and stylistic innovations in a different language unleashed Chinese and Chinese diasporic writers' creative imaginations differently? Comparing and contrasting the reception of these often-associated European Modernist authors in a different cultural context such as China would open up another fascinating area of scholarly enquiry. One particular strength of my morphological approach to this 'Proustian constellation' lies in its fruitful and continuous methodological as well as epistemic negotiation between the more traditional critical approach built on historical or philological relations among literary texts *and* the more 'speculative' planetary criticism advocated by Wai Chee Dimock and Gayatri Spivak, which emphasizes the global readership and the randomizing, extra-territorial morphology of literature that outlive the 'finite scope of the nation' and disrupt 'dimensions of space and time' and the 'synchronic plane of the geopolitical map'.[6] For David Damrosch, such a critical negotiation is what essentially defines world literature, as he formulates: 'world literature is not an infinite, ungraspable canon of works but rather a mode of circulation and of reading' (2003, 5).

Proust disliked C.K. Scott Moncrieff's English translation of 'A la recherche du temps perdu' as 'Remembrance of Things Past' (a phrase borrowed from Shakespeare), as he criticized in his correspondence: 'cela détruit le titre' ('it destroys the title') (Proust 1993, 476). Had he lived long enough to know the Chinese title for his novel, Proust would in all likelihood have disapproved of 'Zhuiyi sishui nianhua' ('pursuing the memory of time/years as water/river', 追忆似水年华). However, he would certainly have been intrigued to observe how his own 'sensation du temps écoulé' ('sensation of time's slipping away') (*RTP IV*, 535; *PT VI*, 266) metamorphosed into a tradition in which time is conceived of as 'fluvial',[7] and is expressed and reformulated both in French and in Chinese—a logographic language that was even more foreign to him than English. Proust in *Contre Sainte-Beuve* (1954, 297–298; 1988, 93–94) famously concluded: 'les beaux livres sont écrits dans une sorte de langue étrangère. Sous chaque mot chacun de nous met son sens ou du moins son image qui est souvent un contresens. Mais dans les beaux livres, tous les contresens qu'on fait sont beaux' ('beautiful books are written in a sort of foreign language. Beneath each word each one of us puts his own meaning or at least his own image, which is often a misinterpretation. But in beautiful books all our misinterpretations are beautiful'). This remark points sharply to a 'good' theory and practice of reading. It seems that there is something inherently 'strange' and 'foreign' in the literary language of great works which robustly invites readers to (mis)translate and (mis)interpret according to their sensitivity and experience. 'Beautiful books' like *La Recherche* are beautiful not for the sake of being susceptible to 'errors' of understanding. If one were to transpose Proust's statement from its original intralingual to our interlingual context, one could say that 'all our misinterpretations are beautiful' because such 'misinterpretations' open up cultural differences that call for creative negotiations and constant reciprocal actualizations of two traditions—a transcultural dialogue. 'Contre-sens' is literally the way we engage with Proust's work in this book, and the 'ensemble de rapports' ('set of relations') between Proust and China, inspired by such 'contre-sens' ('misinterpretation'), offers a beguiling 'progression de beauté' ('progression of beauty') (ibid., 298; ibid., 94). A 100 years after the publication of *Du côté de chez Swann*, Proust's work will no doubt continue to effect such intercultural transaction that exemplifies our sense of tradition and its becoming.

NOTES

1. I reappropriate Derrida's following remark: 'what is written as *différance*, then, will be the playing movement that "produces"—by means of something that is not simply an activity—these differences, these effects of difference' (ibid., 11).
2. Following Bush's use of the term, 'topoi' is understood 'both in the sense of commonplaces and locations' (Bush 2005, 166).
3. 'Horizon of expectations', 'horizon of change', and 'aesthetic distance' all derive from Hans Robert Jauss's reception theory (1982).
4. Bush (2005, 178) employs this expression rather playfully, and notably with a question mark. He clarifies: 'in Lacanian terms there can't be an Other of the Other because the very formulation assures the unconditional singularity of the Other. [...] The Other of the Other is the other'.
5. This remark is informed by Thomsen's more general observation: 'migrant writers have been historically good at creating new positions in the literary field, because they bring in an intimate knowledge of other traditions and cultures [...] Creating new positions does not guarantee that they will succeed, but the chance of coming up with something new is enhanced by existing between cultures of which the author can be equally critical' (2008, 71).
6. These expressions are taken from Dimock's article. Dimock (2001, 173–188) clarifies: 'a literary text becomes a new semantic template, a new form of the legible, each time it crosses a national border. Global transit extends, triangulates, and transforms its meaning.' She further characterizes the act of reading as 'a global process of extension, elaboration, and randomization' which 'turns literature into the collective life of the planet'. For planetary criticism, see Spivak (2003) and Moretti (2000).
7. The expression is redolent of the exchange of words between Véronique and Tianyi in *Le Dit*: 'Tu es un vrai "fluvial"'—'Comment ne le serais-je pas, en bon Chinois que je suis!' ('You are a real "river person!"'—'How could I not be, good Chinese that I am!'). (*Le Dit*, 267–286; *RB*, 185)

REFERENCES

Appiah, Kwame Anthony. 2006. *Cosmopolitanism: Ethics in a World of Strangers.* London: W. W. Norton & Company.

Bowie, Malcolm. 1998. *Proust Among the Stars.* New York: Columbia University Press.

Bush, Christopher. 2005. The Other of the Other? Cultural Studies, Theory, and the Location of the Modernist Signifier. *Comparative Literature Studies* 42 (2): 162–180.

Damrosch, David. 2003. *What Is World Literature?* Princeton: Princeton University Press.

Derrida, Jacques. 1982. *Margins of Philosophy,* trans. A. Bass. Chicago: The University of Chicago Press.

Dimock, Wai Chee. 2001. Literature for the Planet. *Publications of the Modern Language Association of America* 116 (1): 173–188.

Jauss, Hans Robert. 1982. *Toward an Aesthetic of Reception,* trans. T. Bahti. Minneapolis, MN: University of Minnesota Press.

Moretti, Franco. 2000. Conjectures on World Literature. *New Left Review* 1: 54–68.

Moretti, Franco. 1983. *Signs Taken for Wonders: Essays in the Sociology of Literary Forms.* London: Verso Editions.

Proust, Marcel. 1988. *Against Sainte-Beuve and Other Essays,* trans. J. Sturrock. London: Penguin.

Proust, Marcel. 1954. *Contre Sainte-Beuve,* ed. B. de Fallois. Paris: Gallimard.

Proust, Marcel. 1993. *Lettre à Gaston Gallimard* [Le jeudi 14 septembre 1922], ed. P. Kolb. Paris: Plon.

Spivak, Gayatri Chakravorty. 2003. *Death of a Discipline.* New York: Columbia University Press.

Thomsen, Mads Rosendahl. 2008. *Mapping World Literature: International Canonization and Transnational Literatures.* London: Continuum.

INDEX

© The Editor(s) (if applicable) and The Author(s) 2017

S. Li, *Proust, China and Intertextual Engagement*,

DOI 10.1007/978-981-10-4454-0

CPSIA information can be obtained
at www.ICGtesting.com
Printed in the USA
LVOW05*0030071017

551544LV00016B/509/P